Paraffin Chronicles

Printed in Victoria, Canada

National Library of Canada Cataloguing in Publication Data

Torrens, Herb, 1948-
        Paraffin chronicles / Herb Torrens.
ISBN 1-4120-0920-0
        I. Title.
GV840.S8T67 2004   797.3'2'09   C2003-904390-8

TRAFFORD

This book was published *on-demand* in cooperation with Trafford Publishing.
On-demand publishing is a unique process and service of making a book available for retail sale to the public taking advantage of on-demand manufacturing and Internet marketing.
On-demand publishing includes promotions, retail sales, manufacturing, order fulfilment, accounting and collecting royalties on behalf of the author.

Suite 6E, 2333 Government St., Victoria, B.C. V8T 4P4, CANADA
Phone   250-383-6864   Toll-free   1-888-232-4444 (Canada & US)
Fax   250-383-6804   E-mail   sales@trafford.com
Web site   www.trafford.com   TRAFFORD PUBLISHING IS A DIVISION OF TRAFFORD HOLDINGS LTD.
Trafford Catalogue #03-1289   www.trafford.com/robots/03-1289.html

10   9   8   7   6   5   4   3   2

Dedication

This work is dedicated first to my dad, James Torrens, who taught me to love and respect the ocean and helped me nurture the craft of writing. To my mother, Catherine, who taught me to see the world with an open mind and cherish life. To my son Ryan, whose short time in life remains my inspiration. Rest in Peace all.

For Brandon, Dustin, and Alexa. Live long and enjoy the journey. My love will always be with you.

Acknowledgements

So many people played a part in making this dream become a reality. Dave Rullo who never stopped believing in the journey. My mentors Mike Marshall and Gordon Johnson, who have taught me so much about life in different ways and who always, sometimes painfully, tell it like it is. Terry Smith for continuing to push the envelope." Thanks to Kevin Nellis and Roger Peterson who brought me back to surfing. To Pat Story for the encouragement and hours of editing. Wendy Holder for her artful design. Richard Graham, Ralph Myers, Tom Keck, and Don Craig for helping me find photography for the book. All my surf brothers, alive and dead, who made this story. Finally, to all those who are not mentioned in this book, I just couldn't get everybody in, forgive me and know that you too were part of the journey.

Note on Artwork

Many of the photos in this work were previously published including the shot on the cover, the two scanned magazine covers, and many of the photos by Richard Graham. The cover shot, by Greg Weaver, appeared on the cover of Surfer Magazine (Volume 12, Number 6 Feb. 1971). The Surfing Yearbook, Photo by Ron Dahlquist, was in Yearbook Number 4 of "Surfing." I'd like to thank and acknowledge the photographers, and Prime Media for the use of these photos. Finally, the author shot (back cover), was by Terry Smith.

Thanks all.

Paraffin Chronicles

By Herb Torrens

Waves are life. Pure, strong, predictable yet unpredictable. Each the same in likeness, but unique in form. Shaped by wind and distance, they march toward an inevitable end on a beach of heaven or hell. Along the way, just as they achieve ultimate mass, those who have taken the time to learn the skill might join for a brief moment with a liquid life force.

It is the surfer who knows the waves. They are nomads of the sea. Endlessly searching for the next defining moment of meeting with a wave. Harnessing the energy before it ends. Riding the force of nature. Feeling the power.

Surfing can be all things to those who choose the wave path. Rewarding, frustrating, exhilarating, humiliating. Waves of life. Sometimes you ride a smooth glassy wall in the shining sun, other times you are tousled like a rag doll in a washing machine. No matter the fate, as long as you paddle back out, there's hope for the future. Redemption awaits, just outside the breaker line.

Beach Party Bingo

Imagine being 11 years old living in Southern California in the summer of 1960. Make that Costa Mesa, a sister city of sorts to Newport Beach. The Ventures' number one hit "Walk Don't Run," blares from every radio within ear-shot. Freshly oiled girls in new-style, two-piece bikinis make the scene at the beach. And the movie "Gidget," is drawing hordes of young teens to a new bohemian lifestyle called surfing.

Okay, you got me. Yes, I was one of those hordes that headed down to the beach after seeing Gidget. Sure, surf historians will tell you that Gidget was akin to the downfall of Rome in its effect on true surfing culture. But I don't see it that way. Surfing would have "happened" without the movie. It was inevitable.

I wasn't quite a teen then, but I'd seen enough of the movie's star, Sandra Dee, in the previews to trade my regular Friday night at the Harbor Roller Rink for a night at the Mesa Theater. Gidget was a happening, and all my friends were talking about it. Actually, I had a brief experience on a surfboard the year before when a friend and I got talked into trying it to impress a girl. It was uneventful, to say the least. Still, since I'd tried it once, I felt I had a sort of connection with this new surfing thing.

And what a thing it was, according to the movie. Cool guys and girls at the beach, riding the waves together in the sun. Having beach parties every night. Living free. Oh yeah, and girls galore for those who surfed. What could be better? We all left the movie that night longing to be like Moon Doggie and the Kahuna.

Newport had surfing. So the next day a couple of friends and I caught the Orange Line Bus to the beach and got off at the Pier. It was July the 4th, 1960, a blue-skied sunny day with lots of action at the beach. Woolly-headed surfers bobbing outside the breaker line, straddling boards made of wood and foam. Morning sun flickering off sparkling walls of water. Surfboards slicing across the waves leaving ivory white trails across emerald faces. We watched, awestruck, from the beach.

In those days, surfers rode The Point in the morning and then had to move closer to the south side of the Pier as the beach became more crowded in the afternoon. Most swimmers went to the north side of the pier where the waves were calm. My friends and I soon found that we were a bit out of our element on the south side. Skating rink hodaddies to be exact. We had Brylcreem in our hair, cut-off jeans for shorts and a wool blanket instead of towels. That was three strikes against us at 19th Street, and we became immediately aware of the looks and jeers from the bleached blond, baggy-shorted gremlins hanging around the fire ring.

Still, I was fascinated by the scene. Out on the point, I watched as real surfers picked up swells and rode almost effortlessly on the faces of waves. It was a revelation to see how it was actually done. Much different than Gidget, which portrayed surfing as a bunch of guys riding straight to the beach hooting and smiling as they cajoled their way to the shore.

The real thing looked much better. Much more fun and exciting, and I desperately wanted to try. Luckily, one of my friends spotted a guy he knew with a board. After some negotiations that included a promise of french fries and soda, the guy reluctantly agreed to let us try a couple of rides on his board. So off we went, dragging a baby-blue Hobie down the beach. We all went out at once, taking turns carrying the board out, and pushing ourselves into the foam. There was no instruction of any kind. Just common sense and a knowledge of body surfing and mat surfing that we all had done growing up. Standing up and riding the soup proved no problem, and within a few rides we were all ready better than the Kahuna and Moondoggie we'd seen in the movie the night before. We had a blast, and stayed out as long as we could.

The next day, I returned to the beach without my sidekicks expecting to find the same guy and maybe borrow his board. Hey, in the movie, a regular guy like me could just go down to the surf spot and in no time, he'd be hanging around with the guys, sharing food and sodas and playing the bongos.

There were no bongos on the south side of the Newport Pier. No guys in straw hats welcoming you into the waves. No welcome at all. In those days you didn't just go out and buy a bunch of gear and transform yourself into a "surfer." Commercialism hadn't yet discovered surfing. The only way in to the in-crowd was in proving yourself in the waves and on the beach. Oh yeah, the individualism shared by those who ride waves is often carried over to life on land. A territorial thing, of course. Like early mans' survival against the elements. An aggressive behavior that questions and tests all who invade new territory.

I was an invader. A roller-skater from another culture. Of course, it could have been a plain case of payback. As a skater, we looked at surfer-types as invaders. So it was fair play. But, not easy for me. Not when all I wanted to do was borrow a board for a few rides in the soup. The stares from the guys around the fire ring in those first days told the story. "Get lost hodad!"

And, lost I got. I fell in with a group of outcasts at one of the fire rings down the beach. In those days the term Third Ringer was reserved for beginners, "kooks," rejects, and those otherwise cast from the ranks of surfing's hierarchy. Banished to the outer edges of surfdom. Denied access to the shapely waves in front of the first ring. That was life on the south side of the Newport Pier for me that summer. But then, it wasn't such a bad life.

Surf, Turf and The Third Ring
In the long hot summer of 1960, I found myself in a carnival-like atmosphere of the Newport Beach season. Tourists mobbing every square inch of sand in the warm afternoon sun. Teenage girls in polka-dot bikinis holding court on oversize beach towels. Red lipped honeys wearing bouffant hair dos sipping "Cokes" from eight ounce bottles and rock 'n' roll music blaring from their miniature transistor radios. Families lunching under brightly colored umbrellas rented from Henry's Grocery Store. The smells of hamburgers and french fries inviting hungry customers to come spend a couple of bucks for a beach-style lunch. I soaked it all in.

The early mornings belonged to the surfers. From the alleys up around 38th Street to down around the Pier, they appeared shortly after sunrise. Walking, or maybe riding bikes with wheeled trailers strapped with foam or balsa-wood boards. Wearing "Bermuda" shorts and oversize white T-shirts. No hats, no shoes, no logos plastered on shirt and shorts. Commercialization of the culture had yet to arrive.

I loved the beach. And I found myself fully taken by this new adventure called surfing. Captured by the way the guys rode on the smooth faces of waves. The turning and maneuvering. Like some strange dance that blended the grace and agility of bull-fighting with the speed and excitement of bobsledding. Not that I'd ever been bobsledding, but I'd seen it on TV.

I picked up on the slang and style down at the third ring. Swimming trunks were "baggies." A "set" meant a group of waves. "Outside," meant outside the breaker line. Or it could also be a warning that a "big set" was coming: as in "outside! Paddle for you lives!" "Phonies were guys who didn't surf, but went for the look. Hodads, or hoddaddies, were guys who put grease in their hair, and were into cars. Of course everything good was "bitchen. "Man, check out that bitchen chick...Went to Do Ho yesterday, the waves were bitchen."

The surf at 19th Street wasn't bitchen too often. There was a better surfing spot up around 38th. But, it had some drawbacks for a former hodad skater and now fledgling gremmie. First of all you had to be able to turn or "cut" as they used to say to ride the peak-like waves that broke up there. The waves were predominately lefts at 38th Street, which for me would mean riding "backside," or back to the wave. Going right, or "front side" was much easier. In fact, I didn't even try going backside until late that first summer.

Of course, there were other reasons I didn't surf 38th Street in those early days. Yes, the waves were bigger, faster and much less forgiving than the south side of the pier, but there was another factor. Fear of getting pounded. The guys who surfed there were all good, big, mean, and a little short on welcoming newcomers. After all, there were rituals to be observed, levels of skill to be achieved, triumphs experienced, and most importantly, respect to be earned before you could ride at 38th Street.

Respect is a part of the culture that comes with the territory. It's as much a part of surfing as it was a part of the caveman culture. Territory, respect, pecking order, all of which are only established by action. In my case, the action could be a 40-pound board slicing over my head. The "kick out" was not just a way to pull out of a wave, it was a surfing lesson. There are unwritten rules in surfing. The best waves are ridden by those who put themselves in a position to catch the swell at its peak. Those that elect to try and ride a safer part of the wave can get in the flight path of those swooping down from the more powerful section. That's a violation.

You learn faster in a culture that doesn't accept mediocrity. And that's what it was like in Newport, and I'm sure in other towns up and down the coast. You had to be strong, both physically and mentally to survive. In those early days, I had no board of my own, so I had to grovel for borrowed boards. Sometimes I'd pay one of the older guys to use a board. Fifty cents could buy lunch in those days, and I'd gladly fork up my weekly allowance for an hour in the surf.

It was heaven and hell, for an 11-year old retired skater. I guess you could say retired. For the last six years, I had been involved in competition skating. Racing mostly, and I was state champ for my age group one year. Had a bunch of trophies in the living room. But, I had grown tired of the training and the fact that my coach didn't want me to go swimming. I loved to swim. My dad taught me the ropes early on. I remember swimming across the bay from 15th street to Lido Island with him when I was six or seven. He taught me how to tread water and float, and the importance of changing strokes to save energy. All of which came into play later in life.

Eventually I made some real friends. Not of the ruling class mind you, but friends who had boards and were there everyday. Tommy Kerwin and Fred Dupree were two of my earliest pals. Tom was two years younger, Fred two years older. Fred had a Robinson-Sweet with a fin that hummed whenever the board picked up speed. No kidding, it actually buzzed. The faster you'd go, the louder it got. I had visions of being a dive bomber pilot zeroing in on a target every time I rode that board.

Tommy had hand-me-down boards, mostly old balsa wood logs. But, he had connections with the upper echelon. His two older brothers, Kenny and Russell were both good surfers.

I made other friends that first summer. There was a girl we nick-named Muffin. She was a couple of years older than Fred, which put her way out of my range of ambitions. But, she was nice look-ing as I recall and well-shaped. Down for the summer. Had a bun-galow on 34th Street. She also had a purple Gordi double-ender. Very cool board. Between Muff's Gordi and Fred's big white hum-mer Robinson-Sweet, I learned to stand up in the soup and "cut" right.

Those early days of going right in the soup at the Pier were supplemented with some nights at a very cool venue. A small theater across from the big parking lot where Newport and Balboa boulevards meet. That's right at the Pier, or Mcfadden's Wharf if you want to get historical. Anyway, this was a little movie house just south of the famous Crab Cooker restaurant, on the bay-side of Newport Blvd. It was called The Projection Booth, and it featured art films, film noir and at least once a week, a surf film.

For 50 cents, you could see films such as "Cat on a Hot Foam Board," "Slippery When Wet," "Surf Crazy," Sunset Surf Craze," and more. They were short, snappy films made by the guys who starred in them. Peter Cole, Greg Noll, Bruce Brown. Soon, names, like Phil Edwards, Dewey Weber and Mickey Dora would become household names at the Torrens dinner table. Soon, their pictures would be plastered all over my bedroom, along with bullfighting posters from Tijuana.

In the early mornings, I would ride my bike down to the Pier from our house on 16th Street in Costa Mesa. It was an easy ride down Old Newport Road. The only hard part was crossing Coast Highway. Made harder once I got my first surfboard, which I towed behind my bike on a makeshift trailer made of two-by-fours and wagon wheels.

My first foam board was a nine-foot Horizon pop-out. A pop-out was a foam blank that had simply been skimmed, sanded and glassed. Not much creativity involved. No custom shape job. Just a standard shape, and no center stinger of wood. Typically, pop-outs were a solid color of pigment. Mine was a light gray with abstract streaks of white. It was probably pretty cool by some hodad's standards, but it didn't hold much status at the Pier. Cool boards were clear, or a light tint of blue, orange or red. They had fancy laminated wood fins and balsa or redwood stringers.

Status was a major concern at the Pier. It was very important to have the right kind of board, trunks and hair. That first year my board was a pop-out, my trunks were "Surfers," and I had a crew cut with a little too much Vasoline. I was a Costa Mesa boy from the roller rink, and I took my lumps.

The day after I saw the film "Sunset Surf Craze" at the Projection Booth, I got a dose of reality. Sunset Surf Craze starred Peter Cole and Ricky Gregg. Peter Cole had actually been there narrating the movie, and I even got his autograph. I was so stoked. Not much hot-dogging in that film, though. No big turns or arches. No nose rides. Just guys riding huge waves with wide big-wave stances in a low crouching fashion. Right up my alley for the two-footers at the Pier.

So I pull up to the beach early in the morning feeling a little winded from negotiating the eight-mile ride from my house to the pier. Crossing Coast Highway with a board in tow was always a harrowing experience, to say the least. I looked around for my little pack of friends, still hesitant about just walking down to the beach with my board. One of the regulars, a guy named Chicky, spotted me on the sidewalk. He was an older guy. Dark olive complexion reflective of his Italian heritage, and bright orange hair. In those days, Chicky was sort of a self-appointed enforcer at the Pier, and I was his prey. I'll never forget the look on his face when he approached. Sort of like a big cat who'd just spotted a mouse. He came swaggering up and told me he'd seen me at the Projection Booth the night before and that I was a "phony." He also told me to go back to the skating rink. With that, he proceeded to kick my board and gave me few hard shoves to the shoulder. He wasn't big, but he was older, and he had a small group of urchins behind him grinning and egging him on.

Fred Dupree came to my rescue. He was bigger than Chicky, and although he didn't have the same "First Ringer," status, he backed him down without loss of face for Chicky. Which was important in keeping beach harmony.

There were other similar incidents in the surf-school of hard knocks. But soon I had proper trunks and my hair, with the help of a little proxide, grew to acceptable surf length, much to the disdain of my parents. And, my surfing improved. My mornings and early afternoons were spent at the Pier, riding waves and collecting pop bottles to buy a Coke or an order of fries.

There was a great hamburger stand on the south side of the Pier in those days. Char Burger. Like so many things in that year, Char Burger was a first. Char broiled burgers with a Thousand Island-like sauce. Good? Oh yeah, they were great and you could smell them cooking from all over the beach. At 35 cents, they were a bit pricey, but well worth a couple of hours picking up bottles on the beach. Deposit for a soda bottle was two-cents, so 40 or so bottles could render a Char Burger, an order of fries and a small Coke.

But the competition for bottles was tough. There were small bands of guys roaming the beaches from 15th Street to 38th collecting bottles. There were other ways to make money, too. You could go to Delaneys Fish Market, which was over by the Crab Cooker, and pick abalone shells out of the trash. We would scrape them clean in the bay and then set up little stands at the foot of the Pier and sell them to tourists. A quarter to 50-cents apiece for a good shell. But that was a tough gig in itself. All that cleaning and then sitting there for hours in the sun selling the shells. Too boring.

For me, the long tedious hours of scouring the beach for bottles, not to mention the bullies who might simply take all your bottles with threats of bodily harm, did not appeal. I mostly starved at the beach. But, I logged a lot of the time in the water.

Peter Cole Goes Right
I remember my first real wave. Not a slide in the soup at 19th Street, but a real green-water wave. It was at Doheny. My dad took Fred Dupree and me down on a Sunday in July. Boards tied to the top of my dad's '54 Chevy, stopping every 15 minutes or so to check the ropes and worrying the whole way.

No freeways in those days, and the Coast Highway meandered forever through the beach towns of Corona Del Mar, Laguna, South Laguna and Dana Point. There were stop signals every block or so through the cities, and we stopped a lot. It could take more than an hour to get from Newport to Doheny, but there was lots to see. Laguna was famous for its "Greeter." He was an old long-haired guy with wild eyes that would stand in the center of town and wave to all the passing cars. Today, he'd probably be committed, but back then people loved him. They even made a statue of him that still stands.

We leaned out the window and waived at Larson with ear-to-ear grins as we passed him. Hey, we were surfers, on a surf trip with boards strapped to the top of our car. I remember feeling something special about that. Part of a select group. A clique of individuals who shared a common bond. We passed other surfers going up and down the coast giving the thumbs-up, or thumbs-down sign as a way of sharing information about how the surf was. The guys coming from down south were all giving us the thumbs-up.

Sure enough, the surf was rolling in over the outside reef at Doheny when we arrived. Maybe four-feet on the outside sets. My dad set up a little camp on the beach as Fred and I scrambled into the surf. I stuck to the inside trying to perfect my style in the soup. Okay, I was just trying to go right. Fred was pretty good and was able to get outside at first break. He got some pretty good waves and was telling me all about his rides when we broke for hot-dogs at lunch. After much encouragement, he talked me into braving the outside.

Once out in the line-up, I was amazed at how tranquil it was. Sitting with other surfers, floating gently up and down with the swells, looking in at the distant shore. I drifted off into scenes from "Sunset Surf Craze." I was Peter Cole, of course, waiting for a 15-footer. When a set came, someone yelled "outside," and the pack was off for the horizon. I was overwhelmed with anticipation and struggled to turn my board and paddle out. I can't exactly remember what was going through my mind, but then I managed something I never thought possible.

I still don't really know what happens in that magical moment when you see a wave that you know you can catch. I am a chicken at heart, always have been. I'd like to be brave, but I worry a lot about what's going to happen next. I see the worse-case scenario and try to block it out. Then, something kicks in and I go on automatic pilot. It's like I separate from my body and become two distinct entities. One, a gutless wimp trying to beat himself out of a wet paper bag, the other an irrational daredevil controlled by an inner voice giving commands. You know: "Captain to crew....all hands on deck....battle stations....Go, go, go!"

Somehow, I found myself turning my board around as the first gigantic swell of the set approached. Of course, it was probably all of three feet, but in my 11-year-old mind, it was 15-foot Sunset and I was (who else?) Peter Cole! I stroked in and stood up. The next few seconds were the greatest, most exciting, seconds I had ever lived. I found myself sliding down a smooth swell, going faster than I'd ever gone on skates. I sensed a strange sort of power from the wave, like it had its own agenda and I was just along for the ride. What a feeling. Pure adrenaline. I'm sure I must have been grinning ear-to-ear, but who knows. More likely I was horrified.

I had the big-wave stance going though. Feet about four feet apart, low crouch that I had learned so well speed skating, and I was going right. I was almost oblivious of the other surfers on the wave, but as I recall there were at least two in front of me and two behind. All cutting toward the shore on an emerald green sheet of glass. Visions of surf movies crept into my mind. I was one of them now. Riding a huge wave and in control.

About 10 seconds later, reality slid back in to my Nirvanic state of mind. The riders in front of me pulled out. Not sure what became of the guys behind me, but all of the sudden I was alone on the wave. About then I became aware of the shoreline creeping up in my peripheral. And the wave seemed to be getting larger as it approached the beach. I froze in my Sunset stance, careening toward an untimely end. I had never pulled out of a wave, never kicked out, I had only bailed off the back. When in doubt, bail out, but even with that bit of wisdom, I was a little late.

The wave jacked up and threw out over my head. I went headlong into the shore break in my big-wave crouch and got waumped. I thought for a second I was going to die. I bounced off the rock bottom, got tousled around a bit and then came sliding up the sand with the shore break. I lay stunned for a second and then jumped up to retrieve my board, which had washed up to the high tide mark. I survived! I must have relived that ride a thousand times. And that was just in the first week.

The Banzai Rider is Born
Back at the Pier, I was slowly making a move at being accepted. I could make it outside and take off on real waves now. I was becoming a surfer. Sort of. Two rides that summer taught me some lessons. I remember both well. Pain has a way of doing that. The first was at the Pier. I'm sliding along on a small right when I catch the outside rail of my trusty Horizon. The board flips up, and in an instant I'm falling like a guy who's just been shot off his horse. But before I hit the water, the wave scoops up my board and hurls it toward my head. The rail hits me right in the Adam's apple. Gack!

Luckily there was no major damage, but it hurt bad for a while. It did make one change in my riding style that summer though. From then on, whenever there was a hint that the wave, or the soup for that matter, was going to catch me, I ran to the nose. I became the classic banzai nose rider. No thought of backpedaling. Just get up on the front and ride to a frothing explosion. A classic lunge forward would separate me and the board without a chance of being hit. It worked well. Guys paddling out learned quick. "Watch out for that skinny kid, he bails out on every wave!" My new style made for long swims and few friends in the water, but I was safe from bouts with my board.

The other memorable ride that summer was up at 38th Street. My friend Tommy Kerwin and I braved the ride up there one day on a whim. "We're getting too good for 19th Street, we can handle the waves up there...right?" Not exactly. The waves were overhead, meaning they were taller than we were. Huge, by our standards. Just getting out was an accomplishment.

Once we got out, we found ourselves in a lineup of older guys. Tommy was more comfortable for two reasons. One, he knew a lot of the guys because of his brothers, so the regulars cut him some slack. And two, he was a goofy-foot, which meant he stood with his right foot forward and could naturally go left on the waves. Did I mention that 38th was predominantly lefts?

In those days, there were no groins, or small jetties, on the Newport coastline. The summer south swells would pour in with peaky lines angling up the beach in a direction that made for sometimes exceptionally shaped lefts. I, unfortunately, stood left foot forward and went predominantly right. Actually, I had never given much thought to going left. I had yet to develop the skill of sizing up a wave in order to determine the best direction to go. A wave was a wave to me. Paddle in, stand up, angle right, and run to the end of the board before the wave broke.

So here I am out with the big guys. Greg Brown, Pete Nickertz, George Adams, Randy Haworth. All goofy-foots, with exceptional skills and little sympathy for third ringers from 19th Street. I was outside when a set loomed on the horizon. Tommy gave me a "go for it" look as the first wave approached so I wheel my 9-foot Horizon around and paddle in. Oblivious to all around me, I concentrated solely on catching the wave and standing up. I accomplished the feat and was ready for my "I'm Peter Cole," mindset to take over when I suddenly realized there is another surfer charging down the wave toward me. A collision course! He's going left, I'm going right, the wave is jacking up and ready to throw out over the both of us. No time to run off the front, and given the circumstances that was a good thing.

I bail out the back. The wave breaks with a resounding blow to my chest. In a flash I'm unceremoniously swept up and over the falls. It was the most violent explosion of water I had ever experienced and it seemed to pull me in all directions at once. The rag doll effect. I was a sock in a Maytag. I smacked hard into the sand bottom, and then the wave got mean and just pinned me there. I had never thought about drowning. Not in water that was barely over my head. Yet there I was pinned on the bottom for like 10 minutes. Seconds are eternities in a wipe-out, and I was there all of two or three, but it was enough to bleed my lungs of the precious air that kept me alive.

I saw black. Of course, my eyes were closed, but I saw black. And I needed air. I felt panic. Then it lets up just enough to allow me to stroke to the surface. My arms were limp, my body sapped from the loss of oxygen. I surface in a frothy white layer of what seems like soap suds. My mouth opens reactively to the air and I gulp in oxygen. Then, unexplainably, the wave sucks me back down. Waves do that. The turbulence left after a wave has broken in the impact zone is almost air-like and difficult to swim, paddle or stay afloat in.

My second trip under was brief. The taste of fresh air had revived my determination, and this time I took a big stroke with both arms and wrestled my way up through the current. I surface again, mouth wide open, bug eyes, flapping arms. The turbulence was subsiding and it was easier to stay on top. For a brief moment, I was safe. I knew I was not going to drown. But, as will sometimes happen in life, just when you think you've got it made, the opposite happens.

My moment of salvation was shattered by a voice. It was something like "You idiot!" Actually, it was probably a bit stronger. Maybe like "I'm going to kill you," with a few expletives thrown in for effect. Either way, I knew my life was in danger again. The big goofy-foot, and I honestly can't remember who it was, was coming at me. All I remember was the rage. He was like a monster in my worst nightmare. A big, red-faced, snorting bull, and he was charging me.

It was a brief exchange. Me backstroking with all my might, blubbering things like "I'm so sorry, I didn't see you, I.....help!" He didn't hit me. He must have realized I was little more than a 98-pound weakling. But, he did give me a verbal lashing and a surfing lesson I've never forgotten. Never go right on a left, or vice versa. This also applies to many situations in life.

Needless to say, I'd did not spend much more time up at 38th that summer. Like none. And, in fact, it was a long time before I got the nerve to go back up there again. I also developed a new-found respect for how powerful a wave can be. Surfing/Life 101: Respect your environment, respect your elders and respect the ocean.

Life On The Other Side
Summers were long back then, at least a year and a half in kid's time. It's amazing when I think back. So much experience packed into one summer. So many changes, It seemed like a lifetime. Those hot days lying in the sand with the smell of the Charburgers mixing with the salt air. Golden sunsets by the fire ring. My mom and dad coming down to watch me surf from the Pier. Precious memories. Sure, there was still the occasional bully demanding to use my board. I'm going to skip the part where Tommy Kerwin and I tried to pigment my board. Let's just say it was a train wreck. By the time fall rolled around, I was a seasoned surfer. In my mind at least.

Going into the 7th grade, I had new status. Surfer. New look. New guy. One of the only surfers enrolled at Kaiser Junior High in Costa Mesa. When school started, my surfing days went from every day, to just two. That was the bad news. The good news was winter in Newport was a whole new ballgame.

The tourists: gone. The beaches: deserted. The waves: some of the best beachbreak waves on the coast. In the wintertime, the northerly swells created a sandbar at 22nd Street that helped shape the waves for surfing. Long lefts starting out in front of Blackies Bar and rolling through the north end of the parking lot. Past 23rd Street on a good day. On the north end of the parking lot, between 23rd and 24th, a natural big peak broke that had both a right and left.

Fire rings dotted the beach, starting at the end of the parking lot. Spaced about two to the block and going as far as 28th Street. No one wore wet suits. In fact, it would be at least another year until the first surfer dared to don a wet suit at the pier, and he promptly received a Newport-style unwelcome.

I spent my first winter of surfing with a small group of friends, exiled to either 24th street, or right next to the pier. We mostly chose the Pier option. The waves were smaller, and we could hang out around the deserted lifeguard stand, which provided some amusement for us. You know: climbing, jumping, king-of-the-mountain type stuff where one's reign was often short lived.

While no one bothered us down there, the lack of a fire ring made for some cold mornings and afternoons. On the coldest of days, we summoned the courage to approach the fire rings. The big guys would let you stand around awhile if you brought wood. So we'd come in from the waves with blue-capped knees and scour the alleys for anything that would burn.

By mid-winter, we had formed a little group. There were guys from Costa Mesa, like Kim Harp and Dennis Goff, and some from the Point, which is down on the Newport Peninsula. George Anderson, Scott Chasin, and Terry Smith were Point guys and had a leg up on us surfing-wise. Together, we had some great times going right in front of the lifeguard stand. I mention these guys here because they were important to me as surfers and friends at the time. But, more over, those of us who are still alive are still the best of friends. Such are the bonds of surfing.

When we weren't in the water, or searching for firewood, we would watch the surfers at 22nd Street. Newport, like other beach communities, represented a microcosm of a larger culture and it had some great surfers. Pure stylists who rode deep and turned hard. Kent Haworth and Mike Lutz were standout regular-foots who rode every bit as well as the guys who starred in the movies of the day like Dewey Weber or Johnny Fain. There's footage and still photos that attest to their skills. And, I can't forget the contingent of goofy-foots. Newport has a lineage of goofy-foot surfers that goes back to the days when boards had no fins and guys learned to surf going left at Big Corona. In that first year, at the Pier, in 1960 and 1961, several stood out in my mind. Randy Haworth, Pete Nickertz, Rick Lowe and Greg Brown were the kings.

In years to come, others would leave their mark. Mike Marshall and Roger Zieger, who introduced me to the Lower Trestle and a much broader surfing culture. But, for that first winter, Haworth, Nickertz, Lowe and Brown were the guys I admired, and stayed away from. Surfing protocol demanded that royalty be treated with respect and that commoners like myself keep their distance. This edict was enforced by scowls, stares and, if need be, a swift kickout over the head.

A kickout let you disembark from a wave. You kicked out to avoid being crunched by a wave and taking a long swim to the beach. A kickout could also let an inferior know his place. Like I've said, we learned quick in those days not to take off in front of a guy with a better position on the wave. And, we learned by watching the show from the beach.

And, what a show it was. Kent Haworth and Mike Lutz driving down big peaks at the north end of the parking lot, turning off the bottom in classic style reflective of Dewey Weber and Kemp Aaberg. Big drop-knee cutbacks off the top of the wave and then quick steps to the nose. That kind of style became a precursor to power surfing.

Dale Velzy came down to the Pier a couple of times and surfed in those early days, and he had a similar style. Off the bottom in a big swooping turn and then a radical drop-knee cutback, which is a way to turn the board back into the wave after outrunning the swell. The surf movies called it hotdogging. We called it soul.

The goofy-foots at 22nd had a different style. They rode the wave in a more parallel fashion, or what we would now call "down the line" surfing. Turning at the top or middle of the wave, two steps toward the nose, quick little knee movements to position the rails for maximum trim and ultimate speed. They rode in the tube, or on the tip of the board according to how the wave broke and then cranked sweeping roundhouse cutbacks changing directions 180 degrees in a split second. Looking back, I can see that the Newport goofy-foots had picked up on a new style of riding. They had broken away from the turn and slash of "hotdogging" and had progressed to a style more in tune with the wave. Again, a precursor of things to come.

Bottom turn — Mike Lutz at the north end of the parking lot making it look easy. (Photo by Tom Jewell)

Off-shore days — When the Santa ana winds blow the waves at the pier got even better. Ralph Meyers in perfect trim on the north side of the parking lot. (Photo by Tom Jewell)

Top Dog

At every beach, there's always one guy who stands above the rest. The top dog. Usually, the guy will have a run at being the best. Maybe a month, maybe a year, maybe more, and then someone else will come along and take over the thrown. Heros go into the annals of local verbal surfing history and their stories are told as long as people remember them, or in some cases, one gets his picture taken and appears in a magazine or movie. In 1961, there were no regularly published magazines. And, even when they came along about a year later, the featured surfers were from the more renowned surfing breaks: Malibu, Wind-an-Sea, and places in Hawaii. Newport, for the most part, was not on surfing's map.

Still, it is my contention that some of the world's best surfing took place right there at those perfect little beach breaks between the Pier and the River Jetties. And, while the names Kent Haworth and Rick Lowe were sure to come up when the subject of who Newport's top dog was, there was one name that would generate a much wider recognition.

Chris Marseilles epitomized the term Gremmie. Small, dark-skinned, long-haired and what every kid learning the ropes at the beach aspired to be. Cool was about a mile down the scale from Marseilles. He was cooler than cool could ever be. When he came to the beach, he was royalty. The child emperor. Young and old alike were in awe. He had an aura of greatness that commanded respect. Marseilles, although not yet 16, was the man in Newport.

As it is with most legendary figures, his reputation far preceded him. I knew all about him before I ever saw him. How he would hang ten on six-foot waves, smiling like it was nothing. How his style made everything look easy. How he turned and walked to the nose as effortlessly as he walked down the sidewalk. The guys around the fire ring made him sound like he could do anything he wanted on a wave. In fact, he pretty much could.

I remember my first time seeing him surf. He picked up about a four-foot wave at the north end of the parking lot, and before any-one said anything I knew it was Marseilles. Small guy on a big board, and that's the way I will always remember him. All the boards he rode were big. Not too big, mind you, for him.

I watched as he faded left catching the wave in a prone position and waiting a long time before he ever stood up. Then he popped up, carved a right turn, and took four quick steps to the nose. First he hung five with his foot dangling over the tip. Then as the wave jacked up, he put both feet together and hung a full ten toes over the nose.

There were no extraneous moves. No waving of the arms or arching. No Matadorian poses to awe the crowd. Just a casual walk in the park. He could have been whistling. So relaxed, nothing to it. As the wave closed out a little in front of him, he took two steps back, slipped the rail out of its groove in the middle of the wave's face, and let the board drop down and around the little section of whitewater. The added speed gave him the momentum to pass through the whitewater as if it were nothing. In a blink, he was back on the face of the wave again as it turned into a right-breaking shoulder. He took two steps back and did a cutback that was so clean and fast that it barely sent any spray. It reminded me of a cowboy on a horse and he was saying "whoa boy, good boy," to the board. The whole time, he had a smile on his face.

I think that's what I remember most about Marseilles. He surfed with pure joy. And, in doing so, he was without a doubt one of the best in the world at the time.

Small world, Small Pack
Of course, ours was a small world then. We watched from the south end of the beach never venturing north of the lifeguard tower. And for good reason. You could get hurt out there! Surfing is a territorial thing. And that's okay, because we had our own territory. We surfed the small rights coming off of the left-breaking sandbar they now call Blackies. The right is called Dorymen's , because it was, and is, out in front of where the famous Newport Dory Fishermen ply their wares selling fresh red-rock cod and spider crab to the tourists.

The waves are always small at Dorymen's. And that was okay too, because we were small. Just a bunch of grems, trying to eke out a couple of waves. (Grems was short for gremlins, which was what they called us back then. I don't know how it evolved to groms now. Go figure. Anyway, we were grems then, not groms.)

I had stopped trying to be Peter Cole and had gone on to the Malibu portal. I was now Dewey Weber, or Kemp Aaberg. Of course, Terry Smith, Kim Harp, Dennis Goff and others were also Dewey Weber and Kemp Aaberg. We would vie for each other's attention and cheer when one of us got to the nose and did a charging arch into oblivion.

On one day, a big day as I recall, one of us pups broke out of the pack. Terry Smith on his orange Ole got a perfect wave. As we all watched, Terry turned and made his move to the nose. He hung five! Better yet, he didn't immediately crash and burn, but kept going. A screaming right, all of about four feet, but definitely a charger wave. Then he did something unexpected. He backpedaled! Unheard of south of the lifeguard tower. With that, he instantly became the top dog of our group. Kind of like the first guy to climb Mount Everest or something.

We were like a little pack of pups back then. All about the same size, with the same amount of bite. And then one of the pups steps out of the pack and takes the lead. The rest destined to follow, until another steps it up and pushes the benchmark out a little further. Fun? You bet!

When we weren't trying to out-do each other in the water, we were watching the show at the Pier. And, we had pretty good seats. Like I've said, the caliber of surfing was pretty damn good in Newport. We had our heroes and our legends, and there were a few guys on the scene that will surely go down in surfing history.

Velzy Makes the Scene

That winter the legendary surfboard maker Dale Velzy moved up from San Clemente. He would cruise the parking lot in a silver Mercedes 300 SL with gull-wing doors. Oh yeah, he was cool. Always had a good-looking lady riding shotgun. He would pull up and get out to check the surf wearing shiny cowboy boots, smoking a Camel and doing a great James Dean. Every once in a while, he would go out and surf. And everyone would gather around to watch. The Hawk, as they called him, commanded an audience.

He liked Newport and that winter opened a shop there. The first was on Newport Boulevard, but within a few months, just before the next summer, he moved to a location right at the Pier. Bob Bermel and Dean Elliot ran the shop and they were classic old guys, probably in their early 20s. Both had been to Hawaii and surfed the big waves at Sunset and Waimea, and they were never lacking for stories.

We loved to hang out there after the surf had blown out and listen to the stories. The Hawk would come in from time to time and check up on sales, but mostly it was Bermel and Elliot. None of us could afford a Velzy, of course, which sort of made us a nuisance for Bermel and the Hawk. But Dean Elliot didn't seem to mind. He was a mellow guy. Years later he would become a master shaper and helped design some of the classic Harbour boards like the Cheater and Trestle Special.

But the stories we heard, or I should say overheard because they were rarely told for our benefit, were great. Big waves in Hawaii, classic days at Rincon, and out-of-control runs to Tijuana. We learned a lot about the goings-on in the world, at a tender age. Oh yeah, we heard it all. But best of all, we heard about guys like L.J. Richards and Phil Edwards, two surfers who rode for the love of surfing and avoided the limelight.

Soul, I think, has a lot to do with the surfing mystique. Doing things for the love of doing it and not for some commercial glory. Newport had a lot of that. In fact, I think that's what set it apart from other towns on the coast. It wasn't cool to be famous in Newport. Why? I don't know. It just wasn't.

I think that's why the Velzy shop was never very successful there. Velzy boards were too "in." Guys in Newport surfed Oles, Gordis and mostly Quiggs. And, the only reason they didn't all have a Quigg, was that Joe Quigg wouldn't make enough of his boards for everyone. That's another story.

By the time spring rolled around in 1961, I had a decent education in surfing. Sort of like graduating from grammar school. I could spell and add and subtract and speak the language fairly fluently. The days at the Pier had taught me the ins and outs in the lineup, nights at the Projection Booth brought the big world of surfing to us. And, the days hanging around the Velzy shop were, let's just say, very enlightening.

History casts Dale Velzy as a pioneer, and rightly so. He drove the change from balsa to foam, and had a penchant for shaping boards that were out of the ordinary. Innovative? You bet. When he was with Jacobs, as the famed "Velzy and Jacobs," he helped develop the "pig" boards and created such features as the "South Bay tail-block." By the time Velzy got to Newport, he was making boards under his own name. Velzys were, if not the Mercedes Benz of boards, at least the Cadillac.

The great thing about the Velzy shop in Newport was there were always some new and different boards to ride. And, Bermel and Elliot were pretty good about letting the guys take them out for a ride. There were "double-enders," round-tails, square-tails, and more. All beautifully laminated with solid colors, tints, stripes, anything you could imagine.

I remember one special board they called "The Potato Chip." It was small, I think about six-foot eleven or so, very thin and wide. It had a scooped-out deck with a nice little kick in the nose, like a ski. It looked like a potato chip and it had a big sticker that read: Surfboards by Velzy and Bell Brand. Do they still make Bell Brand Potato Chips anymore? Probably not, but they were big in the 1960s.

Wow, what a board. Everyone loved it. It was the talk of the beach. Easy to turn, easy to ride the nose, just plain easy to ride. Velzy or one of his guys, would bring it down to the Pier and let just about anybody ride it. Well, just about anybody. Not the gremmies from south of the lifeguard stand. We were like that caste in India, The Untouchables. So we mostly watched while guys went out and rode, never failing to come in with a smile on their face. "Great board!" They would all say.

Finally, one Saturday after the wind kicked up and the crowds had thinned, I got my chance. Joey Gallant had the Potato Chip. Joey was an older guy and established in the ranks. He had the respect of the older guys, yet he was nice enough to acknowledge that we were alive. Of course, most of his communications with us ended up in an exchange that mostly favored Joey, money-wise that is. "Hey how you guys doin'? Saw you out there today, you know you're getting pretty good." Then he might add: "Hey does anyone have a quarter, need to get some smokes..."

On this afternoon, Joey comes walking up the beach after getting some nice rides on the Potato Chip. He was all smiles. I asked about the board, and sure enough, I could ride it for a half hour if I could come up with 75 cents. That was a lot of dough for me. I mean, you could go to the show and get a coke and a candy bar for 75 cents. An evening's entertainment. Better yet, you could get a Char Burger, or a Scotty's Fish Burger, with fries and a coke, and still have change. It was a lot of dough for a short spin on the Potato Chip, but I had to do it. Even if it meant starving that afternoon and staying home with my parents on Saturday night. Oh boy, Lawrence Welk!

I scraped up the cash, by borrowing a little from my friends. I hoped I would catch a couple of waves at least after going into debt. So I hand over a fist full of coins—we used a lot of pennies in those days, pennies and Buffalo Head nickels and thin Statue of Liberty dimes. Who knew they would be collectable? Gallant handed me the board and I set out to the south side of Blackies.

The wind was blowing hard on-shore and I struggled to carry the board down to the water. It was at least 24 inches wide. No way I could get it under my arm, and carrying on top of your head was strictly for kooks. And, I was no kook now. I was going to ride the Potato Chip. Somehow, I carried it awkwardly with two hands to the water's edge and waxed it up with my trusty bar of paraffin.

It paddled fine for such a small board. I don't remember much about my first couple of waves, other than the board seemed almost magic. It caught waves and turned so easy. I took a couple of lefts, then a couple of rights. It was magic. Then, sitting outside, an afternoon set rolled in. I maneuvered into about a chin-high wave, stood up and turned right. Looking down the line, I instinctively took a step up to the nose, then without thinking about it I shuffled up to hang five. The Potato Chip started flying and it was the best feeling in the world. A magic carpet under my feet. I remember the wave turning translucent green in the afternoon sun as I rode across its face, hanging five.

It wasn't the first time I had hung five, but usually my tip rides ended in a huge splash with, you know, that dive thing off the front. But the Potato Chip wasn't crashing, and I wasn't about to dive off. The board just kept going along with me on the nose. Again, without thinking or planning or even realizing I was doing it, I backpedaled. You have to know, that for us hanging five and backpedaling was akin to breaking the sound barrier. A major accomplishment.

Like so many things in life, you struggle to attain a certain level or accomplish a goal. When you do, guess what? It's much easier the next time. In fact, I don't even remember the second time I hung five and backpedaled. All I know is once I knew I could do it; I just kept doing it. A walk in the park.

Without a doubt that was the highlight of my first winter. It's funny, I don't remember ever being cold, or getting tired. We ran on fumes then. No worries, just the pure stoke of being at the beach and getting better with every wave we rode. Always looking forward to that next wave, or the next day.

Changing Seasons, Changing Lives

June arrived too soon. June meant back to the south side of the pier for us. No surfing allowed at 22nd Street, but then the change in seasons brought the change in swell direction. The south swells of summer pass by 22nd Street. Newport was one of the first beach cities to enact surfing laws. From May 31 to September 30, surfers had to stay in restricted areas, and could only ride from 6 a.m. to noon.

The year before, we could surf all day on the south side of the pier, but they changed that. Things seldom get better, you ever notice that? Beaches don't get less crowded. The water doesn't get cleaner. Surfing spots don't get created. What's up with that?

But, back then, few of those things burdened our minds. We moved like gypsies, or migrant workers, wherever the waves beckoned. Wherever we were allowed to surf. The upper echelon took up summer residence at 38th Street. The bourgeois set up shop at 19th, where the waves were smaller, and there were more tourists to contend with. That was okay, because that meant more bottles to collect, girls to oggle and more lunches at the dozen or so places to eat. Life wasn't all bad in Newport's surfing ghetto.

Thirty-Eighth Street had no stores. The best they could do up there was when the Good Humor man came by, or the Helms Man. Do you remember Helms? If not, you missed something. Helms Trucks were from the Helms Bakery and they drove neighborhood to neighborhood selling fresh bread, rolls and a host of donuts and treats. Man, the smell of those glazed donuts in the morning.

The Helms Man had a little horn on top of the truck. Not a loud honk. More a soft whistle blending two or three tones. It had a nice sound, like the nice smells that came from the truck. Music to the ears of the hungry. Oh sure, we ran some scams on the Helms Man. Like two guys with a hand full of nickels keeping him busy on one side of the truck while a third guy swooped jelly donuts from

26

the other side. If he got wise, we'd run down the alley and slip away. Urchins? Oh yeah, the poor and starved gremmies of Newport Beach!

With school out for the summer and a winter's experience behind me, surfing took on a whole new meaning. No third-ringer me! I had survived almost a year and had earned some respect. Plus, I was going into the eighth grade. A major status upgrade. Top dogs of junior high. Of course, girls had taken on new dimension in our lives, and surfing was pure gold when it came to girls. Yep, it was going to be a good summer.

Still, riding the waves took precedence over all other interests. Going right, and walking to the nose. Going left with a drop-knee turn. Everywhere we went we were surfing. Surfing the sidewalk and hanging five on the curb. Surfing in your mother's kitchen. Surfing the walls in the living room. The world became our waves and life was all about riding the waves.

Our days began at sunrise. I hated getting up so early, but once I was up there was a lot to love. The way the early morning sun gave the seagulls a golden sheen. The sound of crisp waves breaking beneath the pier. The smells of coffee, bacon and donuts beckoning to us from the Char Burger and The Coffee Haven. A cup of hot chocolate and a cinnamon twist was an excellent way to start the day.

That was the good thing about the south side of the pier, there were lots of places to eat and interesting people to see. Like the baggy-suited bums that lived under the pier. Fishermen gathering at the end of the wharf early in the morning. And just people in general, coming to the beach, going for a walk on the pier. It was a lively place. And while the summer surf on the south side of the pier wasn't as good as 22nd Street, the waves were still fun for our little band.

We had firm control of the second ring now, and were moving toward a take over. Our group had bonded during winter days in front of the lifeguard tower. We were about a dozen strong and all about at the same level of ability. On any given day, one of us would break out and do something to become king for the day. A nose ride, a head dip, or a bad wipe-out. Fun stuff.

Masters of the Wedge

Some afternoons, after the wind had come up, we would ride our bikes down to The Wedge and go bodysurfing. I never liked The Wedge. Oh sure, it's a place to make a statement. To show your guts. To swim in troubled waters and reap the thrill of life. But, not me. My time in the water at The Wedge was focused on survival. Those waves broke hard. I mean hard. It's a wonder more people haven't been killed there.

The fun for me at The Wedge involved watching those who had mastered the art of bodysurfing. Joe Quigg, Carter Pyle, and Mickey Munoz took bodysurfing to a whole new level at The Wedge. They could catch the side-wash off the Newport jetty and surf it into the wedge-like peak. A true backdoor take-off and guaranteed tube ride. The classic deal was watching all these macho guys try to take off on the apex of the wave, only to get pitched into oblivion. Over the falls is a term that aptly describes the fate of those who shoulder-hopped the masters. Flailing? Oh yeah. Wipe-outs? The worst. Meanwhile the masters cruised in using the side-wash to gain speed and elevation to make the wave, while the beef cake want-to-bes got pitched over the falls.

We mostly hung out on the beach and watched. At least I did. I had my butt kicked enough times by waves there to render a lot of respect. Although, I have to say that certain things, physical and mental, that I learned in those tumultuous waters prepared me for later years in island surf, and I'm thankful for the experience.

The best part about going to The Wedge was, well, going to The Wedge. The bike-ride down the boardwalk checking out all the girls at 15th Street. Letting them know that we "were going to The Wedge." Yep, we were cool. Sometimes, they would buy us a Coke or some fries at the little hamburger stand on the beach at 15th. If not, we'd stop in at Terry Smith's on 14th Street. His parents were teachers and every day of the summer they were out on their boat, The Adios, fishing for Albacore.

The Smiths were good fishermen, and the cupboards at Terry's house were filled with cans of Albacore. We'd pop open two or three cans apiece and make a slew of sandwiches. Wash them down with fresh whole milk right out of the quart bottle. Mrs. Smith must have wondered about it, but she never said anything. Those were great lunches, and food was an important part of life for us.

In the evenings, we'd be back up at the pier for the LEGO, that's late evening glass-off. I've always loved surfing at sunset. The golden color of the waves with the sun shining through gives pleasure to the soul.

The Quigg Connection

On one such evening, we were out doing our little hotdog thing in some killer two-footers, when one of the guys noticed two older guys watching us from the pier. Somebody said that they were John Reynolds and Mike Marshall, both of whom worked for Joe Quigg Surfboards. I'd heard the names, but wasn't overly impressed. After all, it wasn't like Dewey Weber was up there. Still, being watched by some Quigg guys was all it took for us to turn it up a notch.

Nose rides into the sand, head dips, island pullouts, quizimotos, and coffins. Kim Harp and Terry Smith were ripping, pushing us all to the edge of our capabilities to impress the guys on the pier. Afterwards, we huddled around the fire ring trying to get warm and they walked up to us and started talking. We welcomed them to the ring and even gave them the prime spots out of the smoke. Hey, they worked for Quigg, and they were older, good surfers whose status demanded respect.

They talked about the waves at Trestles, Malibu and other far-off breaks. I hung on every word, seeing the perfect waves of places beyond our reach. Suddenly, Newport was a smaller place, and our reign at the south side of the pier was diminished. Sure, we were the kings at 19th, but that wasn't good enough. I wanted to go to Trestle in the worst way, and so did everyone else.

Terry Smith came up with the plan. We'd hitchhike, without boards, and hopefully borrow boards when we got there. Of course, we didn't exactly know where Trestles was, but it was south and we would find it. Can you imagine? I was 12, Terry and Kim were both 13, and we were hitchhiking off to a place we'd only heard about. Sure enough, the next morning at dawn we met at the pier and then walked up to the Arches, that classic old bridge over Coast Highway 101. With our trunks in our back pockets and about a buck-twenty-five between us, we stuck out our thumbs. I remember our first ride was from a lady, a mom, who picked us up because she was worried. She gave us a ride about a mile, just long enough to tell us to go back home and "don't ever hitchhike."

Oh sure, we'd heard the stories. You know, the "nice" guy who picks you up and then offers to buy some beer. Shows you pictures of things you really don't want to see and then starts to unzip his pants. As soon as you try to jump out the door, the handle comes off in your hand. It's kind of like those hook stories.

But, that didn't happen, and we, of course, ignored the nice lady's advice. Hours later, we found ourselves tired and hungry in Laguna Beach. No surfers ever stopped to pick us up, and there was no way we were going to find Trestles. Not that day. We did see Brook Street, and that was sort of famous. And, we met some sort of friendly locals at Thalia Street. It wasn't what we set out to do, but we did have an adventure, and made it back unmolested.

After that big trip "South," we stuck to 19th Street. Although we did make one variation in our routine that ultimately changed my life. Instead of going to The Wedge everyday after the morning surf, we went over to Quigg's shop on 31st Street.

Joe Quigg Surfboards and Sailboats is the stuff of legends. A small, stucco industrial building on the bay side of 31st Street where magic happened. The smells of resin and wood, the sound of a planer screaming away at foam and redwood, the fiberglass dust hanging in the air illuminated by thin shafts of afternoon sun became elements in a fascinating world.

Joe Quigg was by all accounts an innovator, master craftsman and pioneer of the modern art of surfing. More than that, a classic individual. The epitome of a man doing what he wanted to do in life. Quigg designed and built sailboats and surfboards that are a marvel to this day. I hope that someday the world of surfing recognizes him for his accomplishments and pays the long-overdue respect he deserves. But, between you and me, I don't think he even cares.

Our chance meeting with Marshall and Reynolds at the pier opened the door to Quigg's world. Well, it wasn't wide open. We were gremlins, urchins from the south side of the pier. Even the Lido Island guys were higher up in the pecking order at Quigg's. Of course, their parents had the money to buy them two or three boards a year.

Not that it mattered. Quigg only made so many boards and money never seemed to be one of his high priorities. You could order a board in June and come back in the middle of July and Quigg would give you this blank sort of look and say that he was working on it. Oh, he was nice about it. He'd even stop what ever he was doing and sit you down on the bench out in front and look at his order book. Then, you would get to go back over the order, length, width, thickness, stringers. When he was finished, you didn't care how long it took, you just wanted that board. And you left happy.

Quigg's will never go down in history as a mass production shop. Okay, understatement. But, the boards that came out of there were all special. Marshall, just a rough shaper back then, learned the craft there and became a true master. He'd rough out the blanks in the mornings, and set them on the racks for Quigg to come in and perfect them. Eventually, the boards would be glassed by a classic guy named Bones, a master in his own right. He was a tall, skinny guy, whose best days were behind him. He wore resin-stained khaki shorts and T-shirts and drank tall cans of Lucky Lager as he worked his magic with resin and fiberglass. Bones loved to talk. He would tell us stories of the early days up at Malibu and South Bay. His classic line was "grits and eggs, stick to your ribs. You want to surf all day? Eat grits and eggs."

In those first days, we were lucky to even get inside the shop. Mostly we sat out on the bench in front and read the surf magazines of the day. And, we'd watch the streams of guys as they come and go in their quest for a Quigg ride. We picked up on every bit of information available striving to become more important in this little world.

We'd say things like: "Hey, I heard Huntington was up yesterday, we should check out The Cliffs." Hoping someone would turn around and acknowledge us. Maybe take us on a surf trip.

Reynolds and Marshall would work in the mornings, then drive south in the afternoons to Trestles or Doheny. Summer nights they'd be back in the shop working. Reynolds cleaned up after Bones and did the final polishing on Quigg's works of art.

An Introduction to The Trestles
One afternoon, Terry Smith and I were on the bench out in front of Quigg's and Roger Zieger, a.k.a. Rat, pulled up in a classic 1940

Mercury. Blond hair slicked back, perfect white T-shirt and shorts. Mr. Cool. He sort of snickered at us and went inside. Awhile later, he, Marshall and Reynolds all came out with boards. There was another guy with them, Yama, who was a carbon copy of Rat. They were all headed to "Lowers." We sat there watching them when the unexpected happened. Rat said "Rim (they called Marshall Coin Rim because of his red hair) why don't we take the grems?"

Just like that we were in. Terry got to ride with Rat and Yama and I went with Marshall and Reynolds. An hour's ride down Coast Highway and another 45-minute walk through the jungle and we arrived at our ultimate destination: Trestles.

We were greeted by overhead waves in the early afternoon. Beautiful peaks outside and great lined up waves on the inside. Heaven. We were so stoked. At first, Terry and I rode the inside trying to stay out of the way. Then Reynolds coaxed us outside. The wind died down and the waves were so good. The best I'd ever ridden. I really only remember one ride. A nice peak on the outside and I did my first ever bottom turn, just like in the movies. I think I was Kemp Aberg at the time, maybe Johnny Fain.

We must have done pretty good, because from then on, we got to go on the afternoon runs. Trestle and beloved Doheny were finally in our world. Better yet, Marshall got me to order a new board. He said by the time it was done, I could sell my old board and save up enough money to pay for the new Quigg. Somehow, I did and by the end of the summer, I had a brand new Quigg. Eight-foot-eight, one-inch balsa wood stringer, clear glass job, and a cool Joe Quigg sticker. I called it "The Jet."

Moving to Newport

The Jet changed my life. Surfboards can do that you know. What a board. It turned on a dime, rode the nose forever and was all mine. I literally slept with that board. I mean it. I had it in my room and on my bed. My mom would come in and I would be standing up on it, on my bed, doing all these moves. She'd just roll her eyes.

Something else happened that summer that helped shape my life. At about the same time we started hanging out at Quigg's, I started looking for houses to rent in Newport. Don't ask me why. A 12-

year old kid has no power to get his parents to move. That is, unless he has some great parents and a dad who loves the ocean.

One day I saw a For Rent sign on a house on 32nd Street. It was two blocks from the ocean. I took all the information home to my dad. I can't remember all the logistics, but somehow we ended up moving in that summer.

That was it for me. I was no longer a roller-skating hodaddy from Costa Mesa. I was a Newport kid. Newport schools, Newport friends and Newport girls. Not that Costa Mesa girls were bad. You get the picture. And, I was two blocks from the beach, and two blocks from Quigg's. Life was good. Oh, was it good.

The house on 32nd Street had a storage room next to the garage and it became our little hangout. We called it The Weasel Room. We'd go in there after a day at the beach and just hang out. It was our own little world, where we were the kings. Sometimes at night, we would sneak girls in there and make out. But, mostly it was a place where we went to smoke cigarettes and just get away.

With my new-found status as a Newport guy and my new Quigg board, I started surfing 38th Street. Actually, the first time I went back since my fabled run-in with the goofy-foot, was one afternoon with Marshall and Rat. Walking down the beach with them gave me the acceptance I needed to paddle out.

The waves were ten times better there than the south side of the pier. Soon all of us became regulars there. My parents' house became home base. My friends all started leaving their boards in our garage and we could actually jump in the bay off of Lake Street and paddle up the channel four blocks to 36th, then walk the two blocks to the beach. That was fun. On the paddle back, after the lifeguards put up the black ball flags, we would play all sorts of games in the bay. Sliding under docks, racing, standing up and sort of wind-surfing down the channel. Not a bad way to grow up.

The First Surf Contest
I started school in September at Horace Ensign Junior High. What a great place to go to Junior High, and more important to this

Waxing up — This photo announcing the Horace Ensign surf Contest appeared in the local newspapers. Notice the quality of the boards we were riding. That's not the Jet, and notice we don't even have any wax. From left: Terry smith, Me, Joe Sanford and Pat Huggins. (Photo courtesy of Pat Huggins)

story, something took place that year that was a first in surfing history. In 1962, Horace Ensign Junior High School held the first-ever inter-scholastic surf contest.

We had a great bunch of surfers there. Kenny Kerwin, Terry Smith, Pete Sellas, Scott Chasin, Ron Bauk, Dale Kinsella, Bill Duff and more. All guys who could hang five and backpedal. We were quite a band. Probably a bunch of misfits, but likable misfits. Our P.E. coach was Hap Jacobson, a longtime Laguna Beach lifeguard. He was a tough P.E. coach, but a nice guy at the same time.

He kept a paddle in his office, and if you got out of line, you got smacked on the butt with the paddle. Once, twice, maybe three hefty swats. Yeah, we listened to what Hap had to say. You better believe it. And our parents never once threatened to sue the school if we came home with a black and blue butt. Those were the days. Oh well.

Anyway, Old Hap, or Mr. Jacobson, came up with the idea to have the contest. He organized it, set up the criteria and got celebrities to judge it. There was like a mayor and a city councilman, and Andy Devine. Remember him? Jingles on the Wild Bill Hickcock show. God knows what any of them knew about surfing, but they probably did as good a job as any damn surf contest judge. Oops, we hit a sore spot.

So we had the surf contest and a paddling race and it all came off great. It was covered by the Newport Harbor News Press and The Globe Herald. There was even a picture of the winners in Surfer Magazine. Yep, the big time. Of course, it wasn't a big picture, but there we were in the mag with Jingles. For the record, Kenny Courtney got first, I got second and Terry Smith got third.

This actually brings us to a point. Surf contests: are they good? Are they bad? Are they fair? What the hell are they about? Hanging around Quigg gave me some perspective. He was dead-set against the commercialization of surfing. He put stickers on his boards to identify them, but he wouldn't sell stickers, or even give them away. He had an advertisement in Surfer once that said: "No stickers, no T-shirts, just surfboards." It took Marshall and the guys years to talk him into making some T-shirts.

If you see a guy wearing a Joe Quigg T-shirt today, it's a guaranteed rip-off. And one not ever authorized by Quigg. Ahhh, commercialization...don't get me started.

You think Quigg ever had a surf team? No way. We got some deals on our boards, but we paid hard cash to ride for the brand. Still, some of the best surfers on the coast were riding Surfboards by Joe Quigg.

So when the subject of a surf contest would come up at Quigg's, there would be some heated discussion. He was all for paddleboard racing and, in fact, was a champion paddler, and paddleboard maker. He said "in a paddleboard race or a sailboat race, the winner is the first to cross the finish line. In a surf contest how can you tell the winner? It's subjective." Wow, I'll never forget that.

Kind of ironic though that about a year later, I was heavily involved in every surf contest I could get in. Maybe it was ego. Maybe I just craved the competition, but it was also away to travel and meet new people. I was one of only a few who ventured out of the Newport crowd to enter surfing contests, and I'm glad I did.

It opened up a new world to me. And, I got to see the best of my age group surf. Eventually, I got free surfboards and got to go to

Hawaii. So speaking of the best in my age group, there was one guy who came out of nowhere and became a legend, and I was lucky enough to see it all.

David Takes Us to School

I first heard the stories about a kid named David from my friends Dave Howard and Scotty Chasin. Each summer their parents took them to Hawaii. They sailed over on ocean liners. They had lots of stories to tell when they came back, but none more riveting than those of a skinny little Hawaiian kid who could ride the nose forever. According to Dave and Scotty, there was nothing this kid couldn't do on a surfboard.

They befriended him, and hung out with him at Waikiki. He showed them the ropes at Queens and Number Threes. In the winter 1962, David Nuuhiwa (pronounced nu-ava) moved to the mainland. First stop, Scotty Chasin's house in Newport Beach.

I'm not sure of the exact logistics, but David stayed with the Chasins while his dad, a renowned martial arts expert, set up a practice in Garden Grove. Ultimately, he formed a life-long connection with Newport, and one that none of us will ever forget. He changed the way we surfed. He changed the way we thought about surfing. And, he led me out on the road of surfing. If it were not for him showing up at that time, I'm sure my life would have been much different. Thanks David.

I remember the first time we met. Scotty brought him over to my house one winter night. We hung out on the patio and talked for hours. He was tall, skinny and was missing a front tooth. He had sort of a street-wise maturity about him. A born leader, no doubt about it.

On the following Saturday the surf was huge. A guy named Chuck Mandell, who knew David from the islands, took us all down to Doheny. It was storm surf, about six-feet and like a washing machine. I watched as David went backside doing nice drop-knee turns. Nothing special, I thought then. Boy was I in for a surprise.

In the days that followed, David started surfing the pier. Blackies more than suited for his style. A perfect, hollow, lined-up left. I watched as he became more acclimated. We didn't wear wetsuits then and the cold water must have really affected him. But then he started doing things on waves that had people jumping up and down in the parking lot, literally.

Middle-of-the-wave turns with quick steps to the nose. Squatting down while still hanging five and getting fully tubed. Big round-house cutbacks, arches, 10-over the nose. He had style, he had grace, and he had incredible agility. It was hard to out-do the Newport goofy-foots, but he did it. He took them all to school, and he was only 13.

Word spread fast up and down the coast, and soon the parking lot was full of guys we'd only read about in magazines. Mark Martinson, Corky Carroll, even Phil Edwards. I remember one day when Mickey Munoz was there with Phil. Mickey was telling Phil about David and then, as if on cue, he catches a perfect left at Blackies. David takes off deep and runs to the nose. Time stops and all eyes are watching him cruise across this glassy, green wall, hanging 10. He's there for an eternity. All of the sudden, Mickey starts jumping up and down yelling "you can't do that! You can't do that!" Well, as it turns out, he could do that, and it was only the beginning.

Big Names from Wind-an-Sea
Late that winter, a guy named Gary Cook moved to Newport from Pacific Beach. Cook, a smooth and stylish goofy-foot, had been in several magazines and won a couple of contests in San Diego. Nice guy, too. He was immediately accepted into the Newport echelon, and like everyone else, was quite taken by David's prowess on the surfboard.

When Easter Week of 1963 rolled around, a bunch of Cook's friends came to visit from La Jolla. Probably came for the famous Newport partying that used to go on during Easter Week. They called it Bal Week back then, because hordes of tourists mobbed every inch of Balboa, and Newport. The main thoroughfare, Balboa Boulevard, would be bumper-to-bumper from morning to midnight. There are lots of stories about the goings-of of Bal Week. Wild parties, wild people, wild music and wild times. And, most of it was true as I recall.

One blown-out afternoon during Bal Week, we were hanging out at my house. David was there, and we were just doing kid things like trying to reshape the nose of this old Gordie with a shovel. There was a party going on next door and over the back fence we could see a bunch of guys drinking and talking. One of them was Gary Cook. He sees us and what we're doing and he motions to his friends. They check us out and start laughing.

Then Cook tells us to come over and meet some of his friends. We stayed on my parent's side of the fence, no use getting in any trouble. Right? So, he says "guys I'd like you to meet a couple of my friends. This is Mike Diffendiffer, Butch Van Artsdalen, Dave Willingham and Mike Hynson." We look at them and say "yeah right." You have to realize, we are a bunch of little smart asses. Anyway, we call bull shit on them and they sort of get mad. Diff even takes out his wallet and shows us his I.D.

We were still skeptical. Plus, we'd never even heard about any Mike Hynson. That upset them even more. So Diff says that if we don't believe them we should come with them to the premier of a John Severson movie that night and see all of them on the big screen. We say: "Is it free?"

Sure enough, that evening we all pile into Diff's stationwagon and go down to Laguna Beach High School to see "Going My Wave". John Severson, himself, let us in. We were all somebody's little brother. Okay, you're probably thinking what kind of parents would let their 14-year-old boys go down to Laguna with a bunch of 20-somethings who had been drinking all day. Well, it was just a different time, that's all. I wouldn't do it today with my kids. No way. But that was the way it was then.

What a heady night for us walking in with a bunch of big-name surfers. The movie, indeed, starred all the guys we were with. The highlight came when they all went out at Pipeline. It was only the second time anyone had ever ridden the wave. Phil rode one wave there for a Bruce Brown movie, but he really just rode the wave in survival mode. This time, these guys ripped it. Willingham and Hynson going backside on huge waves. And, of course, Butch getting the tube ride that defined tube riding at the time. When the movie was over, we were all believers. And, Hynson became one of our new heroes.

That night helped set the stage for what came next. Actually, it took a while. It was the following summer, when those same guys and their friends formed Wind-an-Sea Surf Club for the first-ever Malibu Surf Contest. No, I wasn't on that infamous bus-ride, nor was David or any other junior for that matter. Good thing too, from what I hear.

Okay, I should explain that for those of you who have not heard about "the bus ride." The story goes something like this. The wild bunch at Wind-an-Sea decided they wanted to surf in the first-ever club contest at Malibu. Hey, it was Malibu! So, they formed a surf club on the spot, and rented a bus to drive them to the contest. What went on during the bus ride has grown to legendary proportion. Let's just say, they all had a really fun time and, miraculously, were still able to win the contest the next day!

Actually, after Wind-an-Sea's success in the contest, the crew got the idea to form a real surf club. A respectable surf club.

This was at a time when surfing was considered sort of a degenerate life style. The whole surf bum thing, probably extenuated by the character Kahuna in the movie Gidget. Society had a rather dim view of surfers in general. Our parents, for the most part, thought surfing was a phase and that we'd grow out of it. So much for that.

Wind-an-Sea Surf Club
Wind-an-Sea Surf Club, a titan at the Malibu Contest, became an instant force. Surf clubs were not yet popular. Mostly cliques of locals who had somehow pooled enough money to buy jackets or sweatshirts. Newport had the Newport Surfers in the early '60s. There were also the Dapper Dans from South Bay, Swami's from Encinitas, and there were a few others.

Wind-an-Sea President Chuck Hasley was quick to see that a sustained effort might help improve the surfing image. Of course, he wanted to have fun, too. And, Wind-an-Sea Surf Club was always fun. Chuck helped organize a junior division. He gave senior members the task of hand-picking a crop of hot up-and-comers to join the club. Gary Cook was one of the Wind-an-Sea Seniors.

Cook, still living in Newport, asked David and I to join. It was a giant step in a direction that led me away from my Newport surfing roots.

Other junior surfers from up and down the coast were asked to join, again hand-picked by one of the Wind-an-Sea seniors. We got word to report to a meeting in Pacific Beach at a restaurant called Uncle Suzie's. It would be a long trip, on a school night if I remember right. My parents were supportive, as always, and somehow my dad arranged to car pool with some of the other parents. I don't remember how David got there, but I rode down with Howard Chapleau and Billy Hamilton. My dad and I drove down to Laguna and from there we all piled into one car with Billy's mom driving.

What a ride. I knew Billy and Howard from the beach, although not that well. Howard was a little older and was one of the kings of Doheny. Great drop-knee cutbacks. Billy was my age. Billy could do it all, and, just to piss guys like me off, he always had this big smile on his face. I remember surfing with him at Doheny, and he'd run up and hang ten, big smile, just looking at the rest of us as if to say "top that!." It was a good show. Yeah, he had style, and still does.

That ride down to Uncle Suzie's took forever. No freeway in those days. Down the coast highway through Blood Alley, the stretch of road from San Clemente to Oceanside. It was three lanes. Cars going either direction could use the middle lane to pass. Oh yeah, it was named appropriately. Head-ons were an everyday deal on Blood Alley. Then you had to go through all the little towns in North San Diego County. Oceanside, Carlsbad, Leucadia, Encinitas, Cardiff, Del Mar. They just seemed to go on and on. Torrey Pines Grade was a big deal back then. It was a giant hill, that cars and trucks had to chug up. Finally, you went over the top and down to La Jolla and Pacific Beach.

We were beat by the time we got there, but then the pure energy of the group took over. Man, what a scene. Here were about 20 or 25 of the hottest kids on the coast all in one room. Peter Johnson, Dickie Moon, David Rullo, Jon Close, Larry Strada, Francis Thompson, Hank Warner, Hugh McIntosh, Ricky Ryan, Denny Tomkins, Mark Hammond and Curt Slater, just to name a few.

What a night. The energy was unbelievable. Probably the most famous junior then was Peter Johnson. He had been featured in the movies surfing Waimea Bay when he was about 11. And, of course, he was known as Phil's protégé. But, in that room, he was just one of the gang. Everybody was hot. Everybody had something to prove. What a great feeling.

We not only formed a pretty good surf club that night, we formed bonds that will forever hold us together. Those of us that are still alive will always have a special feeling for each other. Like I've said, the bonds of surfing last a lifetime.

Under the direction of President Chuck Hasley and advisor Thor Svenson, we created the Wind-an-Sea Club Junior Division. Jon Close was elected president. Our agenda was to dominate the USSA surfing contest circuit, and for awhile we did just that. Contests became the focus, and my parents would drive me up and down the coast every weekend to surf. Everywhere we went, the Wind-an-Sea juniors made an impression. And, we had fun.

The Juniors Take Makaha

The highlight of that year was going to Makaha to surf in the world's most prestigious surfing contest. Makaha, of course, is the world famous big-wave surfing spot on the west shore of Oahu in Hawaii. Thor Svenson organized a raffle and we all sold tickets to earn our way there. It was kind of hard for those of us up the coast to sell tickets for a raffle in San Diego. I think I only sold two, so my parents chipped in, as did Dr. Nuuhiwa. In the end, both David and I got to go. Oh what a trip that was.

It started at old Lindbergh Field in San Diego (Now San Diego International Airport). My parents dropped me off in the care of our chaperones, the Senior division. Butch, Hasley, Root Swan were all there. Not all the juniors got to go, but most of us made it. Peter, David, Dickie Moon, Huey McIntosh, Ricky Ryan, Rullo, Close, Strada. We took off about midnight headed for Honolulu on a chartered Saturn Airlines propjet.

Jet, my ass! It was what they called a rubber-band airplane. Fourteen hours of drowning propellers and tight accommodations. Can you imagine? All of us kids having pillow fights and food fights up front, while all the seniors sipped cocktails and flirted with the stewardesses in the back. It was a scene. Nobody got any sleep.

I remember being glued to the window all the next morning trying to catch a glimpse of the islands. Sometime the next day, we landed in Honolulu. Aloha. Yeah, the Hawaiian girls were all there in hula skirts, putting leis around our necks and giving us kisses. You should have seen Butch lay a huge kiss on this one hula girl.

They piled all of us juniors on a school bus and headed out to the west side. That was about a two-hour ride in itself. Still, with the adrenaline pumping, we were feeling no pain. In fact, even though we were staying in Wainae, we talked the bus driver into driving us straight out to Makaha, just to check it out.

When the bus pulled up in front of the surf spot, we all ganged to the windows. The surf was just like I'd remembered in the surf movies. About six-foot, beautiful aqua green waves, with a huge backwash. It was crowded. Really crowded. We watched a couple of waves and then saw this one guy really ripping, super style, radical cutbacks. Petey Johnson immediately identified the rider as Phil Edwards. We were impressed. Actually, later we learned that Phil hadn't even made it over yet. The rider was a young Australian nobody had ever heard of, Nat Young.

Later that afternoon, we arrived at the Wainai Church Camp and got word that getting to and from Makaha was going to be a problem. There would be a bus once a day. Other than that we were to hitchhike out there two or three at a time. Thor gave us small tokens of a little wooden foot, with the big toe sticking up. Hawaiian good luck charm for hitchhiking. Can you believe it?

That first afternoon there was no way any of us could get to Makaha, so we went exploring. Sure enough, we found surf. Pokai Bay was some type of military installation that had a nice beach. It had a little reef break outside. Kind of mushy with not much shape, but we attacked. The waves were thicker than mainland waves and they moved to the beach with more speed. We all had a little trouble judging the waves at first. It wasn't good surf, but there was something about the place, the warm water, the color in the afternoon that was way different, and very exciting. It sort of set the tone for what was to come.

Dave Rullo got the wave of the day. A clean four-footer on the outside. He ripped it up pretty good and the next thing you know, we were calling him the King of Pokai. After we all surfed, we gathered on the beach. I remember everyone kind of checking each other out. Most of the guys had new boards, made just for the trip. Many were already sponsored by board makers.

I wasn't. I was riding my second Jet board, which I'd had for about six months. It was nine-two and a little beat up. Actually, Quigg had done a little remodel job on the nose. He cut about two feet off the front and shaped a new, more pointed tip. It had some additional belly to it as well as some more kick in the front. I was stoked when he did it, but that afternoon, looking at all the new boards, I felt like I was wearing hand-me-downs. There was some comments, but I shrugged them off. Tough crowd.

There was an odd feeling that afternoon. Here we were a bunch of guys from all up and down the coast who hardly new each other, thrust into a situation 3,000 miles from home. Youngsters from different tribes, come together. Mark Hammond and Erik Murphy from Santa Barbara. Denny Tompkins from the South Bay, Jeff George from Malibu and David and I from Orange County. Most were from San Diego: Dickie Moon, Dave Rullo, and Larry Strada from the Shores. Francis Thompson, Curt Slater and Steve Jenner from Pacific Beach. Brad Owens and Hank Warner also from PB. Hugh McIntosh and Ricky Ryan from Ocean Beach.

We stayed at the Wainai Church Camp sleeping five or six to a room. It didn't take long to form alliances and give each other nick names. Soon we were banding about, playing pranks on each other's rooms.

Dinner with the Duke
On the first night, they bused us all to Waikiki to eat dinner at Duke Kamanamoku's famous restaurant in the International Market Place. Man, was that fine. Duke was there and the Martin Denny Band was playing "Quiet Night." The food was Luau style and really good. That night, they passed out our team gear: Wind-an-Sea T-shirts, red trunks with club patches and a whole bunch of other stuff, like the little wooden foot I mentioned. It was a grab bag full of goodies.

Thor Svenson gave the juniors a talk about conduct and how we were representatives of surfing. I didn't know what to think about Thor then. He was a small guy, probably in his 40s. He had dyed blond hair and wore a crew cut. Obviously not a surfer, but some how drawn to the surf culture. He was very good at what he did, and that was to organize and direct.

He orchestrated us. Told us what to do, how to act. He was the one who gave us the schedules, planned field trips to "Town" and the North Shore. He was strict and he had a way of talking to you that was very serious when you screwed up. He was a good guy though, and worked well with what had to be an outrageous band of wild kids.

The tone was set that first night at Duke Kamanamoku's. We were going to be a well-oiled surfing machine and we were going to show the world that surfers were good citizens. That, according to Thor.

The next few days we split our time between Pokai Bay and Makaha. The days at Makaha were great. The surf was usually about head high to slightly overhead. We watched as Buffalo, the legendary Hawaiian surfer, and his family of friends just ripped the place. I've never seen one guy have one spot so wired as Buffalo at Makaha. It was like he and the wave were of the same energy. He just flowed with the wave and knew exactly when to do things. Unbelievable.

We saw a lot of great surfing. Nat Young, Barry Kanaiapuni, Fred Hemmings were all in the outer limits, and guess what? They were all surfing in the Junior Division! Yep, Makaha Juniors were 18 and under. Maybe 17 and under, but whatever, all three of them were in the Juniors.

That kind of dampened our spirits a little. Even David was out-classed by these guys at Makaha. So we set our sites on having fun, and that we did. Learning how to turn around the back wash, and just enjoying the great speed of the Hawaiian waves. It was like the board became alive under your feet. Turning, nose riding, everything was easier.

Then the day came. Contest day. We arrived at Makaha early in the morning, the waves were the biggest we'd seen all week. A solid 10 foot. Point Surf as they called it. A whole new ball game. We watched in awe as Fred Hemmings rode a huge wave all the way from the outside point through the infamous Makaha bowl.

I never even knew what a "bowl" was, but I found out quickly that it was a place in the wave caused by a shallow spot in the reef. A bowl typically jacks up higher and throws out further than the rest of the wave. At Makaha, you had to rush through it before it broke, or straighten out in the soup. Nothing on the mainland had prepared us for a 10-foot Makaha bowl looming like a giant claw at the end of the wave.

Somehow we mustered up the courage to go out in our heats. I should say I mustered up the courage. Many of the San Diego guys were ready for it. I'd never been in waves this big. My big surf experience was limited to one day at Sea Side Reef in Cardiff that was about eight feet. Still, in the spirit of the day, I went out when my heat was called.

Francis Thompson became a close friend that day. He was experienced and so damn funny and relaxed about it all that it helped me forget my fears. There were lifeguards out in the water. Big Hawaiian guys on huge tandem boards. Some were in the channel and some were out on the point. They told us where to go, and what to watch for on the horizon.

I listened to them and managed to paddle out around the bowl. I didn't want to go way out on the point, my plan was to sit as far outside as I could get and then paddle in when the heat ended. Good plan. But then a set came cranking around the point. I just remember these huge green walls. I paddled over the first one. There were a couple of guys outside of me and two of them swung their boards around to take off. I thought the wave was going to break on me, which wouldn't have been a real bad thing. Hey, if I survived the wipe-out, I could swim in with no shame.

The guys paddling for the wave couldn't catch it, and one of them yelled at me to go. I don't know what exactly happened except that I was suddenly turning my board around and stroking in to the biggest wave I'd ever even seen. That out-of-body thing again. A little terrified voice inside of my head screaming "what are you doing?" Then the body just taking over. "All hands on deck...battle stations."

I couldn't believe the feeling of catching that wave. The speed, the wind. I did my Peter Cole stance, this time it was entirely appropriate. The drop was iffy. Like jumping off a two-story building and trying to keep your balance through the air. My trusty Jet board hung in there and I made it to the bottom of the wave in tact. I turned and was flying—I mean it—flying across this big wall. A few seconds of pure ecstasy. Oh what a great feeling. Then I see the famous Makaha Bowl waiting for me at the end of the line like a big cat, ready to reach out and smash me with its claw. I slid down the face and made it as far as I could before straightening off.

Makaha Rules

The rules of the contest, Makaha Rules, took points off if you touched your board so I remained standing and widened my stance. The soup hit me and knocked me back, but some how I made it out still on my feet. I could see the calm water of channel ahead so I leaned in and bombed the whitewater in that direction. Somehow I emerged on this really nice eight-foot shoulder. I made a cutback, then a bottom turn and another cut back. Hey, this was fun!

Wind and Sea at Makaha — This is one of my favorite pictures. Taken by Tom Keck at Makaha, this is most of the team that went to the contest that year. It included some of the best surfers in the world. Thor asked us to wear our T-shirts backwards for the photo. The seniors went without shirts, and our rebel, Jon Close, didn't turn his around. (Please forgive any misspelling of names) From top left: Princess in chair, Hank Warner, Steve Jenner, Dave Rullo, Dickie Moon with Thor behind him, Peter Johnson, Butch Van Artsdalen, Ricky Ryan, Denny Tomkins, Joey Hamasaki, Rusty Miller, Linda Benson, Rod Surprizio Second row from top, from left: Loren "Root" Swan, Mickey Munoz, Joey Cabell, The Duke, Jeff Geroge, Mark Hammond, Herb Torrens, Judy Dibble, Marilyn Malcome, Curt Slater, Francis Thompson. Front row from left: Larry Strada, Howard Chapelo, Dale Keeler/Dobson, Jon Close, Brad Owens, Mike Brner, Huey Macintosh, Don Schmidt, David Nuuhiwa and unknown.

I rode that baby all the way to the shorebreak and even walked up and hung five before the end of the ride. It was the greatest feeling. I stroked back out the channel, actually hoping to get another ride. I was about half way to the bowl when another big set came through. One of the lifeguards in the channel looked at me then told me to paddle over toward him. I did, and then he instructed me to cut across the break a little and pick up one of the shoulders if no one was on it.

That was scary, but I followed his instructions and sure enough I got a nice big shoulder and rode it in. Drop-knee cutbacks and big bottom turns. It was great. I got one or two more just like it and never did get back outside again. At the end of the heat I came in and was very stoked.

A couple of the guys came up and I told them all about catching the inside waves. At the end of the day, we got the heat results. Four of us had made it into the semi-finals: Francis Thompson, Curt Slater, Mark Hammond and me. It was pretty cool, for a brief moment there, actually about two days, we were the kings of the juniors. No one was making fun of my Jet board anymore.

On the morning of the semis, I remember waking up and thinking about what I was going to do. I was laying in my bunk when someone came in to the room and said that the surf had come up. Come up? Oh man, how big was it? It was big.

When we got to the beach, we saw solid 15-foot point surf. They were talking about postponing the juniors, which I was all in favor of, but I'm pretty sure Fred Hemmings talked the judges into running the heats. It was his kind of surf and he was a local boy.

I'll never forget putting my jersey on and waxing my board that day at Makaha. I had to piss really bad. Nerves? Heck yes. I peed my pants and it was all I could do to try and hide the big wet spot as I was running down the beach to jump in the water.

This time I wasn't even going to try and make it outside. I didn't want any part of those monsters out there. Francis Thompson was with me again, and I had told him about my plan. I was going to hang in the channel and when a set came in, I would cut across in front of the bowl and catch a big shoulder. Good plan, right?

Well, Francis thought so. We were there straddling our boards when this huge set comes around the point. We made our move, but miscalculated the size and power of the waves. When surf gets big, the whole line-up can change fast. So, here's Francis and I paddling across in front of this big set. We were smiling and all stoked. Then the first wave looms out of the deep water. I looked over at Francis and his eyes are bugging out. I'm sure I had a similar look on my face.

We both realized that we had made a huge mistake. The wave exploded about 20 yards in front of us. We were definitely screwed. There was nothing to do but dive off our boards and get as deep as we could. The classic move for that was to stand up on your board and then dive off. Francis was about 20 feet further out than I when we both stood up on our boards preparing to dive. The last thing I saw was Francis standing up and then tripping on his foot. He fell on his board and got eaten alive by the soup. I dove and swam as deep as I could. The soup was killer. It was like a monster with huge arms coming down from the sky and grabbing me. Then I was being tossed about and dragged. My lungs were exploding. The pure violence of nature.

After an eternity of being thrashed around, I flailed up to the surface. I looked around and no Francis. Then a couple of seconds later here comes this brown head popping out of thick foam, and its Francis. Man, you should have seen his eyes. Like silver dollars! Then we both laughed. The next soup got us again, and it wasn't as bad as the first. I guess we'd been swept in a good distance. We made it to the beach, and saw both our boards being swept out to sea in a huge rip. They were headed for this big point south of Makaha called Clausmeyers.

Somehow we managed to swim out and get our boards, but that was all for the contest. We were out, but we had some stories to tell. The surf kept coming up and up.

The next day they planned to run the men's division. It was huge. Twenty-foot Makaha Point Surf, what a sight to see. We all climbed up the judges towers to get a view. Oh man, it was scary. That point I mentioned, Clausmeyers, it had morphed into what they call a cloud break, because the waves break out so far they look like clouds. We heard that Phil Edwards had lost his board on a big wave and that it had drifted all the way out to Clausmeyers and broken in half. Phil was out.

The one guy who really ripped that day was Mickey Munoz. He caught some huge waves. Joey Cabell was good, too. They both surfed for Wind-an-Sea, and Joey ended up winning the men's division.

The junior final was held days later in smaller surf, the kind we all would have loved, and Fred Hemmings won.

The day after the contest, they bused us all into town and we got to surf Waikiki. It was wintertime, of course, and there wasn't much surf. But we had a great time just being on hallowed ground. Diamond Head reaching up to a dark blue sky. Clear, warm water. The hotels lining the beach. We were charged and ended up paddling all the way out to Number Threes, just for the fun of it. It didn't take much to make us happy, and the occasional three-footer that came through would be attacked by a dozen whip-cut gremmies with red trunks.

That night, a famous local photographer, Clarence Maki, had a party for us at his house and Duke Kamanamoku was there. I'm assuming you know who the Duke was. If not, let me just say that he was a Hawaiian legend. Make that surfing legend. Oh hell, he was legend of legends. I mean it. He helped introduce surfing to California in the first part of the 20th Century. He won Gold Medals for swimming in the Olympics. He made movies with Johnny Wisemiller, who also was a Gold Medal Olympic swimmer and played Tarzan. The Duke. One of a kind. Real man. Real surfer.

Anyway, there we all were with the Duke himself holding court. Great party. Hawaiian style. There was kalua pig and lome lome salmon and poi. And, we all got to wear lava lavas. You know, those little wrap-around skirts. Okay, they made us wear them. Clarence took our pictures with Duke, a couple of which made it back home to appear in the local newspapers. Pretty cool. I remember Duke being very soft spoken and humble in a way. Yet, he had an aura of royalty. The look in his eyes when he smiled, the smooth texture of his voice, his wavy white hair, the Duke was an icon and we were all honored to be in his presence.

A couple of days later, we got to go to the North Shore. Thor rented two vans to take us there with our boards. We were charged, but when we came over the top of the hill and caught our first glimpse of Haleiwa, our excitement turned to shock. It was closed-out. Meaning, the waves were breaking out so far that none of the regular spots would be rideable. A huge north swell on a blustery side-wind-type day. Pete Johnson told us the only place we would be able to get in the water was, you guessed it, Waimea Bay. Oh man, I already had enough of big surf.

Of course, that's where Petey Johnson had made his name. So it looked like we might all be talked into going out there. We looked at Haleiwa first. No way. It was closed out, and outside there was this big cloud break they called Avalanche. Yeah, they surf it now, but this was before jet skis, and cords. You had to be crazy to go out there. Maybe you still do.

We made our way out to Waimea and were kind of surprised to find a sort of peaceful little bay with just a few waves breaking off the point. It didn't look so bad, at first. A closer look showed a horrendous shorebreak, which meant the waves outside were bigger than they looked. Much bigger.

Petey was Right

We hiked out on to the point and gathered at a spot where we could see the outside waves. There was no one out, so it was hard to tell how big they were. Petey said they were 15-plus, but then someone said no way. An argument broke out with Petey getting really mad. We must have been arguing for about 15 minutes out there when some one suddenly jumped up and said there was a guy paddling out.

A set came wrapping around the point and we strained our eyes for a glimpse of the lone surfer braving Waimea. We saw him paddle up a wave that had to be four or five times overhead. Then someone said, "Hey, that's Strada!"

Strada? We looked at each other. Larry Strada had been with us when we started the argument about the waves, then he just sort of disappeared. So, here's Strada scratching to get out over this set. And we were all jumping up and down. Petey was yelling "I told you so."

Luckily Strada made it out without getting caught inside. Then one of the seniors, Mike Burner, grabbed a board and paddled out. We couldn't believe it, Larry Strada paddled out alone at Waimea, and Burner went out to see if he needed any help. Burner got outside and then they both ended up paddling in without catching a wave. I always wondered what they said to each other out there.

There was no way anyone else was going out, so we went up the valley to Waimea Falls and jumped off the cliff. It was fun, but man that water was cold. Colder than the mainland water in winter.

That afternoon, we were on our way back to Wainai when we saw that the huge surf on the North Shore was also wrapping down the west side of the Island. We stopped at a place called Maili Beach, made famous by Phil Edwards and Mike Hynson in Bruce Brown's "Surfing Hollow Days." It turned out to be the best surf of the entire trip. Perfect four-to six-foot rights with the sun shining through the back of the waves. We surfed until dark. That was what Hawaii was all about.

Those two weeks in Hawaii seemed like a lifetime. We all returned to the coast with a different attitude. Some how much older than when we left. We'd seen the big waves, felt the majesty of Hawaii and shared times that none of us would ever forget.

Team Rider
Back on the coast, Wind-an-Sea Surf Club continued to set the benchmark for contest surfing. As members, we were required to surf in as many contests as possible and conduct ourselves accordingly. Well, for the most part anyway.

Looking back, I've always had mixed emotions about surfing contests. But, in that era, contests were part of life on the surfing path. They took you places, introduced you to people, and gave you opportunities that you wouldn't have otherwise.

On one such weekend, I was at San Clemente. A town close to home for me. My dad took me down on Saturday, and much to my surprise, I actually won my heat. That meant another trip down on Sunday, but my dad was busy. I talked a couple of Newport guys into taking me. Bob Bouchard and John Humphries were older guys, good surfers and tried-and-true Newport surfers. And, like most Newport surfers they didn't care much for surf contests. Still, they were up for seeing friends and checking out the action. Girls mostly.

I wore my red Wind-an-Sea shorts, but I didn't wear my club T-shirt. I didn't want to piss my friends off. They lectured me on the way down about not getting a big head. I wasn't worried, I'd never made it out of my heat before. Well, except for Makaha, and that really was pure luck. Being in the right place at the right time. That's kind of what life's about, isn't it?

David Nuuhiwa had started winning most of the contests he rode in by this time, and he was the favorite at San Clemente. Of course, the week before at Huntington, he lost to an Australian named Rodney Sumptor. I guess Rodney was actually a Brit, who had moved to Australia, but he was good. No matter where he came from.

I remember watching David do this new maneuver that morning. He called it a Roller Coaster. Off the bottom, hitting the lip and then floating down. In my mind, he was the first to do it. Maybe not, but he was doing it all day that day and everyone was amazed. You have to remember, we were all riding these 30-pound logs, that just didn't whip around. Unless you were David Nuuhiwa. Then your surfboard did what ever you told it do. At least that's the way I remember it.

My semi-final heat was held in the late morning and there were some good guys in it, including Greg Tucker from Long Beach. Tucker was a fun guy. Older and bigger than me, and yeah, better too. Somehow I ended up taking the heat that day and low and behold I was headed for the final.

An interesting course of events occurred that day. Before the semi final, Tommy Leonardo, a red-hot goofy-foot from Huntington, asked me if I'd like to meet Dewey Weber. He said that maybe I could get on the Weber Surf Team, meaning free surfboards. I still had my Jet board, which I loved, but she was getting old. So Tommy takes me up on the Pier and we walk up to Dewey. He's all smiles for his rider Tommy, but barely gives me the time of day. I eventually got to know Dewey and he was a good guy, but that day he didn't have any time for a skinny little no-name gremmie like me.

So, I go out and win my semi-final and am headed for the finals. One of the guys I'd recently met on the contest circuit was Mike Stevenson. He rode on the Jacobs Surf Team and man they had cool shirts. All white, with a blue competition band going around the chest, big Jacobs Surf Team logo on the back and your name on the front. Mike asked me if I wanted to meet Henry Ford, captain of the team. I thought "Oh no, here we go again," but I went along with him anyway. Hey, I was star struck because I'd seen Henry in the movies.

We found him on the beach, and guess what, he was actually really nice. He said that he'd seen me surf and was impressed. Then he asked me if I'd like to be sponsored by Jacobs. I couldn't believe it. Jacobs. Free boards, cool shirt, and trunks. I agreed immediately and made arrangements to come up and see him in South Bay the next week. I'd find a way up there, no matter what.

Before the final, one of the funniest things I've ever seen happened. Corky Carroll and his partner were in the tandem finals. All the finals were on the north side of the pier and I was on the pier watching, mostly checking the waves out, but somewhat interested. Now, if you don't already know, Corky has always been known as much for his showmanship as his prowess at surfing. He was a great surfer of the time, and he was something of a clown on the beach. He went on to star in several beer commercials and has made quite a career out of being a celebrity.

So Corky and tandem partner are out bobbing in the waves when a set comes in. They pick the last and largest wave of the set and he goes to hoist her up when he misses his grip and drops her. Well, she falls into the wave and gets swept in with the soup toward the beach. But, instead of going in to get her, he lays on the board and motions for her to swim back out.

He's got his head resting on his elbow and his feet crossed, like he's lounging in a chair, playing it up for the crowd. Everyone was laughing and he was eating it up. Meanwhile another set of waves was sneaking in behind him. He's focused on his act and oblivious to all else around him. Good old Mother Nature. A four-foot wall breaks right on his head and he gets slammed. Talk about being upstaged.

I can't remember everybody in the junior final that day, but there was Rodney Sumpter, David Nuuhiwa, and Steve Slickameyer. All hot. I just went out to have some fun, and I did. I really didn't pay too much attention to how everyone else was doing, so when it was over, I figured I got fifth or sixth. Hey, I was happy just to be there.

Later, just before they started the awards ceremony, Thor comes up to me and says "Don't forget to wear your Wind-an-Sea Surf Club shirt when you go up there. I thought "up there?" What was he talking about. Then he tells me I got second, I couldn't believe it. He sort of took the fun out of it, but still, I was in shock. In retrospect, Thor seemed to always find out who won a contest before they announced it. I think that was part of his job.

Rodney Sumptor won it, and I think Slickameyer got third. I don't know what happened to David, he got like fourth or fifth that day. Go figure.

What a day, I got asked to join the Jacobs Surf Team and won a trophy to boot. So I get my trophy and no sooner than I get off the stage and guess who runs up to me? Dewey Weber. "Hey Herbie, why don't you come up to the shop and we'll fix you up with some boards." I can't remember what I said, but I remember thinking "No way." like I said, I got to know Dewey better years later and we was a great guy. But back then, he was in the surf business, and the surf business was a hustle.

The ride back to Newport that day was bitter sweet. Bouchard and Humphries made me sit in the back seat and totally ignored me. Especially after hearing that I was going to get a board from Jacobs. Almost a sacrilegious move in Newport. It made me feel a little weird. I was breaking the mold.

The next week, I went up to the Jacobs surf shop with David. He had started riding for Jacobs a couple of months earlier, and Donald Takayama made all his boards. Donald was there and took me through the showroom. It was huge and there were boards of every shape and color. He said "pick out one you like." Man, talk about a kid in a candy store. It was almost worth all the commentary I'd been getting from my friends at home.

David helped me pick out a pretty cool board. It had brown rails and a competition stripe. Big Jacobs sticker. It was a pretty good board too, but it didn't come close to riding like my Jet board. I made do with it though, and hey, I had a couple of Jacobs Surf Team shirts with "H Torrens" on the front. "Hey, look at me, I'm H. Torrens."

Going-Right — Late afternoons at the pier were heaven for a kid who could think of nothing but the nose. This picture of me was one of the first published in "Surfer Magazine." (Photo by Brian Lewis)

Baking at Lower Trestles

Before long I started getting pictures in Surfer, and I was making a name for myself on the USSA circuit. It was a good time. I got to go surfing almost everyday. And people were nice to me. Guys I never even knew were asking me If I wanted to go to Malibu or San Diego. For the most part I stuck with my Newport crew. I did make lasting friendships, with out-of-town guys, including Mark Martinson and Corky Carroll.

Before David came over, Corky was pretty much the hottest guy around. He was never a stylist, in my mind, but he could walk the walk. I remember seeing him up at Anderson Street in Surfside. Man he had that place wired. Hanging ten like it was nothing.

Mark was much more of stylist, and every bit a technician. More than that, he was a really cool guy. He had the name and the talent, but he was always modest. Just one of the guys. He had this old red Chevy station wagon that he would drive to Lower Trestles.

He would show up at my house unannounced, and ask "want to go to Trestles?" I'd say sure, and off we'd go. Sometimes Greg Tucker would be with him, other times Bubby Hill, or both. We would always stop in South Laguna to see if Billy Hamilton wanted to go. Man we had a good crew.

We'd come down to Lowers and get everybody going. Hamilton and I would be dueling on the inside, Mark and Tucker hogging the outside peaks. It was fun stuff. The crew at Trestles were no slouches. The good surfers mostly came from either Newport or Huntington or Long Beach. Sure there were exceptions, but day in day out, it was guys like John Reynolds, Roger Zieger, Chris Marseilles and Mike Marshall from Newport along with Martinson, Steve Pezman, Tucker, the Kuntz brothers, and others who dominated. I spent a lot of great days at The Trestles.

I remember one day someone said there was some hot new kid out from Huntington. Herbie Fletcher, I checked him out and he was pretty good. One-of-a-kind style. For some reason, I always wanted to be called "Herb" instead of Herbie. Fletcher didn't care about his name. We became friends and ended up surfing against each other in contests many times. One year I took fourth in the Triple A division, and he finished fifth. The following year, he was fourth and I was fifth. Of course, David was always first, and rightly so.

Did you know there was another famous Herb at the time? Well, he didn't use his real name, which was Herbert Peter Johnson. Yep, Petey Johnson was really a Herb too.

 But, back to the Trestles. The thing about that place was, it always had waves. And, when the waves were good, they were really good. Not perfect, mind you, not Malibu or Rincon perfect. You had to pick your wave, and ride through long sections, and get caught inside while paddling out. It made you surf better and know the ocean better than any of those perfect spots on the coast.

And, like many a good surf spot, there was a price to pay for surfing. At Trestles, the price included a long walk with a heavy board and the constant threat of being caught by the Marines. Never-the-less, on any given day, there would be 20 or 30 guys in the water and on the beach.

The Marines tried everything to stop us. They came by jeep up the beach or they'd launch surprise attacks from the jungle behind the beach. And, occasionally they would be successful in catching a couple of stragglers or neophytes. Mostly, we'd just all paddle out and wait for them to leave.

Low tide was the worst. If you were on the beach and they got a good jump on you, it was tough getting over the rocks and out to safety. Especially when they had on their boots, and you were running, barefoot, with a 30 pound board.

In those days, there were so many different ways to get in. You could park up on Old 101 by the Del Cannon shop and walk down the road. They would put fences up, but we'd just climb over. Or, if you could walk through the old Cottons property and then down the beach. It seemed like the way in was always changing. Someone would have a key to a gate and you could drive on base and stash the car in the Jungle. Or get dropped off by the overpass, slide down the hill and make a straight run for the beach. Of course, that meant the driver would have to go back and park the car and then walk the long way in.

I got caught a couple of times. One day when they came at us from the jungle at low tide, I slipped and fell. They got me and a bunch of others. Busted at the Trestle. Not good. They impounded our boards, and to add insult to injury, they stabbed them with their bayonets. Yep, they stabbed my cool new Jacobs right through the middle. It got worse, though. If you were a minor, they made you bring your parents to Oceanside and meet with the Provost Marshall before you could get your board back.

Worse yet, they would show your parents, in my case it was my mom, pictures of guys "browning out" the train. You know, I really don't remember anybody ever dropping their shorts when the train went by, but I guess it happened. Hey, they had pictures. My mom made me promise to never go back to Trestles. Sorry mom.

One time, we were leaving in the late afternoon. Our car was parked deep in the jungle, and we were going out through this newly made trail, when we heard the whine of a Marine Jeep coming down a nearby road. We stopped in our tracks and were silent, and then the jeep stopped. They had seen our trail where it crossed the dirt road. We heard them talking and then they started coming down the trail. I was with three other guys, and the two closest to the beach beat it for the safety of the water. I was stuck, so I jumped into some bushes. Turns out the bushes were nettles. Here I was huddled in a briar patch of stickers and thorns trying to be quiet while the Marines passed. It was pure hell. Somehow, we all got away. And not without a good story to tell the boys back at Quigg's.

The Marines and the long walk to Trestles did not deter us from sharing some of the best waves on the coast. And, like I said, it seemed there were always waves at Trestles, especially in the summer time.

I had a summertime routine by now, and it was a good one. I'd surf 38th Street in the morning. Then go home and either meet up with Mark and the boys or slide over to Quigg's and try to put together a crew. We'd pool gas money, and if we could afford it, go over to the Market Basket and by a couple of loaves of bread and a jar of peanut butter. If we were living high, we'd even get a couple of sodas. But, they were added weight for the walk. Not good.

This would land us at Trestle in the early afternoon, maybe even after the wind had come up. We'd establish a little camp and make some peanut butter "sinkers" and chow down. Sinkers were traditionally one piece of bread with a large amount of peanut butter. You fold it over and then wolf it down in one bite.

Meanwhile, the guys who had been surfing all morning would be starving and they would leave. Then it would be early afternoon and we would have the place to ourselves with a full tank of sinkers to keep us going.

We traveled light. No towels, no hats, not even T-shirts. Just trunks, board and bags full of sinkers. In the summer afternoons, it was show time. The major players would come out and shine. Roger Zieger, Bob Lemaker, Mark Martinson, Mike Marshall and a full supporting cast. Guys like Herbie Fletcher and Billy Hamilton established themselves as contenders to the throne.

Then, every once in awhile, a guy would just show up and rip the place to shreds. I saw L.J. Richards do it one day. On another day a little-known Hawaiian named Barry Kanaiapuni showed the locals how a bottom turn was really done. You never knew when somebody would do something nobody had ever done before, but you knew it would happen.

One summer day in 1965, one of my Wind-an-Sea brothers joined us for an afternoon session at the Trestle and ended up stealing the show. Dave Rullo had been staying with me in Newport for a couple of days. We surfed the beach breaks that morning then headed down to Trestles with John Humpheries in the early afternoon. The waves were really good, about six plus. Glassy walls. Rullo was always a stylist out of the Hynson-Fry mold. He wasn't a flashy nose rider type, just smooth turns and perfect trims. Making it all look so easy.

On that day, he had on these new type of shorts. Jams. So he kind of stood out anyway, but it was his surfing that got all of our attention. He would sit outside and wait for the biggest waves. When he snagged one, he would do these beautiful carving bottom turns and then just rocket down the line. He did what we used to call the "up and drop" and it was all about where surfing would be going in the years to come. Hard driving turns, trimming the board for maximum speed always with ultimate control. Oh yeah, he ripped that day and I was proud to be his friend.

I have to say that the surfing I saw in those days at the Lower Trestles far surpassed any I've seen in films of the era. I have images etched in my mind of Barry Kaniapuni proning out all the way to the bottom of an eight-foot wave and then standing up and carving a turn where all you could see from the beach was the bottom of his board. Roger Zieger hanging ten backside on huge green walls. Mark Martinson and Bill Fury getting fully tubed in the outside peak. Mike Marshall fading into huge peaks and cranking beautiful drop-knee backside turns, and so many more. Yeah, those were the days.

Dawn of the Red Fins — Mr. Style Dave Rullo with his Mike Hynson Model. Yes, they were ahead of their time and so was Mr. Rullo.
(Photo courtesy of D.B. Rullo)

Wheels

When I turned 16, I went right down to the DMV to get my license. I had a good $75 saved from my job as a dishwasher. I'd been working at the Lido Castaway Restaurant. It was a cool little place favored by the upper classes including a lot of movie stars. It had old movie star photos from the 50s hanging all over the place, red leather booths with a little lamp on each table. It was famous for its prime rib. Every once in a while the chef would slice off a thin piece for the crew in the back.

The job paid $1.35 an hour, plus we'd get some tips from the waitresses. I rode a Honda 50 to and from work. A couple of us had them. They were little mini-motorcycles that weren't much of a ride, but got us around. I remember summer nights with three our four of us cruising down Balboa Boulevard on these little mini-motor bikes. We thought we were cool.

Of course, you couldn't take a board anywhere. And forget about girls, they went for guys with cars. I needed a car.

I passed the driver's test in my dad's '54 Chevy. With my license tucked safely in my wallet, I sold the Honda 50 and bought my first car, a 1949 Dodge. I got it for, you guessed it, $75 bucks. It needed everything. Brakes, tires, engine work, you name it. Still, I managed to drive it around, using milk as brake fluid. It was a kind of primer gray, but it had classic lines. I'm sure someone could have restored it and made it a show car. But, not me. I was, and still am, strictly a driver. Transportation, that's it. Oh sure, I like a nice ride as well as the next guy, I'm just not into doing all the work myself.

I'd rather drive. And drive I did. To school and back. Down to the pier after school. Board in the trunk. I was afraid to take the car out of town, it was strictly a Newport car. Needless to say, it didn't last too long. It died in front of my parents house on 32nd. And I just left it parked there until they towed it away. I know, that wasn't good, but it's just the way it happened.

I managed to save up some more money, and bought myself the first of a long line of VW Bugs. They were dependable, cheap on gas, and they went anywhere. Mine was a cool little brown one with a canvas sun-roof. I put racks on top, and I was set. I drove that baby to Trestle, to San Diego, even all the way to Santa Barbara.

Island Tales
One late summer afternoon at Quigg's shop Mike Marshall announced that he was going to the islands. It came as a shock to all of us. He was one of the guys that was always there. Part of the routine. A fixture at Quigg's. I couldn't image him leaving. Of course, it also sounded like a great adventure and as much as I would be saddened by his going, I knew some day, I would be doing the same thing.

In the months to come, Marshall wrote letters that would arrive at Quigg's shop. We'd all gather round and John Reynolds or somebody would read them aloud. The stories were great. They talked about North Shore life. Harold Bloomfield blowing up cars, Paul Gebour making 15-foot Sunset look like a hot-dog wave, Buzzy Trent psyching guys into huge waves at Waimea. Great stuff.

Then one of the letters described a trip to an outer island. Maui, and a place called Honolua Bay. John Lindsey, from Newport, had joined Marshall in the islands and made the trip over to Maui, along with Dick Brewer and Rick Irons. Images of long green rights peeling off of a steep cliff. Waves that were so fast that all you could do was turn off the bottom and hang on for dear life in the tube.

A couple of months later, the pictures of that trip appeared in one of the magazines. Oh man, it was all so true. Rick Irons doing a cheater five on a perfect wave, Marshall cranking a backside drop-knee. John "Wicker" Lindsay getting the tube of his life ala Butch at the Pipeline. It was great. I remember going to bed at night and thinking what it would be like to surf Honolua. To race a big Hawaiian ten-footer through the bowl.

Makaha Take Two

The next fall, Wind-an-Sea put together another trip to Makaha. Although it had only been a year in my life, so much had changed. My friends and I now had jobs and cars, and girlfriends. We considered ourselves "adults." That was it back then, once you got a car and a job, it was like a coming of age. It was the same up and down the coast. Rullo, Strada, Close, everybody had grown up. So when it came time to go that year, things were way different.

Somehow, I managed to pay my own way. Jacobs may have helped a little. This time Terry Smith would join me and we'd put together our own itinerary. No church camp in Wainai for us. No way. We were going to stay on the North Shore, and just go over to Makaha for the contest. Can you imagine? A couple of 16-year olds planning to be on their own thousands of miles from home. But, we put it together.

We even had island-style semi-guns made for the trip. Terry was one of Velzy's boys. Dale Velzy had sold the Velzy name and was now making Surfboards by Dale in a shop on Cedar Street in Newport. Terry was part of a crew of guys who surfed Cedar Street and hung at Velzy's. Terry will be the first to say that the board Velzy made him to take to the islands that year was one of best ever. Velzy will go down in my book as a magic shaper.

Donald Takayama shaped my board, a 9-6 semi-gun with pulled tail and pointed nose. Both our boards were rockets for the times, and we were ready for the North Shore. We knew a couple of Newport guys who had moved to Haleiwa, Larry Fletcher and Chuck Moyer. They both worked for Dick Brewer at Surfboards Hawaii.

Mike Marshall had worked for Brewer and had enriched our lives with stories about Sunset, and Velzyland and Rocky Point. He'd written us about Maui and Honolua Bay. Those stories, combined with the fact that we knew guys who lived on the North Shore, were enough to hatch the plan. And it went pretty well. Sort of.

We flew out of Lindbergh Field with Wind-an-Sea. It wasn't as rowdy as the year before. There were a lot of new guys in the club, and those of us who had gone the year before were now seasoned Island veterans. At least we thought we were.

Terry and I flew over with the club, but were picked up by Larry Fletcher, Chuck Moyer and a Filipino guy named Carlos who lived across the street from them in Haleiwa. I remember saying good-bye to Thor and some of my friends from the club and feeling a little strange. Maybe even a little scared. I knew the club was going out to a nice church camp, eating great food at the Stroll Inn and pretty much falling into a routine that wasn't all that bad. Terry and I were giving all that up for the unknown.

We got our boards and put them in the back of Fletch's old Plymouth station wagon. Man it was a real North Shore beater car. The kind you used to see in the movies that they were always pushing off cliffs. It reeked of beer and I don't know what else. Exhaust fumes crept in from the floor boards adding to the nausea I was feeling on the long ride out. By the time we hit the "airplane bridge" in Wahiwa, I was longing for home.

We rolled into Haleiwa well after dark and turned down a dimly lit street. Fletch pointed out Brewer's shop, or Surfboards Hawaii, as we turned the corner. I remember feeling a loneliness I'd never felt before. Something about the lack of people around, no cars on the road and the thick, pungent night air. It got worse.

We pulled into a yard in front of a dark rambling old cane house. I thought "oh no!" Fletch and Moyer weren't exactly homebodies. A dining room table, and a refrigerator were about it for amenities. No furniture, no lamps, no lamp shades just bare light bulbs in bare rooms.

Fletch showed us our room, empty except for a cardboard box that served for a table. Luckily we had brought sleeping bags. He gave us a couple of mosquito punks, and we needed them. I hadn't realized it but I'd been getting bit ever since I got off the plane. Going to bed that night was hell. The hard floor, no pillow and the mosquitoes were driving me crazy. I missed home, like never before.

The next morning, our world changed. We awoke to the sounds of a rooster crowing. We were in "The Country," In Hawaii, they called just about everywhere outside of Honolulu the country. Honolulu was known as "Town." The sounds and smells of the country in the early morning were enough to wake the soundest sleeper, which would be me.

My body ached from the long hours of travel and short intervals of sleep on a hard floor. Then it hit me: The North Shore! All the stories I'd heard, the movies I'd seen. I was ready. This was going to be fun after all.

We went outside to look around and found that we were in a beautiful place. The dark road from the night before had been transformed into a beautiful tunnel of huge trees. The yard surrounding the house, was now a jungle teaming with life. The fresh smell of grass and foliage hung lush in the air. Oxygen, pure and sweet, was being created all around us, and it felt so good to breath it in.

After a while, Fletch rolled out of bed and took us to breakfast at Miriam's Café. Fletch was sander for Brewer, and adhered to that old "Bones" school of eating a hardy breakfast every morning. We had eggs over-hard with Portugese sausage, scoops of white rice with gravy. Hawaiian-style breakfast. Great stuff. Especially the sausage, spicy hot and tasty.

Fletch took us out for a cruise after breakfast. We checked out a couple of spots, determined that the surf was small, and went back to get our boards. We ended up at Chuns Reef, a place I'd always heard about, and wanted to surf.

Style Master — Tommy Leonardo was one of the best goofy foots from Hunington. Here he is doing a perfect PSJ on the south side of Hunington Pier. (Photo by Tom Jewel)

All the way with a PSJ

The waves were about four feet, maybe a little overhead on the sets. What a beautiful wave, at least it looked beautiful paddling out. Riding the waves was a different story. Coming from the mainland, where the waves are much slower, the North Shore waves were harder to judge and catch. Frustrating for a couple of boys just off the plane.

But, then Terry got a good ride all the way through the inside, and he came out jazzed. That got me going. I managed to roll into a nice four-footer on the outside. A quick turn up on to an emerald face and I was moving down the line. The big-money move at the time was the stretch five, or cheater five, or as we used to call it a PSJ, as in the legendary master of the move Paul Strauch Jr.

So I pull it off pretty good, and Terry is paddling out, and things suddenly start to fall in place. The water is warm, the sky is a vibrant blue, fluffy white clouds drifting by and the waves are just about perfect. It was one of those moments. Then it got even better.

I'm paddling back out, taking my time, when I see this guy fading left. He makes a middle-of-the-wave turn and takes two steps up. At first he reminded me of Chris Marseilles, so smooth and effortless. Hands held in just the right way. He was like a bull fighter

65

with a cape and the wave was the bull. I stopped paddling just to watch. As he got closer to me, I recognized him. Paul Strauch, the man himself.

For the next two hours we surfed and watched the master. He was everything that I heard and more. What a fluid style, he made everything look so easy. But, you know, I watched him ride dozens of waves and he never did do a PSJ! So much for calling-card moves.

Over the next few days, we got to surf small North Shore waves at Chuns, Laniekea and Haleiwa. We ate breakfast at Miriams and dinner at a little shop by the pool hall in Haleiwa. The theater in Haleiwa had samurai movies. We saw The Seven Swordsmen, and The Blind Swordsman and a couple of others.

The shop next to the pool hall sold what they called Barbecues, which were teriyaki beef and chicken on a stick. They cost a quarter, and four or five of them would fill you right up. Wash it down with two or three dime Cokes from the machine and you were set.

The days and evenings introduced us to a whole new culture. Country style Hawaii. Warm sun, gentle breezes, friendly people who seemed to have no sense of hurry. The locals were a blend of Filipino, Hawaiian, Japanese and Portuguese. Some looked very Asian, while others looked just like us with better tans. All were friendly, even the guys in the pool hall.

It all sort of made up for the uncomfortable sleeping and the starkness of our quarters that we returned to every night. Still the mosquitoes were hell and the night noises sometimes made a mainland boy long for home. But, then morning would come and we'd be off a new adventure. And every day there was an adventure.

Hanging with Uncle Butch
As the weekend approached, we prepared to go over to Makaha. Fletch would drive us over, but then we'd be pretty much on our own. I figured we could stay at the church camp with Wind and Sea, or find some other place to sack out.

We left on a sunny Friday afternoon. Butch Van Artsdalen rode over with us. What a great guy. The year before, he had been one of the seniors that had chaperoned the juniors. We called him

"Uncle Butch" then. He was really just a big kid and such a real person. Talk about unpretentious. Butch was just one of us grems. He laughed with us, wrestled with us and hung out with us at the church camp.

He had moved to the North Shore after the rest of the club went back to the mainland. Hawaii became his home. He would become the most respected haole in the islands. "Mr. Pipeline." But, it didn't change him a bit. Nothing would ever change Butch, he was a classic rouge, living life by his own set of unique rules.

We took the short cut over to Makaha, through a pass on the military base. The same pass that the Japanese had flown through when they bombed Pearl Harbor. Fletch was in the Army before he became a surfer, and used his military I.D. to get us on the base.

Terry and I rode in the backseat. Fletch and Butch had a box of San Miguel beer in the front, and let us have a couple after we got on the base. We had a great ride over, talking and laughing all the way. Then as we came out of the pass on the west side, we started noticing a change in the weather. The sky had turned dark with thick clouds moving in from the southwest. Butch told us it looked like a Kona storm.
It was. By the time we turned up the west-side highway, it had started to rain. Not just the typical Hawaiian shower, but full-on rain. The windshield had a thick film of red dirt and oil. The windshield wipers were basically useless and Fletch had to stick his head out the window to see where he was going. What a scene.

It was late afternoon, when Butch suggested we stop by one of his friends' house on the west side and take a break. We were all for it. When we pulled up at the house, which was way up one of the valleys, it was pouring rain. There were a bunch of cars out in front, and Fletch remarked that there must be a party going on. Butch smiled.

Oh yeah, it was a party all right. An all-Hawaiian party. Fletch told us to stay close to Butch and we'd be okay. Haoles were not allowed at this type of party, but we were with Butch. They loved Butch. In fact, they really loved Butch, so we went in.

The next thing I know, we are inside this house with all these Hawaiian guys, and they are slapping Butch on the shoulder and getting us all beers. Primo beers. I wasn't much of a connoisseur in those days, but that was some crappy tasting beer. We stuck close to Fletch as he pointed out some of the guys to us. Dynamite, Rabbit, Blue Maku, Bobby Achoy, The Pattersons and Bla James. Oh man, I'd heard of these guys and some of the stories were a little unsettling, to say the least.

Here we were the only haoles in the place, with all these notorious Hawaiians. We hung in there for a couple of hours and the party raged. They were playing slack key guitar and singing. A table had been set out with a bunch of strange food. The Hawaiians basically accepted us and we loosened up, but I could tell even Fletch was nervous.

I had on my Jacobs Surf Team T-shirt and was standing there when Blue Maku came up and started talking to me. I could barely understand his thick pigeon, and he was pretty well blasted. I just smiled and nodded my head to everything he said. He was wearing this grubby yellow and green InterIsland Surfboards T-shirt. When he took it off and handed it to me, I didn't know what to do. Fletch elbowed me in the ribs and said "he wants to trade shirts." I was about to say "no way," but Fletch gave me this look. So I took off my cool clean white Jacobs Surf Team shirt and traded it for a sweaty old InterIsland shirt. Then, Bla James spotted Terry with his "Dale" T-shirt. When Bla found out it was a Dale Velzy shirt, that was all she wrote. Bla traded his shirt for Terry's.

The exchange wasn't all bad. Soon, we were one of the "bras," which I learned was short for bradda, or brother in pigeon English. If you were a bradda, you were okay. So we were bras for the night, eating, drinking and singing away. Fun stuff. Scary fun stuff. During the course of the evening Fletch and I lost track of Terry and Butch. Fletch asked around and somebody said that Butch may have gone to another party out at Makaha.

We decided to slip out and see if we could find them. It was still pounding rain outside, which made for a very slow ride out of the valley. Somehow we found our way out to Makaha and located the party where we thought we'd find Butch and Terry. Actually it wasn't that hard to find, it was a big party and you could hear it for blocks. We parked and went in. There was a mix of Hawaiians and local haoles, or Kamainas, as they called themselves. Whites who had grown up in Hawaii and talked with pigeon accents.

Fletch and I mingled. He knew a few of the people, but it didn't matter, everyone was really friendly. We looked in vain for Butch and Terry, but other than that, we had a good time. Again, plenty of beer and food and music. Hawaiians can party. Oh yeah.

A giant Army tent had been set up in the back yard and somebody said we could stay there if we needed a place. By this time, it was late and we were tired. A drive back down the coast was out of the question.

The Kona storm howled through the night. Rain, wind, the works. Almost like a hurricane. We ended up in the tent with about 10 other people. We had our sleeping bags, but it was still rough. The ground was wet, the air thick with humidity and there were bugs. Lots of bugs. Not the pleasantest of evenings.

I did manage to get a little sleep just before dawn and awoke with the sun shining through a crack in the tent. I had a killer hangover and the inside of my mouth felt like sand paper. My body ached from sleeping on the ground and I itched everywhere from mosquito bites.

The gale wind and white-capped sea left little doubt that the Makaha meets were canceled. The rain had stopped, but the ocean looked like a huge washing machine. I walked down to the beach and saw what must have been 50-foot waves breaking every which way. There would be no surfing that day. Then I remembered Terry. Where was my bro?

I went back to the house and got Fletch and we drove back to the first party house. There were still cars out in front, and the party was still going pretty much like it was when we left the night before.

But unlike the night before when Fletch and I had been welcomed, the guy who opened the door told us "no haoles, go home." We knocked again and said we were just looking for our friend, and again they slammed the door in our face. It was getting ugly, so we turned to leave. Then, a guy came out and asked "Where's Butch?" We said that we didn't know. He said, "You bring back Butch, you can have your friend."

Terry was still there! I was glad to hear that, but now we had another dilemma: where to find Butch? We drove back out to Makaha and checked all around. He wasn't at the beach, and he wasn't at the party, which had started back up again.

Finally, we got one of the Hawaiian guys to go back with us who knew the crew at the first party house. He was successful in getting Terry out after a long conversation. Terry was no worse for wear. He had partied with them all night, and there was never any threat to him. Actually, he had a pretty good time, and could probably write a book about all the stories he heard that night.

We never did see Butch, I think he left the party with a local gal and just disappeared for awhile. We spent the rest of the weekend at the party out at Makaha. The "Meets" were cancelled, but that didn't diminish the party spirit. We met lots of people and it gave us a chance to interact more with the Hawaiian culture than I'd experienced the year before. We played guitar and ate the food and learned about "Hawaiian Style." That was sort of a me casa, su casa, where everything from your last beer to your last smoke was handed over without a thought. What's mine is yours, and so on. Terry and I spent the rest of the trip out on the North Shore. I never did make my heat at Makaha. They held it during the week and I couldn't get a ride. Thor was pissed. We got some good days at Chuns and Haleiwa. Nothing big. Well not real big. There was one day when Chuns started closing out at about eight feet and we went over to Laniakea. I only rode a couple of waves there that day, it was hard to figure out for me and once you rode inside, it was hard to get back out.

We flew back the following weekend. I can't remember who finally won the contest that year. Thor gave me a long lecture about accountability on the flight back. It wasn't anything like the year before for me, but I had gained in experience. And, despite seeing a whole seedier side of life there, I knew I would be back.

The Hobie days
I continued to ride in the contests, and started to win heats with some regularity. One day, I got a call from Corky Carroll saying that Hobie was going to form a surf team. He asked if I'd be interested. I wasn't sure at first, Jacobs had been good to me. But then Hobie was closer to home, and there was a major incentive. McGregor clothing was going to co-sponsor the team and actually pay us!

McGregor Hobie — The McGregor Hobie Surf Team was, I believe, the first-ever professional surf teams. We were paid something like $250 a month and we got lots of free clothes. This is a photo of one of the posters they made to hang in department stores. From top left: George Weaver, Herbie Fletcher, Dave Willingham, Billy Hamilton, L.J. Richards. Bottom from left: Corky Carroll, Bobby Patteson, Hobie Alter, Herb Torrens, and I don't know! Hobie, of course, on the right. (Photo of poster by Don Craig)

At that time, the only guy getting paid to ride boards was David. He and Donald had left Jacobs and gone to Bing. Dick Brewer had sold Surfboards Hawaii and also gone to Bing. That was one hell of a company. Brewer launched a design called The Pipeliner and Donald introduced The David Nuuhiwa Nose Rider. The stuff of legends.

I decided to make the move to Hobie, and Corky put together a pretty good team of riders that included Herbie Fletcher, Mike McClellan, George Weaver, Darrel Diamond and others. The best thing for me was the boards. Herbie and I both went right for Phil Edwards models. Oh yeah, the main guy. Phil boards. And, they were great. In fact, it was almost like being back on a Quigg.

My closest friends from Wind-an-Sea, Dave Rullo, Jon Close and Larry Strada, were all riding Hynson Models by then. They were long, thin and pointy affairs with three redwood stringers and big red fins. The Hynson Models were known as "Red Fins," and those boys all ripped on them. Rullo, Close and Strada were all multi-dimensional stylists out of the Hynson/Fry school of soul surfing. You knew that.

Herbie Fletcher, George Weaver, Mike McClellan and I all got Phil Boards and nick named them "Pine Fins" after their distinctive reverse fins made of wood. They also were long, thin and pointy, and they had three redwood stringers, but different from the Hynson Models. My Phil Board was a great joy. Maybe it was the shape, maybe it was the mystique. I remember picking up my first one at the Hobie factory in Capistrano.

Bubby Hill was with me. I really didn't know Phil Edwards, I'd met him once when Mike Marshall took me down to Oceanside and Phil had shaped him a board. Bubby and I found the legendary Phil in the shaping room covered with foam dust and looking like some sort of snowman. His smile was quick and genuine and he had this glint in his eye that reminded me of Sean Connery as 007. I remember thinking "this guy is immortal."

He helped me find my board in a finishing rack waiting to be polished. He took it down and rubbed it out himself. Wow, what a moment, Phil Edwards polishing my board and then handing it over. I was in heaven.

Corky organized the Hobie McGregor team and set us all up with boards and plenty of gear. The big kick-off was at Cottons and we all had to wear McGregor outfits and surf on boards that matched the outfits. It was a photo shoot for an ad campaign, and we were all duded up in these trunks and jackets that matched boards made just for the event. We'd gone from hot-dogs to corn dogs!

I sported a blue jacket and trunks with a red competition stripe. The board matched perfectly. Just right for the ad campaign. I was glad there was no one around to see us though.

The boards were total junk. Just popouts with fancy pigment. We had to surf them for the photo session that day, and they were pure hell compared to our Phil Boards. But, they paid us $250 apiece and bought us lunch. Big juicy cheeseburgers, fries and large Cokes. I didn't surf well enough to get my picture in any of the ads, but my buddy George "Little Wevo" Weaver made it.

Little Wevo and MacClellan were Newport guys, and we hung out a lot back at home. MacClellan was older, Wevo younger, but we were united by our new ties to Hobie. And what great ties they were.

I always remember Hobie as being such a nice guy. He'd be in his office working behind his desk, but always take time to come out to the showroom and talk whenever one of us walked in.

The Hobie label had lots of pull in those days and it was fun being part of that. I don't know if it was the Hobie influence or my improved surfing, but all of a sudden I started getting my picture in magazines, and I started doing much better in surf contests. I was even featured in a "Surfer Magazine" article called "The Hot Young Crop." Of course, Corky wrote it, but I didn't complain.

Herbie Torrens is probably the fastest rising junior to hit the competition circuit this year. He is rated Triple A by the USSA and won numerous contests last year. Herb hails from Newport Beach, California and is a member of the Newport Beach Surfing Association. He is also sponsored by Hobie Surfboards and McGregor Clothing Company. Watch for him in the Junior Division this year.

CORKY: Herb, you're a pretty hot surfer for being only seventeen years old. How did you get started surfing?
HERB: Well, I met this girl surfer who was super-boss, and she asked me if I surfed. Naturally, I said "yes." So she asked me to go surfing with her. Like a champ I rushed out and bought a twenty dollar backyard special. But the romance was snuffed out when she saw what a kook I was. That was the year of my 12-year-old broken heart misery. So it ran off with big surf hero Mike McClellan. Love was blind and she really missed out on my true worth.
CORKY: What true worth is that Herb?
HERB: I was a hot tennis player, and besides that I was voted the skinniest kid in the seventh grade. That carries a lot of social significance you know.
CORKY: How do you feel about surfing contests?
HERB: Competition is really a lot of fun and I like it. It gives me a chance to see all of the other guys from up and down the coast that I don't see very much.
CORKY: Judging from your Triple A rating for 1966 you must be a pretty fierce competitor. Who do you feel will be your main competition this year?
HERB: Well, there are a lot of good surfers around. Denny Tompkins, George Weaver, Billy Hamilton, and David Nuuhiwa are always good. Guys like that are hard to beat.

CORKY: After this year, you will become a senior in the competition. How do you feel about this?
HERB: Naturally, the competition is going to be a lot harder. It is hard for me to imagine myself surfing against guys like Mike Doyle, Rusty Miller, and well, you're fairly lukewarm at times, too.
CORKY: Thanks Herb, you really know how to make an old kook feel good. By the way, what do you plan on doing when you get older?
HERB: I am thinking about becoming a literary critic. So it looks as though your career as a writer is shot. Get the rub, dad?
CORKY: Yeah Herb, you really know how to hurt a guy (sob). You're a member of the newly formed Newport Beach Surfing Association. Could you tell me a little about that?
HERB: Sure, Newport is the fastest rising club on the coast right now. We have already beaten San Clemente Surf Club, Swamies Surf Club and Hope Ranch Surf Club. Our win over Hope Ranch was a big step forward. They are one of the major clubs. I think that within a few years Newport will be right up there in the number one spot on the coast. Right now we have the best goofy-foots in the world, although our club is restricted to people who live in Orange County.
CORKY: What do you think of the new USSA ruling where a club can only

register members in its own area to compete for it?
HERB: It is great for us in Newport. Too bad about Windansea, though. It sure looks like their downfall. Dogsure go it, just when they were getting gone it, just when they were getting ready to take over the world. Tsk Tsk Tsk.
CORKY: You were a member of Windansea once. What made you join Newport?
HERB: I really like all of those guys in Windansea. They and the rest are really good guys, although Windansea is just trying to get too big. They started taking in members that were nowhere near good enough to rate membership in a club of that caliber. The purpose of that was to just completely dominate the coast. And in doing this they have lost the surfing for fun element that a club should have. Newport is limited to a small area and all of the members are there for fun.
CORKY: What do you think about surfing styles?
HERB: I really don't like those phoney put-on styles where a guy will hold his hands a certain way just to try and look smooth. Most of the guys that do that think that they are trimming when they are really just posing. A good label for that sort of style would be the "Pseudo-Trim Pose."
CORKY: Well, then, what style do you prefer?
HERB: I think that Phil Edwards is the best surfer and has the best style. Bill Fury is also good and has a good style. Those two guys just surf and don't try to pose and their surfing speaks for itself.
CORKY: What do you think about J. J. Moon?
HERB: He's got guts. Actually I think that he is really Mickey Dora's brother. Dora is a classic and really adds color to the sport.
CORKY: I guess that I could ask you what your favorite spots are. But that is a fairly sterotype question.
HERB: Well, my favorite spots are pretty sterotype anyway. Like "The Boo," "The Con," and "The Poe." I really dig the lefts at The Poe.
CORKY: Yeah, those lefts at The Poe really have a lot of class. Well Herb, I guess I'll be seeing you at the beach.
HERB: What beach? Are you kidding me? I just met a zambowangakeen ski bunny, and I'm going out and buy a pair of skis.

HERBIE TORRENS
"I don't like phoney put-on styles..."

99

There I was right alongside David Nuuhiwa, Denny Tomkins and a guy by the name of Jock Sutherland. Jocko was such a classic. I'll have a lot more about him later.

Success at the Shores

I've found that sometimes in life, when one part gets going the other parts get going, too. Success breeds success. That's the way it was for me along about that time. I seemed to have it all going.

I got a second place at Santa Monica and then won the Hermosa Beach Contest a few weeks later. That was big for me. I remember walking down the beach with Jimmy Irons just before the final. We were talking about life and how much better it would be if we could just surf for fun instead of being pitted against each other in a competition. Jimmy was so soulful, and man was he a good surfer. So here we are two soul guys telling each other how we didn't care who was going to win, and that when it was time for the final, we would just go out and do some soul surfing.

Then we both go out there like rabid dogs and fought for every damn wave that came through.

Afterwards on the beach waiting for the awards ceremony, Thor comes walking up and pulls me aside. He says, "Here's what I want you to say when you get your trophy..." I swallowed and asked what place? He said, "You won, of course." I was back in the good graces of Thor.

My biggest day in contest surfing came later that year at La Jolla Shores. That was, of course, a hot bed of soul surfing back then. Dickie Moon, Dave Rullo, Larry Strada, Curt Slater, Hankie Warner, Jon Close, the list went on and on.

The year before, when David Nuuhiwa was still in Wind-an-Sea, we went down together with some older guys and managed to get ourselves in trouble. Well, not exactly trouble, but we both screwed up our semi-finals and didn't make the final. We had stayed up late, and basically missed our heats. It wasn't like we were totally out-of-control teenagers. Well, maybe just a little out of control.

So the following year, my parents drove me down. They stayed for my heat and drove back. I would have no problem getting a ride back, I thought, and I would stay with my good friend Huey MacIntosh in O.B.

74

I won my heat and had a great day surfing with all the guys. We had a total jam session just outside the contest area. I mean, it was show time. All the shores guys on their Red Fins surfing with such style. The master was Jon Close, who held the title "King of the Shores," at the time. He was the odds on favorite to win, even with the likes of David Nuuhiwa, Billy Hamilton and Dale Keeler (now Dobson) in town.

Rullo had been in some sort of accident and couldn't surf. He watched on the beach with this big white bandage around his head. He would have been a contender, too. Dickey Moon was no slouch either, and Erik Murphy. Man there were so many hot guys there and everyone was just taking it up another notch. David had all he could handle to stand out in that crowd. But, of course, he did.

So on that Saturday afternoon as I was leaving to go down to Huey's in O.B., Thor came up and gave me a big lecture about getting to bed early. I took it with a grain of salt, but down inside, I didn't want a repeat of last year. I was in rare company, and wanted to do my best.

Huey and I went to his parents house, a great little California style bungalow atop Coronado Street in Ocean Beach. His mom was a great cook and she made us dinner. Afterwards we just sat around and played guitar. Huey was a good musician and played bass in a band. I'd been plunking around at guitar since I was about seven. We always had fun when we played.

The next morning, we arrived early. Thor had an ear-to-ear smile for me. I got through my semi and made the final. That was all I had even hoped for. To make the cut.

When the final came, I was psyched. It would be David, Dickie Moon, Close, Dale Keeler, Billy and myself. Somehow, I'd made it. I remember paddling out to perfect glassy three and four-foot waves. When La Jolla Shores is on, it's as good as any beach break on the coast, and that (forgive me) includes Newport.

I got some good set waves and seemed never to stop paddling and riding. Rights, lefts, tubes, nose rides, it was just a blast. When I came in, I thought if I could just beat one guy, I'd be happy. And, that would have been an accomplishment.

So there we are standing up on the makeshift stage waiting for the announcement. Thor hadn't come up to me, so I knew I didn't win. Billy and I were talking and he was thinking the same thing I was: "Just let me beat one guy."

The judges assembled, Skip Fry and Mike Hynson were both judges, and handed the announcer the results. I think it was Chuck Hasley, but I can't be certain. I remember him saying that this had been one of the closest competitions ever, and that's why it took so long for them to tally up the points.

So there we are all lined up and they start announcing from sixth place. I sort of blanked out and was just standing there when I realized that Billy, Dale and I were the only ones left standing. I looked at Billy and he was flashing that famous smile of his. "Trophies! Oh yeah." Then they announce Billy as third. My heart starts to beat as I realize that I got second. I figured no way I was going to beat out Dale. Then they call my name as the winner, I was genuinely surprised beyond belief.

The trophy was huge. The biggest of any of the contests. Oh, I loved that trophy, it really did mean a lot to me. I don't know how it happened that I won. Like I've said, I've never come in from a final saying "oh boy I smoked 'em." In fact, I've never felt I really won any surfing contest. But, I have learned to take the trophy and run.

Cruiser — Dave Rullo going left at inside PB Point. What a stylist he was, never an extraneous move, just ride and glide. (Photo courtesy of D.B. Rullo)

That was the highlight of my contest surfing career. Not that it all went down hill from there, but I still get some mileage joking around with my good friends Rullo, and the "King of the Shores," Jon Close!

As the World Turns

Meanwhile, the world was changing around us. The Viet Nam "conflict" had escalated to a war. The Beatles had changed pop music. A generation of college students were dropping out and joining in protest marches. Yet, here we were, going in almost an opposite direction. Cosmetically, of course. Inside, we were all still non-conformists at heart. Individuals that really just wanted to ride the waves.

While the rest of our generation were tuned into the likes of the Rolling Stones and Bob Dylan, most of the guys I hung out with were listening to jazz. Wes Montgomery, Herbie Man, Dave Brubeck, and the many other great "cool jazz" artists of the time. It went with our style of surfing. Long boards, smooth walks to the nose, quiet drop-knee cutbacks. Soul surfing had come of age.

The Short John

Along about this time, something came along that gave us more range. The Short John wetsuit was a big step up from the long-sleeved beaver tail diver suits guys had been wearing. For the most part the beaver-tail style wet suits were frowned upon in the ranks. They looked funky, and they were constraining when it came to paddling. I never owned one, and can't recall anyone worth a damn that did. Then O'neil introduced the Farmer John, or Short John as they later became known.

The Short John caught on quick, and soon we were all wearing them everyday in the winter. This innovation in attire allowed us to stay out longer, and go out in conditions that we would have thought twice about without them. They also made the cold waters of northern points more attractive.

Up until then, I had only surfed Rincon a couple of times. And, they were short go-outs. I was a warm-water kind of guy. But when I got "the suit," the first thing on my mind was a trip up north. One day, we loaded up the boards in a couple of cars and set off for Rincon at about four in the morning. What a great day it turned out to be. We pulled up at Rincon early in the morning to see perfect eight-foot lines wrapping down the point.

We had Mike McClellan, George Weaver and John Lindsey in our car, and it took us all of two minutes to jump into our new wet suits and hit the waves. What a day. Phil Edwards showed up and Paul Strauch was there, both just ripping. Even Matt Dillon was out! No, not Mat Dillon today's movie star, the real Matt Dillon. You know, Gunsmoke? Okay, his name was really James Arness, and his son, Rolf, would someday be a world champion surfer. Anyway, Matt Dillon was a pretty good surfer. Had his short john on and was looking pretty smooth on those glassy walls.

We clocked a lot of hours in that day thanks to the wet suits. Good waves and a good show. Phil Edwards and Strauch were the kings. They pretty much could ride every wave they wanted without a bunch of dummies taking off in front of them.

Looking back, I think this was the hey day of longboard surfing. Before it got real ugly with noseriding and grandstanding. Phil and Strauch were absolutely the epitome of style and finesse. They had it all. Power turns and cutbacks, smooth speed trims, and way of surfing that melded with the wave. Man and nature in harmony. What a day.

We surfed Rincon for all it was worth and by the end of the day we were famished. That's when a little bit of luck kicked in.

I had ridden a wave in from the outside and milked it as far as I could to the inside. The tide had gone out, and after the wave petered out, I had a long, slow, rock dance to shore. Of course, this requires watching every step you take so you don't slip or step on something sharp. So here I am walking in, step-by-step, and I see a $20 bill in a little tide pool. Man, I scooped it up and just looked up at the sky. What a great way to end a perfect day.

We had pooled all our money for gas and had just enough to get home. I think we had some "sinker" material and sodas to eat, but that was about it. When I found the twenty, it was like hitting the jack pot. So, once everybody came in, we piled in the car and headed down to this all-you-can eat smorgasbord in Ventura. It was like three or four bucks apiece for all you could eat.

The guy gave us a funny look when the four of us came in. Okay, we may have been a bit grubby, and our hair wasn't combed, but we were clean. Anyway, we set about filling up plates with spare ribs and chicken and mash potatoes and anything else that looked edible. And then, of course, it was on. Who could eat the most? Who would walk away as the biggest eater? Who could eat the most pie?

Well, between the four of us, we put a significant dent in the guy's smorgasbord buffet. And, we might have wedged out a few regular customers, too. But, we were having fun. The guy finally came over and said that we couldn't go back for anymore food. This didn't set well with the boys. We were about to see who could eat the most banana cream pie. So the guy comes over and cuts us off and gives us the bill, which was just about twenty bucks. We were kind of bummed, so Lindsey gets an idea. He says "give me the twenty, I'll be right back."

Ten minutes later he comes back with a bag full of pennies. Yep, he took the twenty to a supermarket and cashed it in for pennies. With that, he puts the check down, and pours the bag of pennies on the counter. Oh, the guy was pissed. He lost it and was yelling at us in some foreign language. We got out of there quick, but we laughed all the way back to Newport. Hey, we were paying customers and the customer is always right. Right?

We made other trips up north and got great waves, but we never went back to the smorgasbord. I think the guy would have had a heart attack if he ever saw us again.

Contests get ugly
There was an event that year held up north that I think sort of changed the course of surfing history. It was a invitational nose riding contest put on by Tom Morey at California Street in Ventura.

Looking back, and considering what Tom Morey has accomplished over the years, I think he organized the event just to see what kind of boards everyone would come up with. Maybe not, but he was quick to see the potential of the nose riding element in creating a new market for surfboards.
The buzz about the contest sent shock waves into shaping rooms up and down the coast. Guys like Mickey Munoz, Mike Hyson and Dewey Weber went to work dreaming up bizarre nose riding

boards. Down in Capistrano Beach, the guys at Hobie had their own Skunkworks. Really, it was like top secret. They cranked out at least a dozen prototype noseriders over a month or so. Some were thick slabs with almost square fins. Some had accentuated kick in the nose and tail to create drag. All were really strange.

Mickey Munoz, Corky Carroll and Bobbie Patterson were Hobie's test pilots. They attacked San Onofre everyday for weeks, coming back each day with feed back and ideas. Then Mickey and other Hobie shapers would go to work in the shaping room. They came up with five or six boards for the contest, all with high profile pigment jobs. One was red, white and blue with stars on the nose, about 9-feet, rounded nose and parallel rails. Very thin, as I recall, with a thick fin and a little ridge on the nose.

Most of us watched all action with mild amusement. Nose riding had always been a factor in surfing. There were guys that were just naturals, like Chris Marseilles and David Nuuhiwa. And there were those who learned it as a skill, who worked at setting the rails, and stalling the tail, and all those little moves that go into positioning a board for a nose ride. Noseriding was not something you did on an easy-riding tanker where all you did was hop up and run to the nose. Well, then it wasn't.

When the contest finally rolled around, David was the odds-on favorite, even though he would be riding backside at Ventura's California Street. Munoz, Patterson, and Corky were all in from the Hobie team. John Peck carried the Morey flag. It was the first of its kind of event, and the surfing world definitely took notice. A bunch of us from Newport went up just to watch. There were some who applauded the event as the definitive test of surfing skill. Finally, an objective way to tell who won.

It threw surfing for a loop, that's for sure. It introduced a whole new concept in board design and probably made surfing more fun for a larger segment of the population. Ultimately, a specialized line of surf boards was born. The Stretch from Gordon and Smith, the 722 from Jacobs, the John Peck Penetrator from Morey, and a whole bunch of others. As I recall, though, the event itself did not generate much in the way of good surfing.

In fact, it was ugly. Guys were taking off on angles and literally leaping to the defined portion of the board considered the nose.

Both feet had to be with in 30 inches of the nose, or something like that. Sure, it set an objective by which surfing could be judged. But good surfing? Not to me. No great turns, no trims or cutbacks, just a lot of posing on the front. Never liked that, never will.

At the time of the Morey Invitational, I was riding for Hobie and Wind-an-Sea Surf Club. On the Saturday of the contest, Thor put together an ad hoc Wind-an-Sea team to surf in an impromptu club surf contest on Saturday afternoon. I had planned to go back home with my friends, but when Thor asked if I would surf for the club, I agreed.

It wasn't a big meet, just four or five surf clubs. I did okay. The one memorable moment was when I was riding a pretty nice wave on my Phil board, and it lines up on the inside. I take four steps to the nose and was just kind of standing there and I hear the announcer counting off seconds: :"three, four, five."

Along about then, my trusty Phil board caught an afternoon chop and I went flying off the front. Luckily, I was pretty close to the beach, but my board took a beating on the rocks, and I was a little disgusted with myself for getting caught up in the announcer counting out the seconds while I was on the nose.

I made the finals along with fellow club member L.J. Richards, yep the legend himself. What a great surfer and great guy. I'd only heard about him up until then. Well, I saw him surf the Trestles a couple of times, and he ripped. But, I'd never talked to him.

A local Ventura guy got first, L.J. second and I finished third. Wind-an-Sea won the club part of the contest, Thor was happy. He arranged for me to stay at Tom Morey's house that night. L.J. gave me a ride there in his VW bug. I found out that L.J. was just a regular guy. Very humble, and likeable.

Tom Morey was a gracious host. There were a bunch of guys staying there, including L.J. Don't remember much about the night, except we all went out to Shakey's Pizza. Pizza and pitchers of beer and soda, what a concept. The next day, it was more ugly surfing. Hey, maybe that's where Con got the name for the Con Ugly. You think?

After it was over, I got a ride back with Tommy Leonardo, who had gotten second and won some pretty good money in the process. Tommy was a great goofy-foot who held court along with John Boozer on the south side of Huntington Pier. David surfed with them and learned a lot about that break from those guys. I thought it was kind of ironic that Leonardo, a guy known for his front side tube riding, got second in a nose riding contest going backside. Don't get me wrong, I was happy for him, and was more than glad to share a pizza and sodas with him, courtesy of his winnings.

School Bound

I continued to surf in contests, but life started getting more complicated. I was seventeen. My grades had been rather poor in high school. Oh, the counselors and my parents kept telling me how I had the potential to do well in school. But, I was distracted. Surfing, girls, hanging out, all of which were better than school. Then I got one of those teachers. You know, a real teacher. One that grabs your mind and squeezes it until the juice runs out.

I was taking Junior English, for the second time. His name was Mr. Young, and he taught English Lit at Newport Harbor High. Mr. Young looked like he should have worked for NASA. He wore his hair in a short-cropped crew cut, his dark eyebrows almost grew together over intensive eyes. His glasses were thick with horn-rims. His limited attire included baggy slacks, funky short sleeve white shirts, and big wide neckties. Style was not Mr. Young's forte. But he could engage you and hold your attention. He could read a passage from Steinbeck or Hemmingway that would wisk you away to another place and time. He found meaning in almost every word, and encouraged discussion.

I found myself looking forward to Mr. Young's class. I started to read. "The Old Man and the Sea," "The Grapes of Wrath," "For Whom the Bell Tolls" and more. And, I started actually doing my homework! I got an "A" on a paper, then another. I started to write my own poems and short stories. I dug in.

That spontaneous inertia that happened in my surfing started happening in school. I improved in math, history and political science. My parents were pleased to say the least. Even my friends were supportive. It's funny, it seemed like all my friends started doing better at the same time. Not that I had anything to do with it, but we were seniors and no one wanted to be a "five-year man."

Terry Smith, Dale Kinsella and I would spend evenings at the public library and talk about art, literature and world affairs. None of us had the grades to go to a university, but we made up our minds to go to Orange Coast Junior College and transfer to a four-year school. Terry did just that transferring to Colorado State and earning a degree in anthropology, and Dale went all the way through Harvard Law!

Me? I went to Maui. But, 30 years later I did finish my degree, although not in English Lit as I would have dreamed. I graduated from the University of Phoenix with a bachelor of science in business and a certificate in marketing. Hey, you have to earn a living. I have no regrets.

Newport Beach Surfing Association comes of age
Along about that time, I was doing better, make that much better, in school. And I was doing okay out on the surf circuit with Hobie. The McGregor deal had kind of gone away, but not before we all made some money and got a bunch of new clothes.

After the Morey Invitational, contests began to change. There was more of a call for nose riding and what I thought was grandstanding. I continued to ride in contests, but somewhere along the line, I drifted away from the Wind-an-Sea Surf Club. The club changed so radically as new members joined. Close had quit surfing and was playing piano. Rullo and Strada took off for Hawaii almost the day after they graduated from high school. The old gang just wasn't the same. And, about that time, some guys in Newport—Gordon Connelly, John Lindsay and Mike Marshall—started up the Newport Beach Surfing Association.

I joined and so did Corky Carroll. Mike McClellan and George Weaver were in, and a whole bunch of others. NBSA in the early days was every bit as fun as Wind-an-Sea. We held interclub contests. We went to official USSA contests in mass. And we had events called "fun days" at Doheny.

Fun Days usually consisted of surfing contests where you'd do things like tandem surfing with a buddy or seeing who could stand on their head the longest while riding the wave. On the beach, we'd pig out with burgers, hot-dogs and watermelon. There were pie fights and watermelon fights and impromptu wrestling matches with two or three little guys piling up on some big bruiser. And there was surfing. Lots of surfing, with no one judging who was best, or who did what. Just riding for fun and in our own way trying to out-do each other with every wave.

NBSA was also sort of a political action committee for surfers in Newport. The City of Newport Beach has always adhered to a rather strict regiment as far as policies are concerned. Okay, make that quasi-Nazi policies. Not in the real sense, of course, it's just that they took the law seriously, and the City Counsel loved to make laws. There were laws against dogs on the beach. Laws how long you could be on the beach. Laws against changing clothes on the beach. And yes, lots of laws about surfing.

From the very beginning of my surfing, they kept us in specified areas at specified times during the summer. Then, in 1966, some Einstein council-person came up with the idea of licensing surf-boards. Can you believe it? We actually had to go down to City Hall, buy a little yellow sticker and have it on our boards just to surf in Newport.

Our surf club turned out in mass to protest, but the law passed anyway. Go figure. A couple of years later, they determined that it was too much of an enforcement problem. Really? Who would have thought?

They even went so far as to propose building a breakwall outside of the pier to create a new harbor. Oh, that upset us. NBSA went into action. We lobbied every business in town and created a coalition of business owners, homeowners and beach people. Unlike the licensing issue when it was just the surfers opposing the council, this involved the whole town turning out in protest. Diverse groups of property owners, business owners and beach-goers of any kind grouped together under a common flag. It worked and the new harbor idea was dropped.

There's a lesson there. Diverse groups working together for the common good. Wonder why it hasn't really caught on?

Newport wasn't the only place where battles were being waged over beaches and the right to surf. The Wind-an-Sea Surf Club, and United States Surfing Association set the model for surfing organizations that would try to improve the image of surfers and protect the beaches up and down the coast. NBSA, like other clubs, encouraged, okay, make that required its members to be clean cut. Gone were the days of shaggy hair cuts and baggy trunks. Surfers everywhere were looking more like Cal Poly graduates than the "beach bum" image that had so stigmatized the surfing subculture.

Changing lifestyles go with changing times. College students became revolutionaries. The beat generation became hippies. Relentless stories about the war in Viet Nam generated a new stress level across America. Everyone grasping for some sort of new reality. Of course, real surfers were still hanging out at the beach and talking about going right at the Trestles, or about the last swell that hit the pier.

As the war in Southeast Asia continued, more and more guys our age were being drawn into the conflict. Not many surfers were keen on going, and for good reasons. People were dying over there. A lot of the surf crew had other ideas. There were stories of guys showing up to get drafted and then jumping out of windows with their records just to get away. Most of us though, chose the student deferment. That meant taking a full-load of 15-units in college to stay out of the draft.

My parents didn't have the money, nor I the grades, to go to a four-year school. I was headed for Orange Coast Junior College in Costa Mesa. But, not before a little side trip to Florida for the summer.

Cape Canaveral and Melting Wax
After graduating from Newport Harbor High School in June of 1966, my friend Dale Kinsella came up with an idea for an adventure. Dale's mom had a business associate that could get us summer jobs at one of the hotels in Miami Beach. Hey, it wasn't Hawaii, but it was a chance to travel.

I got Hobie to chip in some money and my parents pitched in a couple of bucks. That, with money I'd saved, bought a one-way ticket to Florida. In late June, Dale and I boarded a flight for Miami. We were both 17 and very green, but on our way out into the world. What an experience. I remember getting off the airplane wearing my Raybands. The cool Triple A rated surfer from

California, soon to be a lifeguard and maybe Beach Boy. Girls, waves, sunny white sand beaches.

The Raybands fogged up the second I stepped out of the cabin. Warm, sticky night air consumed me. A stark feeling of being alone in strange place hit me like a ten-foot wave at The Wedge. Odd looking people stared at us like we were freaks. They spoke with strange accents. They dressed in strange clothes. Welcome to reality in Miami Beach. What the hell was I doing three thousand miles from home?

We took a Yellow Cab from the airport to a Howard Johnsons hotel in Miami. Down well-lit thoroughfares and over arching bridges to a city of lights. Still, it seemed like an awfully dark night to me. Our driver was dark too. Thick lips and a thick southern accent that was hard to understand. He chuckled when we told him we were surfers from California. We listened to stories about the city. The murder last night. Muggings. People who'd disappeared. Miami was like a different planet for a couple of California boys.

Dale's mom's friend was putting us up at Howard Johnsons and we were to await for him to call us about the jobs. Dale's mom was Cass Daily, a famous comedian in the early days of TV. The guy who was supposed to get us jobs in Florida was a Hollywood agent. Nice guy, but, well, a little flaky.

After a couple of days of not hearing from him, we got bored. We had done nothing but walk around Miami and eat at Howard Johnsons. Our boards were still at the airport, but from what we could tell there was no surf in Miami anyway. I'd brought two boards, a lighter version of a Phil board, and that funky red, white and blue noserider that was used in the Morey contest. I think we called it Stars and Stripes. Corky had talked me into taking it, and he was the captain of the Hobie team. He made me do it!

So there we were stuck in Miami, no surf, no girls we could talk to, no friends. Corky had given me the name of the local Hobie dealer in Miami and we looked him up. It was more of a boat yard than a surf shop. They sold all kinds of boats, and had a few pop out Hobies stuck in the corner. Not much of a surf shop, but the guy who owned it had a son about our age. I think his name was Bruce. We hooked up with him, and he took us cruising in his Corvette.

Bruce was all Miami. Hawaiian shirt and Bermuda shorts, cool wrap-around shades and penny loafers with no socks. We'd really never seen anything like him, but he turned out to be a regular guy. We went up the coast to Fort Lauderdale and all around, but still no surf.

After awhile, Florida started looking all the same. I was shocked by the flatness of the place. No mountains, not even any hills. Sure the lush greenery was cool, and there were lots of palm trees, but this was no Hawaii. And from all the views of the bright green ocean we took in, there wasn't a ridable wave in sight.

Bruce told us if we wanted to go surfing, we'd have to go up to Cocoa Beach, that was where it was all happening. We spent a couple of more days at the Howard Johnsons and one night at Bruce's house with still no word about our lifeguard jobs. That night at Bruce's we hatched a plan.

We'd hop a bus north for Cocoa Beach. Bruce made some calls and arranged for someone to meet us at the bus terminal. The next day we happily boarded a Greyhound, although without our boards. Those old long boards were a no-go on the bus. We left them at Bruce's and he promised to drive up the following weekend. It was a long bus ride through all these little towns. Oh we saw Florida all right. Too much of it.

We finally departed the bus to a hot, muggy terminal with a thousand bugs flying around. Did I mention Florida is in the South? For me it was like being in some old movie like "Long Hot Summer," or "Porgy and Bess." The terminal was something out of the 1940s. Old tile floors and wooden benches, ceiling fans slowly rotating, a refreshment stand with a waitress who wore a little crown-like hat and a pink uniform. And there were all these blue electric zappers that seemed to buzz and spark every few seconds.

Through the maze, a cute little surfer girl emerged and greeted us with hugs. A sight for sore eyes, you bet. Long sun-bleached hair, dark tan, pale blue eyes and lots of freckles. She wore a one-piece mu-mu style shift that belayed a shapely body and well-toned, tan legs. Sunshine said that we could stay at her friends' house for the night. Oh boy!

She drove us through the thick night air in a VW convertible. The Beatles tune "Hard Days Night" was playing on the radio and we all sang along. Things were getting better. Then we turned in to a dank little trailer park that had a half-lit neon sign. The pungent smell of septic tanks overtook the VW as soon as we stopped. Mosquitoes, sensing fresh meat, attacked in mass. Sunshine just smiled and pointed out our lodgings for the night: a ramshackle old, travel trailer-lean-to strung with Christmas lights and fishing nets. Suddenly, I missed Howard Johnsons.

The guys who lived there were a couple of seasoned surf-types who seemed happier to see Sunshine than us. One was named Bains and I think the other was Skip. They were older guys, probably early 20s. They went through the motions of showing us where we could crash and then adjourned to a hatch-cover table that served for dining room, living room and catch all counter for the abode.

The smallish interior was decorated, and I use the term loosely, with tapestries and Indian-looking posters. There were assorted lamps, all turned to the lowest setting. Shadows danced on the wall as an Indian-sounding raga played from the stereo. Hmmm, different world.

We settled in on two mattresses that were in a corner of the trailer's adjoining patio. Dale and I were out of our element. Where was the TV? Any peanut butter sandwiches available? Soda? Not a chance. An eternity seemed to pass before we were invited back into the main room. We talked, and gawked, and basically played it by ear like we were a couple of hip guys from the coast.

Bains turned out to be from Oceanside originally. And that broke the ice. We traded stories about the Oceanside surf crew. Guys like Phil Edwards and LJ, and Jim Sleggle, Chubby Lopez and Petey. Soon, Bains and Skip were telling us about the scene at Cocoa. Who was hot, where the best waves were, and what the parties were like. I remember sitting around that rough-wood hatch cover table on hard wooden boxes for a couple hours just trying to be accepted. A candle stuck in a Matuse wine bottle served as entertainment. We talked and watched the wax drip slowly down the side of the bottle. I was stuck between boredom and fascination, and there was a part of me thinking, "Oh man, I just want to go home."

The highlight of that first night was going outside to see a rocket getting launched from Cape Canaveral. It was impressive. The roar of the engines and the sight of intense flames blasting through the dark night sky was almost as good as TV. Bains and Skip quipped about the launch, which I gathered only happened once every few months. It was definitely a big deal for them and it was the first time I'd ever heard the word "psychedelic" used as an adjective.

The next day, Dale and I set out on our own to get the lay of the land and ended up eating breakfast in this little greasy spoon. We were way out of our element, and money was running low. The waitress, yeah that stereotype gum chewer everyone remembers, picked up on our situation and suggested we talk to a guy who was sitting at the counter. We did, and indeed, he offered us jobs and a place to stay. Yeah, I know...scary. But, we jumped on it.

His name was Johnny and he was some kind of southern hustler. He rented rooms at his house and put people to work mowing lawns and delivering stacks of papers to news stands at three in the morning. Johnny was what you might call a full Southern redneck and he gave us a view of life we'd never heard about. His vocabulary was even more limited than ours. It was all of about a week before we had all we could take of Johnny.

We left by buying a 1950 Studebaker from a guy who lived there. Classic ride. We tore out the back seat so we could put our boards in. And, that also made it a semi-camper once a beat up old mattress was thrown in. That fact that we were destroying a classic never crossed our minds.

We hooked up with the crew at Canaveral Pier. Bruce showed up with our boards. We had a car to stay in and get around. And, we could go surfing. The Florida trip was taking shape.

I'd never really thought about surfing as a lifestyle, or a culture. It was just something you did, that other people didn't do. Sure there were those who tried to imitate it. Like the guys who grew up in inland cities and were more into cruising around with their boards than actually getting in the water. Guys who were influenced by songs from the Beach Boys. Most of us hated the Beach Boys songs. Made fun of them. In fact, the group was even booed by many when they came to play the Rendezvous Ballroom in Balboa.

In Florida, I got a whole new perspective of what it was like to be a surfer. Florida guys had latched on to the look and the language, and had made it their own. Like the guys from inland back in California, the surfers in Florida went a little over the top with it all. Bleached blond hair, baggy trunks, Woodies covered with surf stickers. The whole bit. Dale and I had to chuckle. But, for the most part, they were all good guys. They absorbed the culture from a distance, through magazines and songs. In their own way, they were establishing a new branch of the surfing tribe, inventing it as they went along.

But the poor guys didn't have the key ingredient: surf. There were no waves! At least no good waves. They were small and mushy. The water was so warm that the paraffin wax would melt off the board. Yeah, this is before surf wax.

Gary Proper ruled the East Coast in those days. Florida's answer to David Nuuhiwa. He won all the contests there and he was the biggest name on the beach. Gary was a slasher, who ripped those mushy waves. But he was no stylist. There were guys I met there who I thought were better surfers. A bunch of them.

It all happened at Canaveral Pier. Sooner or later all the good guys would stop by and do their thing. The pier was a show spot. Sort of a Coney Island deal with hot-dog stands and carnival-type games, a real picnic on the ocean.

The highlight of the trip was the Canaveral Pier Contest. Dale and I were asked to judge the event. I couldn't believe it. I guess the fact that we were from California automatically qualified us as judges. But the best part was, they flew Butch Van Artsdalen in to be a judge, too.

I remember the contest as the equivalent to the Huntington contest for the East Coast. Maybe not. But, all the big names were there. Dick Catri, who ran Surfboards Hawaii in Florida, had arranged for Butch to come. Catri knew Butch from the North Shore, where they had ridden Waimea and Sunset together. How Catri ended up in Florida, I don't know. But he was a king of sorts there, a legend. And, a fun guy.

Butch was in true form from the minute he showed up on the beach, an hour or so late for the first heat. I'll always remember him with a big smile on his face. Nobody had more fun than Butch. I remember being up on the judging stand with him laughing the whole time. He did a running commentary on the surfing, and it was funny. Oh man. None of us were very serious about the judging. We just sat up there drinking beer and enjoying the show. Afterwards, we were asked to go out and give a "surfing exhibition." What a scene. Butch did a bunch of spinners on one wave and the crowd went wild. That was one day that I was glad to have the Stars and Stripes. It was the perfect board for those junky little waves, and we actually had fun putting on a show for the crowd at the pier.

There was a huge void when Butch left, and I got homesick. The sleepless nights in back of the Studebaker. The lack of steady income, and food. And, just the lifestyle in general took its toll. Dale and I decided to go back home. He called his mom for money, and I ended up begging Corky to send me a plane ticket. He came through and I was able to get home, albeit on standby all the way. Dale and I got split up somewhere along the line, in Atlanta I think, but maybe Dallas. It was a long travel day.

I arrived back in California somehow feeling a bit older. I had experienced being on my own with no parental supervision, actually no adult supervision. I had crashed in houses and apartments never knowing who lived in them. Stayed out all night at parties. Lived with the first wave of a growing counter culture of Bohemian lifestyle. Felt what it was like to be hungry and not have any money. As the song of the times so aptly put it: "to be without a home, out there on your own, no direction known, like a rolling stone."

I remember the plane making its final bank coming into LAX and looking down at those beautiful peaks of the California coastal mountains. Home at last.

The Music Connection
August of 1966. The Rolling Stones released what would be their biggest hit "Satisfaction." Bob Dylan introduced a new sound with The Band, and a new-be rolling stone had just returned from an albeit misadventure from Florida. It was good to be home, but times they definitely were a changing. The "conflict" in Viet Nam raged to new dimensions. The draft became a part of reality. And,

Music of ilfe — This is me in 1963, about the time Terry Smith and I had formed The Argons. That's my dad and grandmother having a moment, while some little smart-ass dreams about being a guitar player. Nice little Les paul knock-off guitar. Wonder what ever happened to that? (Photo by Mom)

the avenues to the future seemed to be shrinking. Like many of my friends, I opted for Orange Coast Junior College.

A subtle change within had also occurred. The apartment on 32nd Street suddenly seemed smaller. My parents omnipresent. A lot of my friends, were getting their own places or going off to college. After all, at 18 we were Adults.

Along about that time a guy named Oakie appeared on Newport's social scene playing guitar and harmonica at impromptu surf parties. He had an engaging personality and became immediately accepted as a guy who was fun to be around. Of course, to be fully accepted, one had to surf. And, Oakie definitely wanted to learn to surf.

We first connected through the guitar. I, anxious to learn new chords and songs, and he willing to teach. Then I gave him a few pointers on surfing and a friendship was formed. He was a couple of years older and was out in California as a lark. His parents sent him money to go to school at Orange Coast, and he settled into the apartment below us on 32nd Street. It wasn't long before I hatched the idea to move in with him in exchange for eating meals at my folk's house. It was a good deal for me. I was out on my own, but still within reach of my roots.

We called him "Oakie," because he was from Oklahoma and spoke with a casual-sounding drawl. Music was his forte, and he had an extensive collection of records. Nothing too contemporary, mind you. Folk artists, jazz and generally stuff that no one had ever heard.

I had been playing guitar since I was seven. Terry Smith and I even had a little surf band for awhile back in the eighth grade. Our biggest gig was one of my Mom's VFW rummage sales in a parking lot up in Costa Mesa. We were the "Argons." Two guitars and a drummer playing The Ventures, and Fireballs. A sort of pre-punk surf band that relied on volume rather than skill.

To me, music and surfing are alike in many ways. I won't even get into the soul versus commercialism aspects. Let's just say the harmony of a surfer on a wave and a musician playing a solo over a score are elements on inspiration. A dance of life. A cerebral journey that exports one's soul from the mundane. A ride on nature's rhythms. Okay, too deep.

How about the commitment it takes to learn the art of surfing as compared to learning an instrument. The hours spent living out each note, or each wave. The time spent alone thinking and practicing just to get to a level of acceptance. Ultimately, it takes the same type of individual, and that's why so many good surfers are also good musicians.

Mostly guitar players. Why not? You surf, take the guitar to the beach, and have a party around the fire as the sun goes down. Beach Party Bingo! Okay, sorry, but even Hollywood's fantasies have some basis in reality. Flamenco guitar has been a mainstay on the beach since the fifties. I started playing electric guitar when I was 13 and was enamoured with Surf Music. Terry Smith had all The Fireballs albums. Actually there were probably only two, but no matter, The Fireballs were gods, and their songs were often used by the likes of John Severson for surf films. I'll never forget the opening sequence of "Going My Wave," with Paul Strauch Jr. doing a perfect stretch five at Haleiwa with The Fireballs song "Vaquero" playing loud over the theater speakers. Now, that was art.

Oakie took us all in a different direction musically. At first he was into folk music: Hoyt Axton, Tim Hardin and early Bob Dylan. He played the harmonica in a rack, like Dylan, and was pretty good. He'd bring his guitar to parties and sing. Soon, we'd all be singing along and having a grand time making music on our own. Forget about playing records, the real thing was more fun. It always is.

There were clubs to go to that played folk music. The Prison of Socrates in Balboa and The Golden Bear in Huntington Beach. We'd see folk singers like Jose Feliciano and Joan Baez. We'd listen to Beat poetry while sipping espresso. That was some bad stuff, but to be cool you had to drink it. I'd order a side of hot chocolate to take the edge off.

Then one day Oakie brought home a new album. The Paul Butterfield Blues Band. The album cover recommended playing it at high volume. So we did. That music changed everything for a lot of us. It was raw, powerful, driving and heavy on the up-front lead guitar. The world took on new dimensions with Butterfield on the stereo.

The album became our surf music and our anthem. "Born in Chicago," "Mystery Train," "Blues with a Feeling," "Mojo Workin'." Great songs to think about when your dropping in a nice six-footer at the Lower Trestle. I heard the album so many times, I had every note ingrained in my head. The only thing better was to see the Paul Butterfield Blues Band live.

Oh yeah! They came to the Golden Bear. I remember going up on a school night, and seeing the first set. Then returning every night afterwards, even standing back in the alley to hear them when we didn't have the two or three bucks to get in. Paul Butterfield on vocals and very electric harmonica, Michael Bloomfield and Elvin Bishop on guitar, Jerome Arnold on bass, Mark Natflin on keyboards and Sammy Lay on drums. That was the original band, it changed a lot in the years after, but that was the line-up that shook our world.

The Golden Bear had a unique atmosphere. Part Beatnik, part Parisian café. Soft candlelit tables with red-checkered table clothes and sawdust on the floor. It stood where the big surf shop is now, across Coast Highway from the pier. There used to be a skating rink at the foot of the pier, bands played there, too. You could see a show at the Golden Bear and then walk across to the skating rink and see bands like Dick Dale, or even Ike and Tina Turner complete with the Ikettes. Oh those Ikettes, they were something to see.

The blues and surfing went right together for me. The driving beat, off-the-wall improvisation and soul of the music were just like surfing. The solos were the surfer and the rhythm the wave. We played out our vision on the wave, just like Bloomfield and Bishop did with ripping guitar solos.

Soon there were other blues bands popping up. John Mayall and the Blues Breakers with Eric Clapton on guitar. The British Blues arrived. Everyone began collecting blues records, especially Oakie, who drifted toward the more traditional stuff like Muddy Waters and Little Walter. All good. All very good, and a sort of revolutionary foundation for what was happening in surfing.

Expression Sessions
Mid-sixties surfing seemed to be evolving in two almost opposite directions. The new-styled nose-riding boards had allowed a generation of guys to jump up to a new level. Meanwhile, the Hynson and Edward protégés opted for styling out on longer, more pointed boards. I found myself thinking more about the expressive side of surfing than whip-and-slash noseriding. I had started thinking about surfing as an art form, an expression on the wave. Each ride a unique experience that could never be duplicated.

Of course, there was still the contest circuit. But as I became more involved with the form and movement of surfing, I was less interested in winning my heat. I started riding longer, more pointed boards that were made for speed. I'd drive Corky nuts at Hobie, because I'd order a board and then a month later come back and order another one. The fact that I wasn't doing all that well in contests didn't matter to me, but it mattered to him.

Finally, it all came to a head and one day we got into a big argument out in front of the Hobie shop in Dana Point. I remember walking away and just saying "forget it" to him. I went home and called up Roy Crump at Harbour Surfboards. He was captain of the team there and they had a good crew. Mark Martinson, Rich Chew, Gregg Tucker, Mike Koontz. Better yet, they had some great shapers. Mike Marshall, Dean Elliot and Rich Harbour.

I told Roy that I quit Hobie and asked him if I could ride for Harbour. He said no problem and a couple of days later I ordered a Trestle Special and a "Cheater." Those were both great boards. The Trestle Special was a lot like my Phil boards. Thin and pointed and very responsive. The Cheater was a knock off of the Reynolds Yater Spoon. A noserider, but without all the wide nose crap. The Cheater rode the nose great and turned on a dime.

My contest surfing improved a bit after that, but I never won any big meets. I did win a couple of Newport contests though, and that meant a lot to me. Hometown and all.

We surfed up and down the coast making trips to Rincon, the Ranch and Sunset Cliffs. There were more guys in the water than ever before, mainly because by now every one was wearing the farmer john-style wetsuit, which was comfortable to wear and allowed you to stay out for hours. As the waves got more crowded, we started surfing more obscure breaks. Trestles and Doheny were packed. Forget about Malibu.

We surfed places that were a little harder to get to, or had more of a price to pay when you lost your board. One such place was Mepees, or Mepees Point. A well-formed left just north of the Boneyard at Doheny. They say some guys from Capistrano named it. The story was they were up on the cliff checking it out and someone asked what the name of the place was. One of the guys, peeing over the cliff at the time, looked up and said "Me pees."

Mepees looked a little meaner than it actually was. It had a daunting shallow reef. Lose your board at low tide and you had a tough time getting it back. We're talking dings in your board and cuts on your feet.

But the waves were worth it. It had an outside bowl-like peak that lined up on the inside. A nice left, not a hollow left or anything, but just enough juice to make it fun. Growing up in Newport, I learned to enjoy going backside. I used to love to hear stories about Paul Strauch going backside at Ala Moana and Phil going backside at Cottons Point. Both noted for deep-in-the-peak drop-knee turns followed by two smooth steps to the trim point. Backside with style. I have to say that the best of my generation, in my opinion, of emulating the classic backside style was Billy Hamilton.

The guys who surfed Mepees were soul artists. Big fades into the peak and bottom turns up into the lip. Randy Haworth and Pete Nickertz from Newport were two of the best there. It was a forgiving wave that never really closed out. You could bomb the soup and always get back out to the shoulder. A large right loomed just north of Mepees and it had an even more treacherous reef. We didn't surf it much, but thinking back now, I bet it would have been a great short board wave. We called it "Unreals."

It's all a harbor now, of course. They mowed down the majestic cliffs and built a damn jetty. I don't remember much of a protest about it, though. They just came in one day and started dropping rocks in the water. I think we all thought the world was going to end anyway. The war was escalating, the Russians had nukes aimed at us. We didn't think much about the future.

We did go to school though, and not just to get out of the draft. In my experience, there has always been an intellectual side to the surfing culture. There is nothing wrong with being smart, and at Orange Coast College we dug in to get good grades. I wanted to be a writer and took English, political science and psychology.

Maintaining a 15-unit schedule is hard work anytime. I know it was for me, especially because I had a night job at a bomb factory. Really! Terry Smith and I and some of the Cedar Street boys all worked at this factory that made parts for guided missiles. The pay was good and we could study on the job. Still, it wasn't easy.

Along about the second semester of my freshman year a couple of the guys I surfed with got wind of an incredible plan. Join the Maui National Guard! Yep, all you had to do was go to Maui, sign up and then do your basic training at Fort Ord or someplace and then you got stationed on Maui. It sounded crazy. Too good to be true. I elected to stay in school, but some of the guys, Tom Gaglia, Jamie MacGlophlin and Eric Eastman, quit school and took off for Maui.

We didn't hear from them for awhile. Then the letters started coming. And, what letters they were. Surfing eight to ten-foot perfect waves at Honolua Bay, hanging around a sleepy little town called Lahaina, that happened to have about a dozen great surf spots. I was skeptical, at first. Still the letters kept coming and they pulled at me. I thought about the stories Marshall told of Honolua. Martinson had been there and ripped it apart. He said it was the best wave he'd ever surfed. Herbie Fletcher had been there. I was feeling left out.

I made it through the semester though, and did pretty well. Dale Kinsella and I teamed up and studied hard. He was a great student and an inspiration. That next summer, I worked and hung out at the beach. The letters from Maui kept coming, now they were about Lahaina and surfing perfect waves at Mala Wharf. Along about this time, Pete Nickertz and Roger Zieger packed up and went to Kauai. They, being goofy-foots, had heard about a left called Infinities.

More letters. More tales from both Maui and Kauai, all about perfect waves and great living. That summer on the coast had been boring. Seemed like a lot of my friends had either gone to Hawaii or quit surfing to concentrate on school. I consoled my friend Roy Crump at Harbour. Crump was a good surfer who had finished his degree at Long Beach State and was set to become a teacher. Marshall was going to State to do the same. Dale Kinsella had his sights set on going to UC Santa Barbara, and that definitely appealed to me, too.

Just one more semester at Coast and then I could transfer. I had pretty much decided on either UCSB or San Diego State, which was easier to get in. Both had great surf close by. Still, I kept getting these letters from the Islands. It was a dilemma. So, I asked Crump for some advice thinking he was going to say to stay in school. But, he did just the opposite. He said I could go back to school anytime, but that the window for riding waves in Hawaii would not always be there. "You're only young once," he told me, "and it's getting more crowded everyday. Go to Kauai, go to Maui and surf before it gets too crowded. "

That was it. Dale tried to talk me out of it. I don't think he ever forgave me; our friendship was never the same after that. Who knows? Maybe he was right. He is probably the most financially successful person I grew up with. All self-made. A pillar in the Los Angeles law community.

I went in the other direction; and you know that window Crump talked to me about? I wouldn't exchange it for all the money in the world.

End of an era — I didn't know it then but we were all in for a big change. The days of cruising with style, like Rullo here at the Shores, were about to come to an end. (Photo curtesy of D.B. Rullo)

PART II

THE WINDOW
Hawaii 1967

I dropped my plans to return to Orange Coast, sold my VW to
Denny Smith from Huntington and bought a one-way ticket to
Kauai. My parents were pretty much devastated. I remember my
dad telling me that I was just going to be a surf bum all my life. It
was really one of the only times I ever remember him being mad. I
had some blessings though. My mentors Mike Marshall and Roy
Crump both said to go for it.

The plan was to go to Kauai first and then wait until there was an
opening in the Maui National Guard. Tom Gaglia said he would stay
in touch about the Guard and meanwhile I could stay with Nickertz
and Zieger on Kauai. Another hare-brained plan with little money
and lots of unknowns. But with that, I bought a one-way ticket to
Lihue, Kauai, and rolled the dice.

I flew out of LAX on the morning jet to Honolulu. I remember buying a Life Magazine in the airport. It had a picture of John Lennon
on the cover done in the psychedelic fashion of the time. The story
was about being free. I thought about leaving the conventional
world behind. No more contests, no more long hours working, just
living life on my own. Surfing.

Things are seldom as you envision them. Kauai sure wasn't, at
first. I landed at Lihue and thought it looked just like the North
Shore, except there was more red dirt. Sugar cane grew all around
the small airport, giving one the feeling of being in a green desert.
I looked around and all of the sudden, I was lonesome.

Lihue was an open-air airport, crowded with tourists at first. Then
busses and stretch limos showed up and whisked them off to their
hotels for Mai Tais and Hawaiian shows. Where was my welcoming committee?

I'd sent a letter a couple of days before and expected to see my
friends there to pick me up. No dice. With the sun going down in
the west, I asked one of the people at the Aloha counter for directions. With "Plan A" a wash-out, I went for "Plan B." A hitchhike
with my board and suitcase out to where my friends lived in

Waimea. Luckily, the first car that came along picked me up. The driver was a young kid of about 16, all smiles as I got in. I said I would give him some money if he could take me out to Waimea. He smiled and said something that I took for a yes.

The adventure was on again. We drove down the sugarcane-lined road to the main highway and hung a left. I noticed only one traffic light as we passed through Lihue. No bright lights and big city here. We drove out the west side and I started seeing more of what I'd expected. Bright green trees crowding the road and creating tunnels. A pleasant ride through quaint little towns, around sweeping curves with lush green ferns dripping off wet, black cliffs. Okay, this is corny, but I was hearing "Bali Hi" the song from South Pacific in my mind as we drove. The island was alive and so was I. Alive, excited, and a little scared.

I could barely understand the kid behind the wheel. He spoke in spurts with a thick pigeon accent. We smiled at each other a lot, I don't think he could understand me much better. I had rough directions to the house. Somewhere on Menehune Road. I gave him directions the best I could and wasn't to sure if he understood. Still he drove right up to a place and pulled in the driveway. I found out later that just about everybody on that side of the island knew of this "hippy" place.

Oh yeah, that good image of surfers we had tried to convey all those years? It never made it this far. Surfers were perceived by the locals to be surf-bum no-goods, out to poison their children. That Aloha spirit you hear so much about? Not too evident in those days.

Certainly not that evening in the fading light. The kid left me at the house and drove away looking a little disappointed. I couldn't' figure it out. I gave him about five bucks for gas, that was plenty. The only sound after the drone of his car faded out was of bugs. Lots of bugs and birds, maybe. Jungle music. The house was dark, obviously no one home. I took a seat on the porch under a set of wind-chimes made of sea shells and driftwood. I remembered someone telling me "look for the mobile hanging from the porch....that's the place." The mobile made sounds like some ghostly vibraphone player as a mystical wind blew up the valley.

I sat there for more than an hour feeling very alone. Every now and then, a car of locals would drive by and yell something. I thought that I might be in for some trouble, but they just gave me looks and kept driving. Finally, a big old black Buick with surf racks on the top rumbled into the driveway and I was very much relieved.

The house on Menehune Road had been a surf house for several years. Larry Strada, who had gone to the islands with Rullo a year earlier, had lived there and was reportedly the one who made and hung the mobile. Like many surf houses on the North Shore there was generally one guy who ran the place and interacted with the landlord. Everybody else paid a little rent and stayed for however long they could. As always, the new guy fresh off the plane gets hit up for cash to buy groceries and pay some bills.

In my case, we made an immediate trip to the Ben Franklin for some brown rice and soup. I was also called upon to rescue the house stereo, which had been hawked to pay rent the week before. The guy who ran the house was named Jerry Faucet. He was from Kailua, a citified local. There were about five or six people staying at the house when I got there. I was given a futon on the floor to sleep on. New guys slept in the living room until someone moved out or was gone so long that they lost their position in the pecking order.

Zieger and Nickertz were there, as was Skip Richardson from Newport. There was a young couple, Victor Lopez and his girl-friend Cheryl Baron, both from Ina Hina. Victor had a brother, Gerry, who had gone to Orange Coast and surfed Blackies. Years later Gerry would be one of the most famous surfers in the world and Cheryl's sister Michelle would marry Jimmy Lucas. Small world.

Infinities a Trek for Perfection

That first night was spent around a Formica kitchen table talking and eating heaps of brown rice with vegetable soup poured over the top. Mostly the talk was about Infinities, which was the main attraction on Kauai in those days. I listened and heard that it was good, but like so many good surf spots, it had its drawbacks. It was on the Robinson Gay Ranch and you had to sneak in. And, the route was a combination paddle and walk. Okay, just like Trestles, I thought. Not really.

Trestles didn't have Kiavi thorns on the trail, or huge mosquitoes sucking your blood. You had to go through a bit of hell to get to a bit of heaven at Infinities. And yes, the waves were good. I have to admit to being a little disappointed with it though. The water was bad. It was all red from the cane run off and it smelled. Some days were worse than others, but it was not the clear blue water that I'd dreamed about. And, the surf would blow out everyday, just like at home. Sure, it would blow offshore for awhile, but sooner or later the finicky island trades would switch around and blow on-shore.

Infinities was actually Pakala Bay. The lefts at Pakala broke off a low-lying, rocky point covered with kiavi trees, cane houses and tall coconut palms. Cane workers and employees of the Robinson Gay Ranch lived there in a little camp-like village. When you surfed Pakala, the sounds and smells of rural island life would float out into the lineup. Roosters crowing, pigs squealing, dogs barking, breakfast cooking on a wood fire.

Getting to Pakala was a daily adventure. The way in was from Waimea River mouth to the north. It started with a short paddle across a cold Waimea River, then a scramble up the embankment, over a barbed-wire fence and a long walk down a cane road. Sometimes a ranch jeep would patrol the road and you had to leap for cover if you heard it coming. Did I mention the Kiavi (pronouc-ned kee-av-e) trees? The Hawaiian equivalent of Mesquite, with plenty of sharp thorns. About a mile or so of that and then a path cut to the beach. The path took you to the northern side of the Pakala Bay. You could walk around the crescent-shaped bay, or paddle across. Neither route was much fun, but both led to Pakala lefts.

On good days, swells from the south would line up out in front of the houses and wrap into Pakala Bay, peeling into a pristine white sand beach. When the trades were just right and the water not overly red with cane runoff, it was well worth the price of admis-sion.

Pet Nickertz and Roger Zieger had the place wired. The days at Blackies and Mepees had prepared them well for this perfection left. Pakala is one of those waves where you always end up taking off on a shoulder. The wave starts breaking way out, around the point, and is basically impossible to ride from the outside, at least it was for us then on the equipment we had. The wave comes roaring down the line at you . As you paddle in, you're looking to your right at the breaking wave headed your way, and to your left to make sure you aren't going to be too far behind when you catch it.

Once in the wave, and provided no one takes off in front of you, it becomes a race for the bay. The wave lines up, spray blowing off the top, a long, steep line. Depending on the size, you could either walk up to the nose and cruise, or carve up and down the face to keep pace with the wave.

It could get crowded, even then. The crew from the surf house was crowd enough. But there were others, mostly locals from Waimea. We made friends with some, and managed to share the waves pretty well. Two of the best were Kalaeo and Lika Boy, a goofy-foot and regular-foot respectively. There were also guys from other parts of the island who would show up on a swell. One was a master of Pakala and great person as well.

The King of Pakala — Carlos Andrade was a master at Pakala. Pure soul in any size waves. Nose rides like this went on forever, just like the spot's name "Infinities." (Photos courtesy of Kit Cossart)

Mr. Smooth — Carlos after a long nose ride glides into a classic drop-knee cutback. Good, oh yeah, he was something. In fact, still is!

Carlos, The King

Carlos Andrade was a legend on Kauai. A local boy, he had made a trip to the mainland and hung with the boys in San Diego. He'd surfed O.B. and Wind-an-Sea and he was the undisputed best surfer from Kauai. What a classic guy. He was Hawaiian and Portuguese and maybe a little Haole too. A stout man, even then, and always with an endearing smile.

I remember the first time I met him. He pulled into the surf house on Menehune Road on a motor scooter with a stock of bananas tied on the back. He was wearing this funky army jacket and looked nothing like a surfer to me. But his smile was so genuine and he offered me a banana without saying a word.

Later, we sat around the kitchen table "talking story," as the Hawaiians say, and eating bananas for hours. I heard all about the wet caves in Hanalei and the hermit living out in Kalalau Valley. Fascinating accounts of counter-culture life on Kauai and stories of surf out on Kauai's North Shore.

That afternoon, we all walked down to Pakala for an evening surf. Carlos borrowed a board. The surf was small, but the wind was off-shore and it was a good session. What a great surfer he was. Goofy-foot with a Hawaiian style reminiscent of David and Donald, but not as flashy. He had all the moves, but just did them a little slower, a little smoother. He was one of those guys that could make any wave look good. He could make the soup look good. Music on the water.

He continued to drop by from time to time as the summer came to an end, always bringing something with him. Bananas, avocados and mangos that he had harvested from some secret stash. When nobody was home, he'd leave the fruit and a note signed "The Black Bandit."

The Surf House — Kauai

The surf house was like a revolving door with people. Guys from Oahu and the mainland would drop in and out, staying for a couple of days or a couple of weeks. Everyone would pay their fair share and we had a steady supply of brown rice and tuna fish. One of the benefits of living in Hawaii then was that the water out of the tap was really good. I mean as good as any I've ever tasted. I got into the habit of drinking a lot of water. Of course, we couldn't really afford milk or sodas. And, the lifestyle pretty much dictated simple food.

I remember after just a couple of weeks thinking "wow, I'm actually keeping myself alive!" Kind of silly, but I had always depended on my mom telling me what to eat. Now, I was out there on my own, and it felt good to know that I could make decisions for myself. Hey, I was becoming an adult! Heaven forbid.

In late summer, we got a visit from a future legend. Gerry Lopez came to see his brother Victor and catch some waves at Pakala. He had lived in Newport and surfed Blackies, but I'd never really gotten to know him. He was small in stature but, like Carlos, had a great genuine smile and a soulfulness that shined through his eyes. Destined for greatness? You bet, but it would be awhile.

These were still the days of the big tankers, and Gerry was good, but he was no David Nuuhiwa or Carlos Andrade. He was smooth though, and had the moves. At Pakala, he was just one of the dogs in the pack. His time was still to come and oh boy, when he broke away, he really broke away. Hey, that's evolution, you know.

Garden Days
Days were spent surfing in the morning, then kind of hanging around or exploring in the afternoons. Carlos turned us on to this exotic botanical garden. A secluded private estate in a small valley near Poipu. The owner, a Mr. Alerton, had landscaped what must have been about 20 acres around his mansion-like home. What a beautiful valley, with a pristine white-sand beach and perfect body surfing waves.

The garden was full of fruit trees nestled in amongst eccentric statues and courtyards. There were little museum-like buildings and ponds, white stone benches to sit on. Like being in some sort of fairyland. And, there was never anyone there, except for the occasional gardener.

We would park our car in the cane field and then sneak in through the jungle that surrounded the estate. From time to time, we would get caught by the gardeners and told to leave. They would try and block off the trails we had made in, so we were always coming in from different directions. I remember once taking a bad route and getting lost in a fierce jungle. Thorns and mosquitoes everywhere. It was pure hell and took us hours to find our way out.

Afternoons in "The Garden" were worth all the trouble of sneaking in. We would eat fruit of every kind and sit for hours in Grecian courtyards listening to the birds and sounds of the jungle. It was probably the most peaceful place I've ever been.

Life on the West Side

When we weren't spending afternoons there, we would be out exploring. There was surf in Poipu. The locals surfed a place called "Long House," named for a restaurant on the beach. It was a not-so-perfect right with a rather mean disposition. Just north of Long House was this big Sunset-like peak that really dumped. No one surfed it much, except for us. Years later they would name it Acid Drops, but then it didn't have a name. Just a reputation.

On a long board, it was a major accomplishment just to make the drop. The winds would howl off shore and just catching a wave was a challenge. But, the water was crystal clear and if you made the drop, you were in for one hell of a ride. There were rumors of sharks, but I never saw one. But, oh did I think about them when I lost my board.

Back then we had the buddy system. When a guy lost his board, someone would always try to help. Most times anyway. Sometimes there wouldn't be anybody around and you had to fend for yourself. Just finding your board was something of an accomplishment. Swimming in looking for it all around, only to spot it headed out in the rip. Did I mention sharks?

Swimming was a big part of the game then. You had to be able to swim like Johnny Wisemiller or the Duke if you wanted to surf in Hawaii. And we all did. I was thankful for all the water lessons my dad taught me when I was a kid. I used them all. Those days swimming across Newport Bay with my dad and learning to float and relax served me well in the islands.

A Working Lunch

After a couple of months, my money had all but run out. Skip Richardson was in the same boat, so we decided to get jobs. The best we could do was to work construction for a local company as laborers. I think we started at like $3 bucks an hour. Good pay back then.

The work was hard. I learned to hammer drywall and frame. One day I'd be working out on the west side, the next day the boss would have me in Lihue. I remember digging a ditch at this one construction site and thinking to myself that my dad always told me I was going to "end up digging ditches if I didn't stay in school."

I about starved to death the first week. I had no money to buy food for lunches. Once I got my first paycheck, I went straight to the market and bought a bunch of groceries. I'd never had to make my own lunches before, but the following week, I managed to throw together some peanut butter and jelly sandwiches and packed some fruit. It worked out okay, but I was envious of how all the other guys did lunch.

The crew were all locals. A mix of Japanese, who did all the carpentry and skilled jobs; and Hawaiians, who did all the dirty work. I, of course, worked with the Hawaiians, whom I discovered to my shock were considered sort of an underclass. Anyway, at lunch time they all brought some kind of main dish, which they would share. It was like a pot luck everyday. Each would have their own tin of rice, which they held in one hand. Squatting in a circle under some shade, they would shovel rice into their mouths with chopsticks and then pick at each other's main dishes which were arranged in the circle. Smiling, talking thick pigeon English and admiring each other's contribution.

And there I was sitting off by myself eating potato chips and a peanut butter sandwich. It was culture shock, but I admired the way they all came together. The food was always an assortment of fish, chicken and beef cooked Japanese or Hawaiian style with a lot of soy sauce and teriyaki. It smelled really good.

One day, probably the best day of my job at Kagawa Construction, the boss Fumio Kagawa took me to lunch. He was a cool old Japanese guy who was fascinated with us Haoles. I think that's why he hired us, not because he needed more laborers. He wanted to know what made us tick.

He mostly spent his time driving from site to site and checking to make sure all was going well. So this one day he comes down to the site where I was working and says he's going to take me to another project. I was stoked because I had been carrying number 12 blocks all morning and was not looking forward to the afternoon heat.

On the way, he stops at this little Japanese place and asks me if I'm hungry. It was about 11:30 and I was starved. We went in and he orders up a couple of Primo beers. I wasn't to keen on having a beer right then, but hey, he was the boss. I took a swig and he ordered up some chow. The waitress didn't even look at me. So I just flowed with it.

She returned with a big plate of what looked like bright red meat. Fumio used his chopsticks to mix up some soy sauce and hot mustard in a little dish. He handed me chopsticks and motioned for me to dig in. I thought, okay, it's that sharing thing. I'm into it. So I make a run at one of the slabs of meat, still a little awkward using the sticks. I pick it up and he makes sure I give it a healthy dip in sauce. I oblige and bring it up to my mouth.

I had no idea what I was eating, but it wasn't bad. The hot sauce was tasty and sort of masked any flavor of the meat. The texture kind of threw me though, it was soft and almost melted in my mouth. He watched intensely as I chewed. I swallowed and took a swig of beer.

He seemed very pleased. Then he took a piece and ate it and motioned for me to dig in. I did, and it was good. He said "I didn't think haole boys liked sashimi." I said "what's sashimi?" And, he said "raw fish."

That was my first taste of fresh Ahi Tuna. I think I blew his mind because I didn't gag or even make a face. I just dug in and powered the stuff. Hey, it was good and I was damn hungry. The sashimi tuna was followed by tempura shrimp and teriyaki chicken, a bowl of steaming white rice, macaroni salad and a couple more Primos. Man, it was all good.

The Fight
My story about those first couple of months on the west shore of Kauai wouldn't be complete without telling you about the fight. It

was a night I will always regret. The last time I would ever see Billy Pond alive.

Bill Pond was a goofy-foot from Newport who had hung with us at the pier for a couple of years. He was a pretty good surfer, not great, but he had some style. A year younger than me, he was a kid who always had a lot of stuff. His folks bought him a cool Volkswagen bus in high school and we used to go up and down the coast in that thing. He was a good guy, but a bit of a smart-ass, too, who was always pushing the limit to being accepted by the gang.

Pond came over to Kauai and moved into the surf house on Menehune Road. He brought lots of stuff and was immediately taken in by the have-me-nots at the surf house. This, in my opinion, sort of inflated his ego and caused a little agitation between us. One day, we were out surfing at Pakala and he kept paddling past us on the outside and trying to take off too far out. He would end up straightening off, which was no big deal except the guys in the line-up kept giving him waves, then he would blow it and straighten off.

I let him get a bunch of waves before I'd had it with this act. A set came in and he goes for it on the outside. I can tell right away that he's not going to make it, so I turn around and paddle in. Hey, it's a clean five-footer and I'm not letting it go through. I take off and he gets to about 15 feet from me before he straightens off. But not before he yells something like "fucking shoulder grabber!"

We exchanged dirty looks the rest of the afternoon, but nothing much was said. That night back at the surf house we were sitting around talking after dinner and he brings it up. I don't remember exactly what he said, but it was enough to get the hair on the back of my neck to stand up and my lower lip quivering. In a room with a bunch of guys, when somebody makes a remark about someone being a shoulder grabber, that someone has to do something. Or let it stand and become something less of a man. Someone calls you out, you got to go.

A minute later we were going at it in the front yard of the surf house. Everyone came outside to watch, even the neighbors. We threw punches and I landed a couple of good ones. I remember almost feeling sorry for him when I hit him in the nose with a solid right hand. He started bleeding, and I thought he'd give it up, but no, he keeps coming.

I dance him out into the street, and keep jabbing at him. The guys watching are all jeering and telling him to give it up. No way. So I figure the only way to end it is to get him down. I jump in with a headlock, my famous move from about third grade on. I wrench him down to the ground and jump on him. I've got both his arms pinned with my legs and I raised my fist to hit him in the face. I say "give up?" He spits in my face!

Bam, I slam my fist unmercifully in his jaw. Bam, bam. Two more to the side of his head. "Give up?" He said something like "Fuck you! I'll never give up." I couldn't believe it. I'm beating him to a pulp and he's yelling insults at me. I punched him a few more times as hard as I could, then his eyes get real big and his face sort of puffs up.

The next thing I know he lunges up with his arms and knocks me off balance. He rolls over and gets me in a head lock! I can't believe it. I remember feeling sort of weak and him rolling me over on the pavement. He jumps on me just as I had jumped on him and starts hammering me in the face. Then he says "give up?" And, I did.

I had my ass kicked in front of everyone. My face was bloody, my shirt—one of my few good ones—was ripped beyond repair. My knees were bloody, my face hurt like never before. It was all I could do to go back in the house and crash on my bed.

Everyone left me alone, which I appreciated. In fact, it was real quiet the rest of the night. I slept late the next morning, the door to the room had been closed. Somebody came in to see how I was doing and brought me some tea. My eyes were both black and my lip was cut and swollen. The guy who brought me the tea said that if it were any comfort that Pond had looked worse. Bitchen, does that mean I won? I don't think so.

I felt depressed. Very depressed. My body was hurt, but my self-esteem had been pummeled. I thought about leaving the islands and going back home. It seemed like a good idea. I would call my folks and ask for plane fare. Then the guy tells me that Pond had left the island. Someone had taken him to the airport early in the morning and he was gone.

It turned out that my reputation wasn't as badly damaged in the group as I had thought. Everyone said it was a good fight, and thought that I had done the right thing by ending it. Hey, Pond wasn't going to stop until one of us was dead. I saw it in his eyes. I think he even said it while I was beating in his face.

That was certainly the most violent fight I've ever been in, and it was the last fight I've ever been in. I won't fight, unless one of my kids or someone I love is in danger. And then get the fuck out of the way, because I'll take the Billy Pond approach.

Sadly, Bill and I had been friends, shared some good times, and it ended like that. I never saw him again after that night. A year or so later he was murdered on the North Shore, simply in the wrong place at the wrong time. Enough said.

The Pit, the Cement and The Fah Inn
The coming of fall changed the color of the Jakaranda trees around the town of Waimea to bright purple. My face and body healed and things got better. New people arrived from the mainland. John Hawley and his wife from Newport, David Grimes and his wife from Ocean Beach. The dynamic changed with women in the mix and I ended up moving in with the two couples in a house that Fumio Kagawa owned just down the road from the surf house.

We called it The Pit. It was an okay place to live, if you didn't mind the smell. I guess that's why we called it the Pit. It was like a large apartment house connected to a couple of other structures where some pretty down to earth locals lived. By that I mean that they raised and slaughtered their own livestock in the yard below where we lived. It wasn't pretty.

I ended up quitting my job. Sort of a combination gut-reaction, culture-clash sort of thing. I'd been doing pretty well at framing and drywall and was making good money. But getting up in the morning and going to work in the back of a pick-up truck while my friends were all marching down to Pakala was hard. Finally, one day it all came to a head.

Kagawa Construction had won the bid to tear down the old police station and jail in Waimea and build a new one. The old station was at the corner of the main highway and Menehune Road. A classic old two-story clapboard building probably built in the 1930s.

Leave it to the Newport guys to stir things up. Just before it was to be demolished, Pete Nickertz and Skip Richardson went through the buildings looking for artifacts and stuff for their new house in Hanapepe. Sure enough they scored big. They found a human skull in one of the old jail cells. No kidding. A human skull, and they took it home and put a candle in it. Used it for a decoration. That kind of freaked the neighbors out, and the rest of us, too.

When the crew I was working with came to Waimea, the first order of business was to lay the cement for the foundation. As you might already know, cement work is no fun. Cement work in the autumn heat of Hawaii is a nightmare. You have to get the mud off the truck and sling it where it needs to go before it hardens up.

I was on one of the shoveling details with a big Hawaiian guy named Donald. He was a good guy, when he was sober, but he would sometimes drink from a pint of whisky at work and then watch out. I remember one Friday night after work when the crew all went down to the park at Nawiliwili to have a couple of beers and eat pu pus. Donald had been swigging his whisky all day and when he had a couple of beers in him he started calling me "fucking haole...you think you're so fucking smart." He actually took a couple swings at me, but I managed to dodge him. The rest of the crew subdued him and he finally went to sleep in the back of the truck. The next Monday morning, he didn't remember a thing. Nice as ever to me.

So that day at the Waimea Police station job, we were slinging the mud and had two or three trucks backed up waiting to dump cement. The pressure was on and Donald was dripping like a water faucet. He'd also managed to get in a couple of belts every time there was a break in the action.

We were in the middle of one of these mad scrambles of trying to get the cement off one of the trucks when a group of my friends walk by on their way to Pakala. Guys in trunks with boards, their girlfriends in short flower-print shifts. They started razzing me; "Hey HT come on with us. Waves are good."

That was it for my Hawaiian buddy Donald. He goes off on me with the fucking haole routine. It was all I could do to keep shoveling. At lunch time, I found the boss and told him I was quitting. He understood. That evening I was back out in the surf at Pakala knowing that I'd done the right thing.

About once a week we would all go out for dinner at this little Chinese place next to where the police station was being built. It was called The Fah Inn. We called it the Fah out, but the food was good. And cheap too. A really nice old Chinese couple ran the place. The wife waited tables and the old man cooked. You could get a great meal for about three bucks and have leftovers to take home. I remember eating Thanksgiving dinner there that year. A whole bunch of us around a long table eating beef brocoli and sweet and sour shrimp. It was one of the best Thanksgiving meals I can remember.

The Road to Hanalei

Being in Waimea was like being in a time warp. The buildings all pre-dated World War II, except for the Ben Franklin, which must have been built in the early sixties. Getting mail was one of the big events for us in those days. We had no telephones or TVs; mail was the only way we got news. General Delivery. People would share their letters, or read them aloud around the table. Pictures from home, money, cookies. All good.

One day I got a letter from Maui. My old friend Tom Gaglia was planning a trip over to Kauai. I arranged to pick him up at the airport and he stayed with us at The Pit. Tom had great stories about Maui. The surf, the town of Lahaina, the mellow locals, it all sounded great. Best of all were his stories about Honolua Bay. Perfect waves peeling off the point of a picturesque bay.

In turn, we told him the stories we'd heard about Hanalei. In typical fashion, we immediately organized a trip out there to check it out. Winter was approaching, and although there hadn't been any north swells yet, there might be some surf.

The road to Hanalei in those days was long and bumpy. We are talking major pot holes. It was only about 60 miles from Waimea to Hanalei, but the last thirty miles took over two hours, and that varied with how many times you had to stop and change a tire. We took Carlos' advice and caravaned in two cars. We headed out in the morning in good spirits. About four hours later, we rounded the last turn and looked out over the most beautiful valley I've ever seen.

We got so enamored with the waterfalls and huge cliffs that we almost forgot to check the surf. Then someone said "look at that!" We could see a silver strand of a river flowing out into the ocean. Waves were breaking way outside. A couple of the guys who had been there before let us know that the surf was looking pretty good.

Arriving at the beach, we were immediately taken by the scene before us. Tall Ironwood trees swaying gracefully in the tradewinds. A little pier jutting about 60 yards into an expansive turquoise bay. Clear blue water lapping at the shore. Heaven. And, there was nobody around. Nobody. Not a car. Not a surfboard. We had it to ourselves.

We stripped the boards off the cars and charged the water. It would be the first of many go-outs at Hanalei for me. A break that you have no idea what the waves are going to be like until you get outside. That's because it's a long paddle out, and waves you see from the beach are mostly just the inside waves. Outside, it's another story.

The consensus was that we were paddling out to two to three-foot "fun surf." When we reached the bowl, we knew it was overhead. The guys who had been there before, Vance Martin and Mike Would, clued us in on the bowl. They had already told us that there were two or three places to take off, and that it only connected up when it was big.

We were content surfing the bowl for a couple of hours. It was a fun wave. Nice A-frame peak, perfect for a turn off the bottom, a cutback off the lip and two or three little inside sections to squeak through. Fun, fun, fun. The sets were consistent and even though there were about nine of us out, there was no problem getting waves. The whole time though, we kept seeing these sets come wrapping around the point, big perfect rights cranking down the point toward us at the bowl.

Finally, Tom, Vance and I paddled out to the point. I remember my first wave. It was a healthy six-footer and all I could do was just point my board down the line and race ahead full speed to stay ahead of the thundering tube. It was a gas! I came paddling back out just screaming about how good it was.

Vance had a really nice Brewer that was just perfect for the place and he was in heaven. Tom Gaglia had a Surfboards Hawaii that was like a Trestle Special. Mine was an Expression Model from Moyer and a good point-and-trim board. None were made for what was to come.

I had switched from riding for Harbour the summer before coming to the islands. Basically, it was a Newport thing. Quigg had retired and turned his shop over to Chuck Moyer, who had worked for him for a while. Chuck was a decent shaper and a bunch of us in Newport started riding his boards. They weren't Quiggs, but they had some of the soul. Anyway, I had an Expression Model, which was our version of a Phil Board, or a Red Fin, or a Trestle Special, take your pick. Okay, they were actually "Herbie Torrens" Expression Models. Only about a dozen or so were ever made, and I don't think anyone ever paid full price for one.

Raising the Stakes

So there I was on my Expression Model on a day that would definitely take it to its limit. As the day wore on, we took a break and some other carloads of surfers arrived. Carlos was in one of the cars and gets out with this big smile on his face and asks us how we like it. It was a rhetorical question.

We made a run to Ching Young Store, the only store in Hanalei, and bought a loaf of bread, peanut butter, honey and some passion fruit guava nectar.

After we chowed down it was back to the surf. Same long paddle out, but this time we went right past the bowl and joined Carlos and a couple of other guys out on the point. What an afternoon, the waves just kept coming around the corner, one after another, each one a little bigger, better, faster.

It wasn't long until we realized that we were in some 10-foot surf. But, it was so perfect that it wasn't scary at all. I remember thinking this is the fastest I've ever gone on a surfboard....this is the biggest wave I've ever ridden. It was great. We surfed until dark loving every minute.

When we finally came in, Carlos was waiting on the beach. He told us he was staying in Hanalei that night and invited us to crash at his friend's house. We didn't have any sleeping bags or gear, but what the hell, we were in. Actually, the other carload of guys went back to Waimea; they were the guys with the girls at home.

So we end up in this big one-room building with a tin roof. The guy who lived there was named Mike. He was a big-wave rider from the North Shore. The place was right behind the Rice Mill, a quaint little restaurant next to Ching Young Store. We ate our peanut butter sandwiches and talked story around candles and mosquito punks and eventually fell asleep from pure exhaustion.

It rained that night. I remember hearing those droplets hitting the tin roof. Winter was coming. Bigger waves were on the way. And were they ever.

The next morning we went down to the beach early. This time there were guys already there. Lots of guys by Kauai standards. There were locals from Lihue, and every surfer we knew from the west side. Word had gotten out. We checked the surf and it looked about the same as the evening before. Without giving it a thought, I just took my board off the top of the car and started waxing up.

Pete Nikertz came up with a couple of other guys and asked if I was going out. I said hell yeah, that I'd surfed the best waves of my life the day before and it was great. Gaglia and Vance Martin were both waxing up too and then I noticed a group sort of gathering around us.

"Are you guys going out?"

We kind of looked at each other and said "yeah, of course, why wouldn't we? The surf is perfect." Okay, we thought the surf was perfect. It looked about the same. We had failed to notice a little change in the weather. The wind was stronger, there were strange clouds in the sky and the air was thick with unstable moisture.

More to the point, the sound from the ocean was louder. Much louder. No biggie, we just went on down and jumped in.

There's the three of us paddling out the channel, just shooting the breeze and thinking about how good the waves are going to be. We paddle and paddle and then we realize, hey, the paddle seems a little longer today. And, we hadn't even got to the inside of the bowl.

Then a huge set rolls in off the point. I see a huge wave, much bigger than the day before. Maybe twice as big. Vance, who had a passion for big surf, urged us on and we kept paddling. Once outside of the bowl, I wasn't too sure of paddling out to the point. It reminded me of that point surf at Makaha, the day I pissed my shorts. I suggested we just go a little ways out. But then a set came through and we were all scratching to get outside. The bowl had somehow moved to our left and we were in danger of getting closed out by it. We dug in for the point. We all made it over the first wave. I remember paddling up that sucker hoping I wouldn't be dragged back over.

I made it over, and couldn't see a thing for like an eternity. The spray blowing back from the wave was like a wave itself. When I finally opened my eyes, I was looking at my worst nightmare. A huge wave about to break about 20 yards in front of me. I had time to look over at Vance and he just smiled and said: "It's time for a bubble bath." You believe it! Time for a bubble bath?

We all stand up and dive off our boards. I stroke for the bottom, eyes closed, lungs full. Two, three, four strokes down and then I hear it coming. A roar of soup. I don't open my eyes, I don't want to see what it looks like. It rolls like a bolt of thunder overhead and for a second I think I'm okay. Then these icy cold currents come down and grab me. Shake me and then toss me around like I'm in some sort of tornado. I go up, then down, then up. I'm lost for a second, but then I remember "don't panic. Just relax. It will all go away."

And it did. But, not for like an hour. Okay, seconds can sometimes seem like hours when the human body is under extreme duress. And mine was. It finally let up and I didn't have any trouble knowing what to do. I put my arms over my head and pulled with all my might for the light. Sweet precious light. And air. Light and air.

And life. I broke the surface and gulped in oxygen. Sometimes the simplest of things are the best in the world.

Two more heads bobbed to the surface, eyes bulging, cheeks puffed. Vance and Tom had made it through. We all looked at each other for a second, all smiles. Then another giant soup bore down on us. I dove as deep as I could feeling like a submarine captian dodging depth charges. There was an explosion of the soup rolling over, then the aqua-quake, then the icy fingers rolling my body over and up and down. Then, I'm stroking again for the light.

There were a couple more soup explosions before the set was over, but none were as bad as the first. I guess the first one had swept us in quite a ways. Miraculously, all three boards were floating together inside of the last bit of white water. Vance actually wanted to go back out, but Tom and I said no way.

I was so glad to feel the beach under my feet. I just went and sat in the car for a long time. How big was it? I don't know, big. Bigger than I'd ever been out in, but nothing compared to today's standards.

We went up to the Hanalei Plantation Hotel before we left to get a better view of the waves. The hotel was built on the point right at the river mouth and looked out over the break. The patio at the top was a perfect spot to check out the surf, but the hotel staff didn't really want a bunch of grubby surfers hanging out there. Still we got to see a couple of sets before they ran us off.

The waves were huge. Long, lined up rights that came around the point from the North. It was odd watching these big perfect waves with no on out. The reality was no one had the boards, or the balls, to go out.

Board Design Comes into Focus
On the long ride back, the talk was all about boards. Vance's Brewer semi-gun was the only board that came close to being a big-wave board. There was some bantering about if we had big guns we would have gone out. But, I'm not so sure we would have. The surf had been coming up all day and was probably 20 feet before we left.

119

We talked about what kind of board it would take. Ten feet long, maybe ten-six, pointed nose and pintail. Lots of belly in the nose to cut through the chop. Long enough to paddle easily into big waves. That was it. Paddle in early, plenty of time to get set for the drop. Big turn and then down the line. Oh, we all wanted guns. But, no one had the money. I decided to write home to Chuck Moyer and see if he would make me a ten-six gun.

The Expression Models hadn't been the big hit that he had anticipated. There was no real campaign to push them. It was just kind of a Newport thing. Word of mouth. I wasn't sure Chuck would be too keen on building me another free board.

There was only one guy on the island who had the boards and the will to go out at big Hanalei. Joey Cabell. He had a house out in Haena, and would come over from Oahu on weekends to surf Hanalei, but he wasn't around on that first big day.

He did come over once in the summer and surfed Pakala. I had met him a couple of times in Newport. He lived there while opening the Chart House. When he came to Pakala, he ripped it. Classic Hawaiian style with all the backside moves. The thing that always got me about Cabell was the way his board was always in trim. He never stalled, or flopped it around. Every move so purposeful. If he ran out of wave, he would slash a cutback and drive the board in the opposite direction.

The day he surfed Pakala, he had his girlfriend with him. Lisa Star. Oh man, she was everything a surfer dreamed about. She was a small girl, very well endowed, tan, brunette, large brown eyes and gratuitous smile. But, more than that, she had this great understanding of surfing and island style. She was so natural and easy going. From that day, Cabell was my hero. He could surf, he had a great business, houses in Honolulu, Kauai and Aspen, and he had Lisa. Oh yeah, I fell in love with her. Who wouldn't?

I hadn't seen any of Cabell's big-wave boards, but the guys described them as long and pointed, make that really pointed, at both ends. Big wave boards like that were called "big guns," and the talk around the table at the surf house was all about guns. Brewer was the guru of big-gun building. Vance Martin had a Brewer and it was a fine piece of craftsmanship. It was like he was driving a Porsche, while we all had Fords and Chevys.

Our boards were made on the coast for coast waves. They had been okay in the summer, but now with the more powerful waves of winter upon us, most of us were thinking about getting boards that could at least handle the waves.

Then one day we all got a glimpse of what those boards might look like. A guy from the North Shore had shown up at the surf house with two new Brewers. His name was Greg Weaver, a friend of Vance's and originally from Huntington Beach. Weaver was one of those vagabond types who drifted about the islands with little or no money, living in the surf houses of Maui, the North Shore and now Kauai. He was a seasoned guy, who knew the island lifestyle and managed to get along pretty well.

His boards were the best I'd ever seen. Both were made from Jackie Baxter Model blanks, which had a redwood stringer down the middle and two blue foam T-bands on the outside. Both were clear, with just the blue foam in the half-inch T-bands for color. The hot-dog board was a nine-six pin tail a lot like Vance's, a real island-style race car. The gun was ten-six and just like we had all heard about. A rocket ship. an X-1, super sonic, intergalactic projectile. It looked like it was going 100 miles an hour just lying in the yard in front of the surf house.

I took all the dimensions down and sent them off to Moyer in a letter, hoping he would come through for me.

In those days, we weren't real tuned-in to how the surf might be on the other side of the island. Surf trips were more a matter of having enough gas money and food to make the journey. Oh, word got around about the surf. Someone would come back from a trip to Lihue and say they had run into someone else who heard Hanalei was breaking. Then there would be discussions about who's car would make it, who had money. Once it all came together, we'd pile the boards on and off we went on a one or two-day odyssey, hoping to get surf.

On the next trip over to Hanalei, Weaver went along. We took John Hawley's Pontiac. It was a cruiser. A 1947 four-door sedan in excellent running condition. He paid a lot for it, two-hundred bucks; everyone thought that was crazy. But, it took us out to Hanalei in style.

Weaver took both his boards, just in case there were waves of any size. As it ended up, it was just bowl surf that day. Pretty good though with some decent overhead sets. He let me try his hot-dog board. Wow, what a difference. From the very first ride, I could feel it grip the wave. And it was so fast, it made everything easy.

The big move back then was what David used to call the roller coaster. Off the bottom with a big turn, up the face as vertical as possible and then hit the lip and ride it down. Weaver's hot-dog board was perfect for it, and was it fun to ride. The trouble was, coming off that board and back to mine was a bummer. Suddenly, the board that I thought was pretty good—my good old Expression Model—was a dog. Such is life.

Those long rides over to Hanalei and back took their toll. It was strictly a two-lane road in those days, and that 10 or 15-mile stretch between Kapaa and Hanalei was killer. You can't imagine how bad the pot holes were in that road. Flat tires? Oh yeah, we had a bunch. The only thing that saved us was knowing that Kapaa had a great island-style bakery with delicious bread pudding and cone sushi. We'd stock up on the way in and the way out. It was like 10 cents a slice for the pudding, and 15-cents for cone sushi. Throw in a quart of guava nectar for 35 cents and you had a meal for under a buck.

There was also the Dairy Queen in Hanapepe. A couple of the guys, Nickertz and Skip Richardson, had befriended a Hawaiian girl there. Goldie. She was a big-hearted girl who had an eye for haole surfers. Whenever she was working she would take our money and then give it back as change. We would order big double cheeseburgers, fries and shakes and not pay a cent. Of course, we all were on the vegetarian/organic path, supposedly. But, after a long day's surf trip, we took advantage of those free cheeseburgers whenever possible. Never mind the guilt trip.

One day, an old Trestles buddy showed up at the surf house. Mike Kuntz. By this time Mike had become a seasoned veteran and had been living on the North Shore and riding Sunset. He came to Kauai because he had a chance to rent a house out in Hanalei. As it turned out, it was the same house we had stayed at behind the Rice Mill Restaurant. Mike had little trouble in recruiting a couple of room-mates. Vance Martin and I had just enough money to make it work. Another guy, Michael Would, joined us.

Kuntz made the arrangements, and within a week we were all packed up and ready to go. Hawley, who I'd been living with at The Pit, drove us over in the Pontiac. At first it was just Vance, Michael and myself. Kuntz had gone back to the North Shore to get more of his stuff.

If living at the surf house and The Pit was a bit Spartan, living out in Hanalei was down right barbarian. It was a one room building on stilts with a tin roof. No bathroom, no electricity and only screens for windows. There was one double bed, some kerosene lanterns and some odds and ends for furniture. We cooked on a Coleman stove that was a real adventure to light.

We did get to use the bathroom at The Rice Mill in exchange for doing a little janitorial work for the restaurant. Red and Milli, who owned the Rice Mill, were great people and were always nice to us. Red was a helicopter pilot who gave tours of the island. Although, we had no car, we were right behind Ching Young Store and were within easy walking distance to Hanalei.

What an enchanting place. A little village of taro farmers and fishermen, right out of South Pacific. Of course, Hanalei was where they filmed South Pacific, and many of the locals had been extras in the movie. The town consisted of the Ching Young Store, which was also the Post Office, The Rice Mill and a little bar called the Tahiti Nui. I think they opened the bar when the movie crew came to town and it's been open ever since.

There were several large vacation homes along the beach, mostly vacant in winter. The people living out there who came from the mainland could be counted on your hands. There were Red and Millie, a guy named Tom and his girlfriend Sherry who lived out in Haena, another couple that were stone-alcoholic painters, and the beautiful Miss Lisa Star, who lived full-time at Cabell's place in Haena.

We did our best to blend in. The locals out there were different than the other side of the island. Much friendlier, more down to earth. There was this old Chinese-Hawaiian guy who basically was the mayor of Kauai's North Shore. Henry Tyhook. If Henry liked you, you had it made. He actually owned the building where we stayed, and he liked us from the beginning.

Henry would stop by and bring us a stock of bananas or a bag of papayas. Then sit for hours telling us stories about the old days in Hanalei, and about the tidal wave that had come through in '48. Most of the houses were built on stilts, some higher than others. There were few, if any, cement foundations.

Tyhook would often use his bulldozer for transportation. You'd be sitting out in front of Ching Young Store reading mail and drinking a passion-fruit guava nectar and up chugs Henry on a D-9. He'd be wearing a steel construction hard hat, and a big smile. Then he'd just sit down on the steps and start shooting the breeze. The Ching Young Store was the focal point of Hanalei social life in those days, and Henry would hold court nearly every morning on the steps out in front.

Brown Rice and Tuna
We sustained ourselves on oatmeal, brown rice and fruit. We would opt for a can of tuna, or soup to liven up the rice on special occasions. Actually that would be whenever a letter with money would arrive from home. At night, we would huddle by the kerosene lamps and listen to the rain on the tin roof. We'd read each other's letters, and play guitar. Cheryl Baron had loaned me her guitar, can't remember what happened to it, but I don't think she ever got it back. Oh well, Hawaiian style.

When there was no surf, we would spend the days exploring. There was so much to see, valleys to hike, rain forests, white sand beaches to walk. We would hitch-hike out to the end of the road and visit Tom and Sherry. They were nice people in their mid twenties. He was from New York and had fallen in love with Hanalei while on a summer vacation. Never went back. He had become friends with Carlos, who knew everybody on the island. Tom was learning to surf and was excited that he now had four new surf buddies to share waves with at the bowl.

And, there were those times when we would run into Lisa. She was so nice, a little bit of heaven on earth. Oh yes, I was young and impressionable and a long ways from home. And she was older, and spoken for, but hey, a guy can dream, right?

We shared a couple of very special dinners in Haena with Tom, Sherry and Lisa. The food, and music were such luxuries for us, not to mention the warm new friendships and conversations. It was a bit of diversity and sort of a coming of age for me. Listening to stories about growing up in New York and Hawaii from Tom and Lisa. So different than where I grew up. The "mainland" with its smog and traffic was so far away, and getting farther everyday.

Greg Weaver came out for a visit and stayed a couple of days. When he left for a trip to the mainland, he left his two boards with us. By now, I was the only one without a Brewer. Mike Would had one and Kuntzy -(coonsie)-boy had a couple. Of course, Vance still had his. I was stuck on my Expression Model, until Weaver left his boards.

What a difference a board makes. I rode the hot-dog board on most days. The Hanalei Bowl was such a perfect, fun wave. Guys from the other side would visit often, and Carlos was spending more and more time out at Hanalei. The crowd, if you could call it that, was about perfect. Everybody giving each other waves, cheering each other on as they rode.

As a group, we progressed. Moving away from a "see me" style of riding to artful expression. Soul surfing, just you and the wave. No flash and dash show-off moves, no judging. And, the joy of playing it back in your mind at night. It was a magic moment in time for us there, light years away from the rest of the world.

Gun Surf, Ride and Glide
It wasn't long before I got to ride Weaver's gun, and oh man, that brought on a whole new dimension. I remember paddling out with Vance and Kim Harp, who was still on a mainland board, but handled it rather well in the larger surf. Kim had spent a lot of time at Sunset Cliffs since leaving Newport.

We rounded the bowl and figured it to be about 10 foot. The Bowl was peaking up in radical A Frames, but it was breaking so far out that the inside sections were all washed over leaving just big sloppy shoulders coming down the channel.

"Impossibles," which was the last section before the bowl, was grinding. We got out to the point, and started getting our bearings. When the first set came through, we were a little inside. So we scratched over it without catching a wave. I remember feeling very confident on the big gun. It paddled so well, each stroke just shot me forward. Even when I was sort of caught inside, I knew I could make it out.

When the next set came through, we were all in the right spot. I picked a wave and turned around. I remember looking back and for a second thinking "oh shit," but once you commit, there's no turning back. I stroked in, feeling the board start to lift up with the big swell and then catching it with no problem. I stood up and put all my weight on my left side.

I was Peter Cole again! Crouching, driving to the bottom, oh the speed. Then just a little lean in and I'm coming off the bottom like a rocket ship. The next thing I know, I'm a jet fighter pilot in the hot seat of an X-15.

I'd never looked down a wall like this before. It was big and blue green with the wind blowing spray from the top of a white-fringed lip. I pulled up on to the face and just aimed the nose down the line. The ride was so fast and smooth. I felt explosive power under my feet. Like driving a fast car and knowing that you could put your foot down with speed to burn if you needed it.

I let the board glide down the first lined-up section and then gunned another turn up the face. Mr. Greenwater? You bet. I was flying and all I wanted to do was make it past Impossibles so I could get back out.

That was the deal. You took off outside and if you made the drop and the first section, you could either pull out and try to beat it back out before the outside wave catches you, or you straighten out and go for the 30-minute excursion around the bowl. Or you go for Impossibles. Once through Impossibles, there was a little channel between it and the bowl.

I came into Impossibles at Mac 10 and just breezed through. I did one of those pull outs like Ricky Gregg in the movies. You know, where you keep standing up for like about 10 seconds waving your arms up and down like you've just conquered Atilla the Hun's army. Pure stoke!

The rest of the day was like a dream. Big long rides, breaking the sound barrier on every wave. It was so addictive. The sets were probably 12 feet, maybe a little bigger. That was big for me. Still, the board made all the difference.

Those few short weeks in December of 1967 were like a lifetime, experience wise. I ended up selling my Expression Model to one of the locals from the West side. The money gave me enough to make it through to January.

From time to time we were visited by various surfers from the outside world. Joey Cabell would come over on weekends and he was always a gas. New brewer gun just about every time, and stories about the surf and goings on from the North Shore. On one such weekend, the surf was pumping. It had been coming up all week and by Saturday, it was just too damn big to go out. Yep, we just hiked up the cliff by the Hanalei Plantation and watched as these perfect 20-foot waves rolled around the corner. No shame, hey we were just kids and these were big waves. No leashes, no wetsuits, no jet skis to save you. No dice!

About mid-morning somebody said "Hey, there's a guy out!" We looked to see a lone paddler rounding the bowl. A tiny speck in a huge bay with cloud breaks going off all over the place. Crazy! There was little doubt about who it was. Joey Cabell, of course.

We watched in awe as he rode monster after monster through Impossibles. Talk about breaking the sound barrier, he was Chuck Yeager and more. Joey had this incredible crouch-like style with powerful legs. He was actually ripping these big waves, up and drops, high speed trims and pulling up into unmakable sections and disappearing. We would all give up on him, and then he'd come flying out of the tube at the end.

I knew Joey was a phenomenal surfer, but this was simply beyond all that. When we talked to him later, he just asked us why we hadn't come out. "It was perfect," he said. Yeah, perfect for you.

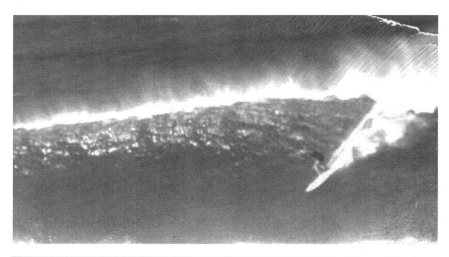

Dropping In — Kim Harp, to my knowledge, never had a photo published in a magazine, but he was one of the hard chargers of the day, for sure. This is a photo of him dropping in at Hanalei. RIP Kim, you were an inspiration. (Photo courtesy of Tom Powers)

Things to Come

That afternoon we all were sitting around talking, and Joey started telling us about some strange things on the North Shore. Not strange, really, but about a group of guys that were starting to charge big Sunset on small boards. They were guys who hung out with Brewer, who had been pushing the envelope on board design. The rumor at the time was that Brewer had been some kind of aeronautical engineer in his former life. It made sense. The foils and curves he was incorporating into his boards were advancing the art of surfing to new levels. In reality, Brewer had been trained as a machinist and pattern maker at the family-owned machine shop in La Habra. He assimilated his roots in surfboard theory from Curren, Shepard, Trent, Diff, Hynson and others. While he borrowed from all those great shapers, the designs he was cranking out in late 1967 were changing the way guys in the islands surfed. And the coconut wireless was alive with tales.

Joey told us about John Boozer, Gary Chapman and Gerry Lopez all riding eight-foot six mini-guns. I couldn't believe it. I knew Chapman well and his younger brother Craig (Owl). Gary was an above average surfer in Newport, but Owl was better. Boozer was always a radical guy. He ripped big Huntington lefts. Gerry, as I

128

said before, was a smooth goofy-foot, but not in my mind an inno-vator. Boy was I wrong. It would be a good six months later when I saw Gerry at Pipeline. Oh yeah, he re-wrote the book on that place.

In late December, we were visited by a group of Australian movie makers. They had a crew with them that included Russell Hughes and Bob Cooper. We spent a couple of days showing them around, but the surf was not accommodating. Mostly blown out Kona days. Still, we got one good day in the Bowl.

It was fun meeting legends like Hughes and Cooper. Both were very hot on this new small board thing. But, their small boards were like hot-dog boards. Big wide tales, with V-bottoms. I had gotten letters from my friend Tom Gaglia on Maui telling about this group of Aussies that had just ripped up Honolua on V-bottoms. Nat Young, Russell, Bob McTavish to name a few.

Looking back, it's hard to say who did what first, or who was responsible for how it all happened. I guess it was a combination of everything that was going on. The Aussies and their V-bottoms, Brewer and his mini-guns were the main factors though.

The talks with Cabell and the others were inspirational. I knew one thing, I wanted new equipment. I wanted to be one of those guys pushing it.

Maui Calls

When January rolled around, it was time for a change for me. My parents wanted me to return home and go back to school. I was also, at age 18, a prime candidate for the draft. I wrote Gaglia about the National Guard and he wrote back saying there might be some openings in the spring. He suggested that I come to Maui and enroll at Maui Community College. That way I could stay out of the draft until I could join the National Guard.

Some how, my parents bought into it and sent me enough money to get started on Maui. I would have to get a job, too, of course. Vance and Kuntz had both spent a summer on Maui and they had hours of stories.

In fact, I'd been hearing Maui stories for years. The perfect rights at Honolua Bay. How if you lost your board on the take off, it could go into a treacherous cave. Most of the time though, your board just broke in half on one of the huge boulders. That sounded fun.

Then there was Lahaina. A crazy, fun town with great surf breaks. The Harbor, Breakwall, Shark Pit and Mala Wharf. I hadn't been there yet, but I knew all about them. And I knew all about breakfast at The Pioneer Inn. Vance had worked there and had described the stacks of macadamia nut pancakes and slices of golden menehune papayas. Every time he told me that breakfast story, my mouth would water. It was time to go to Maui.

A Walk to Remember
Before I left Kauai, and the enchantment of Hanalei, I took a walk down to the little pier. It was a day like many I had experienced, when there was simply nobody around. I walked out on the pier and then back into the forest. Back amongst the towering ironwood trees was a hut made of wood and palm-fronds. It had an open pit barbecue with tables and benches all around. It was known as the Black Pot, and was a gathering spot for all locals on that side of the island. There was a big iron pot, hence the name. Hawaiians on the island were the keepers of the Black Pot. They would have big parties there on Sunday. We were cautioned not to invade on their privacy, especially after they'd thrown down a few cases of Primo.

On this day, though, there was no one at the Black Pot. I sat down at one of the benches and thought about the three and a half months I had just experienced. The long walks into Pakala, Alerton's Garden, trips up to Kokee and hikes up beautiful valleys. And Hanalei, the most beautiful place I'd ever seen. Kauai had been all I heard about and more. It was hard to leave.

I wrote some poems that day, and a couple of letters home. Then a long walk down the beach toward the beach break called Pine Trees. Spent a half a day diddling around the beach and never saw one person.

The Smooth Hound
The next morning, a guy named Greg Baxter gave me a ride to Lihue and I caught an Aloha flight to Maui. Actually, I had to change planes in Honolulu. I didn't have a board, so that made it much easier. I landed in Kahalui about 11 a.m. and Tom Gaglia was there to meet me. He was driving this old '49 Chrysler he

called The Smooth Hound. It was just about as cherry as Hawley's Pontiac back on Kauai. A nice ride for the islands.

It started to rain as we left the airport. A Kona storm had kicked up that morning. Gaglia said as long as we were on the east side of the island we should check out some spots by Kahalui Harbor. There were a couple of spots actually inside the harbor. Swells would come through the entrance and break on a shallow reef near the beach. Weird waves, big thick deep-water swells, that ran into a shallow reef shelf. The bottom just dropped out creating a very thick hollow wave.

We checked out another spot called Pakukalu, a big wedgie left with two or three bowl-like sections. It sort of reminded me of an island-style Cottons Point. When we arrived, the parking lot was full of cars with boards. I was surprised to see so many surfers. Maui was not like Kauai. Gaglia introduced me to a couple of guys, including Buddy Boy Kaohe. I remembered him from the old magazines and had heard stories about him surfing. He was thick around the middle but in good shape. Great smile, that emulated his Hawaiian heritage.

I borrowed a board and went out, just to get wet. Fun surf, about six to eight feet and it had some juice. I had borrowed a Jackie Baxter Model, which had the same stringer design as Weaver's two Brewers. Looking down at the board, I knew that priority number one was to get a new board. A gun!

In the Pakukalu parking lot, the talk was all about boards. I listened to a couple of stories about the Aussies and their V-bottoms. Bob McTavish ripping the bay. Still there were some that said they ripped, but they didn't have the style of Buddy Boy. Buddy Boy had a new brewer. A 9-6 pin tail, which was small for him. Everyone was talking about shorter boards, and I started to wonder how long my next board would be.

I had written Moyer, and asked for a ten-six. But I was thinking of Hanalei. I wasn't so sure I wanted a ten-six anymore. Maybe smaller was the way to go. Most of my boards had been in the nine-foot ten-inch range. I had heard that Phil Edwards always had boards that were nine-ten and three quarters.

Gaglia had invited me to stay at his place in Lahaina. Actually, it wasn't his, he was just staying there with a bunch of guys. Like the surf house on Kauai, it was one of those places that had about two or three permanent residents and the other five or six people who stayed there were temporary. The revolving door theory of life.

Tom Schooley and Mark Monroe were the mainstays where Gaglia was living. The place was just south of The Banyan Tree, which placed it near town, near the Pioneer Inn, and within an easy bike ride of all the Lahaina surf spots. It was a rambling single story affair, painted blue and white. It had probably started as a two room bunk house for cane workers and then rooms were added as needed. It did have plumbing and, oh boy, a hot water shower. Like almost every other surf house in Lahaina, it had one room dedicated to glassing and ding repair. I would soon find out why.

Lahaina was a quaint town, with a mish mash of architectural styles. Everything from the east coast seaport look to Hawaiian country, and there was a little 1960s Costa Mesa thrown in too. Front Street was a clutter of ramshackle two-story buildings. Hop Wo Store, The original Lahaina Bakery, and the Okazuya were the places to go for food. It was a crowded little town, much different than the sleepy towns of Kauai. Newer cars, more tourists, and many more California surfers.

And there were hippies. Gaglia told me how about a month before, the town was loaded with hippies. They would hang out in front of the library at Lahaina Harbor or under the Banyan tree smoking dope and shooting-up speed. I guess the locals got really upset, but there weren't enough police in Lahaina at the time to round them all up. So, the local gambling concern, some said they were the Hawaiian Mafia but I'm not so sure, got the job of cleaning up town.

The way it was told, Takeo, the guy who ran the gambling and his big bruiser body guards, packing heat, ran all the hippies out of town. Buddy Boy went along with them and got to decide who stayed and who left. He let most of the surfers stay. All the rest were told to be out of town with in 24 hours, or they would pay the price.

By the time I got to Lahaina, there were still hippies around, but they weren't shooting up dope in front of the library. Most of them had been exiled to the other side of the island. There was a hippy camp there called Banana Patch where people lived in treehouses made of plastic and canvas. Lots of stories about that place.

It rained the first couple of days I was in town. A Kona storm that blew out the whole west side. We mostly just hung out and it gave me a chance to meet the crew. I already knew a lot of them, Leslie Potts, Jackie Baxter, Jim Turner, Larry Strada, John Fletcher and more.

Maui Daze — Photo of the Carthaginian and the Pioneer Inn from the Harbor looking in. The restored ship was a center-piece in town until it sank after being used in a movie. "The Hawaiians." (Photo by Dick Graham).

Welcome to Honolua

I awoke one morning to find the trade winds had kicked back in. Lahaina was sunny, and the town was buzzing. I saw a car loaded with boards, and I knew something was up. Even though I didn't have a board, I hitched a ride out to "The Bay" to see what was going on.

I had been out there a couple of times just checking it out. It was a beautiful drive, and the setting at Honolua was something to see.

The tight little bay with two jagged points of black lava. The Northern side was where it happened, of course. At the time, everyone parked in the bay and paddled out from the boat ramp. It was a neat place, with a thick jungle. With the longer boards, the paddle was no big deal. Where as getting down the cliff at the point with a long board was hairy.

The Bay parking lot was full of cars. A traveling circus. The waves were not the best quality. The days of Kona had left the ocean bumpy and the trades were blowing more out of the north, so it was almost a side shore condition. Still there were big green tubes out there. I could see that.

Brewer was there. I had heard that he was on the island and was making boards in the old pineapple factory in town. I talked to him, and he actually loaned me a board. I found out later that it belonged to Jackie Eberly, who I had met years before. It was a nice nine-eight or nine-ten, pin tail, and it was a Brewer. I jumped at the chance.

You have to remember, guys didn't lend their boards out at the bay. I was lucky. I paddled out from the boat ramp taking my time to get the line up and make sure I knew where the channel was. I was in awe of the bowl. It was not like the Makaha Bowl or Haleiwa, or Hanalie, this bowl came much more in play. By that I mean it was more connected to the wall than the others. The wave just peeled into it. More than that, it was hollow, inside out, and shallow!

Mike Hyson was out, as were Bill Fury and Buddy Boy. I watched them rip a few on the way out and could feel my heart start to pump out of my chest. This was it! This is what I'd been waiting all my life for. I had this vision of making it through the bowl and getting tubed and then making this big cut back. Oh I wanted to do that.

I chugged around the bowl and angled out toward the point. I had heard enough stories to know that the take-off spot in the peak was right in front of the cave. If you blew it there, you were screwed and your board was history. I didn't want that to happen, especially on a borrowed board, so I held up inside the peak and decided to wait for some kind of a shoulder. There were probably about 20 guys out, and most everything that came through had somebody on it.

I watched and waited, watched and waited. Then, when I saw some poor guy get blasted on the take off, I turned and stroked in. It was a white-water wave, the third or fourth in the set. Overhead, of course, everything was overhead. It had to be, just to break on the point. So I stroke in and stand up. I knew right away that this place was like something I had never experienced before. Steeper, more power, it made the board just accelerate right from the get go. I did a sort of middle of the wave turn because I wanted to get down the line a little. Good old green water, you know.

Looking down that line was like looking down the barrel of a gun. The wave was a hand extending its fingers up in the air and daring me come on down. I was sort of mesmerized for a second and then I knew I had to kick it up to full speed or I was going to be toast. I was a bit late with that judgement and my only way out was to straighten off. Bonk! I caught an outside edge and off I go. I fell into the face of the wave and was suspended for a brief second before getting sucked up and tossed over the falls.

I knew what was going to happen, I was going to bounce. As in off the bottom. So tried to keep my body attitude at an angle that I would hit feet first. I felt my feet hit a grassy flat surface and I bent my knees to absorb the impact. It was okay, then up and over again. Of course, the second time over is not quite as violent as the first, but then there was the matter of having enough air. My lungs were exploding.

This time the bottom was much closer. I hit with my butt, and it sent a jolt up my spine. More thrashing, more thoughts about air, but the damn wave just wouldn't let go. Finally, I got my legs under me and pushed off the bottom. I made the surface and breathed in that wonderful oxygen. If that was what a Honolua wipe-out was like on small wave, what would it be like outside?

Those thoughts were quickly replaced by visions of that Brewer board hitting the rocks. I swam like hell for the shore, taking advantage of the white water and surge where ever possible. A couple of guys along the rocks were holding up the board. But it

had already taken a thrashing. At least three major dings.
Welcome to Honolua, Herb!

I was bummed. Dejected. And hurt. I had managed to step on some
tube coral and my feet were bleeding. I didn't even bother to look
back outside, just took the board and paddled into the boat ramp.

Brewer was cool. He had an all-knowing smile on his face as if to
say "so kid, how did you like having your ass handed to you?"
Some hot shot surfer I was. Jackie was cool, too. He said not to
worry, he would patch the dings in no time. I offered to give him
some money, but he declined. True Hawaiian style.

I spent the rest of the afternoon watching from the cliff out on the
point. I studied the way Buddy Boy and Fury positioned themselves. Hynson was putting on a show. He was riding a very long
pointed gun and was doing all kinds of weird flop turns. That's the
only way I can describe them. They weren't carving turns, they
were more like ski turns, where he sort of jumped the board
around.

Fury and Buddy Boy were more the classic style. Sweeping bottom
turns, trimming the board down lime-green walls, pure speed. It
was something to watch. The waves got better in the evening. It
always gets better in the evening at Honolua. I left, vowing not to
give up. I needed a board!

Surf, Food and Friends
Back in Lahaina, a bunch of us got together for dinner at the
Pioneer Inn. They had an all-you-could-eat salad bar there for
$1.50, and if you really wanted to live it up you could get Mahi
Mahi for $3.50. It came all seasoned, wrapped in tin foil and you
cooked it yourself on a gas grill under a gazebo-like canapé. Throw
in the free ice tea, and bread, and you had a great meal.

We talked surf. There simply were no other subjects worth discussing. The Viet Nam war, the latest in acid rock, even chicks,
were not issues. We talked about the ride Jackie Baxter got, or
Fury or Potts. There were a lot of good surfers on the island at the

time. Jeff Hackmen and Jock lived on the other side. They were going to a private college up in Kula, which was the "Up Country."

John Boozer had moved over from the North Shore and had brought his 8-6 mini gun. He wasn't out that first day I saw The Bay break, but he had already ridden his little board there and ripped it up. He was there that night at the Pioneer Inn and I got a chance to talk to him. I asked him how hard it was to ride a little board in big waves, and he said once you made some adjustments and got the paddling down, it was no problem.

He told us about other guys on the North Shore riding mini guns at Sunset. It was exciting stuff, and the fact that Brewer had moved his operations over to Maui was even better. Intrigued, I listened as Boozer described a new way of surfing where you rode deep in the pocket and worked your board up and down to go faster. There was no nose walking or drop-knee cutbacks, it was all flat-footed power surfing. He talked about Cabell taking a small board out at Sunset and just powering through the inside section. I went to sleep thinking about what it would be like.

During the next week or so I got organized. Took a job washing dishes at a place called The Captain's Chart House out at the Kaanapali Resort. My buddy Dave Rullo had the job before me but had left to go back to the mainland a couple of weeks before I got to Maui. John Barbeau, another La Jolla guy, was the cook. The job didn't pay much, but the perks were worth it all.

The cook and dishwasher shared a closet-like kitchen with a grill and oven on one side and a sink and refrigerator on the other side. We worked back to back talking about waves the whole time. The waitresses were all good looking older women (25 to 30), and they wore these Hawaiian print dresses that showed a lot of cleavage. But the best part was the food.

The Captain's Chart House served steak, lobster and fresh fish. They had a house salad with green goddess dressing and croutons. It was a specialized place with a limited menu, but the food was simple and really good, so it got packed with tourists. We would eat a meal before our shift, which was usually fresh fish and salad. Then during the course of the evening, John would make a couple of mistakes, like cook one too many lobster tails or steaks. Naturally, we had to eat all the mistakes.

Here we were poor starving surfers by day, eating steak and lobster every night. It was a good job. Some nights after work, we would sit at the bar and drink with the waitresses. On good nights, they would give us each a couple of bucks from their tips.

New Dimensions: The Railer is Born

I went for about two weeks without a board. Moyer had written and said my new gun was in the glass shop, so I hoped it would arrive soon. In the meantime, my friend Tom Gaglia and I decided to do something a little crazy. We decided to strip down his Surfboards Hawaii board and make a mini gun. Bruce Jones was in town and was doing some shaping. We talked him into shaping us a board.

We used dimensions that we had heard about. A 13-inch nose, 20 inches wide, a 12-inch pin tail, and all of eight-foot six inches long. Bruce was skeptical about the dimensions and he really didn't want to work with a stripped down blank, but somehow we talked him into it.

The main surf house in town had a shaping room and a glassing room. It was a big two-story house owned by Takeo. As many as 15 guys lived there at a time. Mostly Huntington guys as I recall. So Tom and I borrowed a sander and went to work in the yard with his board. We sanded the fin off then split the rails and peeled the glass off the deck and bottom. It was grueling work, and left us itchy as hell. But stoked.

Jones arranged to use one of the shaping rooms and went at it. Tom and I and a bunch of other guys watched, as the master craftsman did his magic dance with his planer.

We weren't the first to strip a board down on Maui. Guys had been doing it for awhile. Mostly because blanks were scarce. Recycling before it became popular. Old boards became new boards with a little bit of island ingenuity. But, most were reshaped into the same style long boards, not these new mini-guns. A shaper had to work with what he had, and sometimes that left a lot to be desired.

Our board came out a little straight. We kind of screwed up the nose when we peeled the glass off. But, she was pretty. A little three-stringer rocket ship. We named her "The Railer," because she was like dragster. It took us a couple of days to get it glassed, but there hadn't been any significant surf, so we weren't stressing too much.

I think it was a Sunday, when a little north swell came down the Molikai channel and sparked up our lives. The Bay was going off about six to eight feet. We loaded the Railer up and drove out there in Tom's VW Bug. After checking the crowd out at The Bay, we opted to find someplace else for our first test rides. Hey, after my first experience, I wasn't all that keen on paddling some strange new creation out there.

We drove back to the Kaanapali area where there was a little spot called Sand Box. It broke well on a north swell, and the minute we pulled up, we knew we had made a good move. There were a couple of guys out, and the surf was two to three feet. Perfect little rights with straight off shore-wind.

Tom was first out on the Railer. I watched him struggle a little bit paddling out and then missing a bunch of waves. He was a good surfer and a strong paddler, I wondered how I'd do. He eventually got a couple of waves and I remember cheering when he finally made it to his feet and turned. Once he did that, I knew it could be done.

When he came in, we did a complete analysis of his go out. From how it paddled to where you had to turn it from. When it was my turn, I used every bit of that information. The first thing was the paddle. I went right to the arm over arm swimming style paddle as opposed to stroking with both arms at the same time. I realized right away that you had to position yourself so that the board floated in sort of a trim.

The nose looked funny. It was so close to my chin, I really felt like I was swimming rather than paddling. Also it was odd being down in the water. When I got out to the line up, I took a position straddling the board. I did a little horsing around with it, spinning around and sticking the tail down to get sort of a pop start. It was a whole new world.

I missed a couple of waves, then sort of figured out a strategy of sitting in a little closer to the beach. From the first wave I caught, I knew we had struck gold. That little board turned under my feet and then started rocketing down the line. I found myself crouching over almost like I was speed skating again. And that was a thought. It felt like skating, so I went with that and started using little turns to generate speed.

Oh it was all new, and exciting. Every wave was a whole new experience. As soon as I came in, Tom went back out. We traded off all day, getting more and more used to this new genre of surfing. It was like we were inventing it as we went along, and indeed we were.

I'll never forget that day. We experienced a totally new feeling in riding waves. Of course, these were not big waves. Just little three-footers. We knew the real test was yet to come.

The Change Was On

That night we celebrated at The Pioneer Inn. Mahi Mahi and all the trimmings. There was a bunch of us there and we were telling everybody we saw about our adventure on The Railer. At the same time, we heard that Boozer had ridden his mini-gun at The Bay and rode some good eight-foot waves. Not only that, but Jock and Jeff had showed up with a couple of new mini-guns from Brewer and had ripped the place up. It was on. A new era was coming about, and no one knew where it was going to lead.

The next day the winds blew Kona, and dampened our spirits. We drove out to The Bay anyway, and then since we were out there, drove a little further around the island to a place called Windmill. It was far enough around the corner to pick up the Konas as off shore. Windmill is a wicked looking place with grotesque black lava rocks at the base of a 100-foot cliff. The wave is a hollow left that spits like the Pipeline. There's a channel with a fierce riptide that separates the left from a chunky island-style right. A pure Hawaiian reef break with lots of juice.

The waves that day were a little overhead, but still scary. I always felt that there was something about the place that's creepy. Sort of a raw energy that made me feel like there were angry Hawaiian gods around waiting to reek havoc. We went out and rode the lefts, taking turns on The Railer.

Again, it was a whole new experience with each ride. This time going backside on a very steep and demanding wave. Still I found myself getting into this skating-like rhythm and making some waves that I didn't think I could make. We had a good morning's surf, and learned more about this strange new craft.

We learned that she could go like a bat out of hell, and ride in places a long board just couldn't hang in. We also learned that she was a bit unforgiving. There were some good wipeouts. But, with the one of us on the rocks watching the whole time, we managed to save the Railer from major damage.

Death of the Railer, No Going Back

A few days later, the weather returned to normal and the ocean cleaned up. When Honolua came around, it was a small-to-medium size swell out of the north west. Six to eight foot, with some occasional bigger waves. When we showed up with The Railer, it was like we were driving a new race car or something. Everyone gathered around and checked it out, measuring it, holding it under their arms. She was still a sort of green color from the glass job, only a couple of shatters here and there. A good looking new stick.

I don't recall who went out first, but I know that we both walked out to the point, because paddling The Railer out from the boat ramp seemed like a lot of extra work. These were the biggest and most demanding waves we had seen so far with the new board and it was quite an experience. I remember having a severe case of the butterflies when I went out.

Tom had a better day of it than I did. He was much more familiar with the multiple personalities of Lady Honolua. Me, I floundered about missing waves and getting caught inside. I did get a couple of rides that made it all worth while though. Some cranking rights where I kept the board turning the whole ride. But, mostly it was a survival deal.

As it turned out, we survived but The Railer didn't. After a day's surf at Honolua, we accumulated 32 major dings, and a fatal fracture right in the middle of the board. She was headed for the scrap foam barrel. The Railer adventure was over, but she had left her mark on us. There was no going back to a long board!

My ten-six Moyer gun arrived at Kahalui airport via air freight from the coast. I had received a letter from Chuck Moyer and then called the air freight place everyday checking. I was excited to pick it up, and even looking forward to taking it our for a spin at Honolua when the surf got big.

It didn't turn out that way though. When we took the new board out of the cardboard box, my heart sank. It was long alright, and it had a pointed nose, and pin tail, but the shape just wasn't up to island standards. It had full thick rails and a round bottom. It was a tank! And, to make it worse, it had this horrible pigment job. A jumble of mostly brown, purple and yellow like some kind of psychedelic nightmare. It was god awful.

No fault of Chuck Moyer though. He was a fine craftsman, who had learned his trade from Joe Quigg and Mike Marshall. But, he was out of touch with the cutting edge of surfing. Actually, I guess everyone else on the mainland was, too. And the psychedelic paint job was just too much.

I didn't know what to do. Strip it and have it shaped down was a thought. But, stripping a brand new board just didn't seem right. I should have just shipped it back, or sold it and sent the money back. Instead, I did a very selfish thing. I sold it and used the money to buy a new Brewer. Looking back, you could say that I was jaded. I had been getting free boards for years, I just took it for granted that it was mine to do what I pleased. I regret not paying Chuck back, but I don't regret getting my next board.

Everlasting
Joey Cabell had come over to Maui to have Brewer shape him a couple of new sticks. Brewer was on his own, and didn't even put stickers on his boards. Just signed the stringer. Even guys like Joey paid him for his boards. Basically, you bought a blank and then paid about $35 for him to shape it. Another $30 or so for glass and you had a new board. Joey was always pushing the design of boards in those days. This time he had Brewer shaping him a couple of spears, 8-6 and 9-0, I think. Joey had Brewer make them with a new template based on his specifications. The

boards had beautiful tear-drop shapes with the wide point way up from center. He also was stressing a very flat bottom. More speed!

So Cabell gets these two new boards and has them glassed there at a glass shop next to Brewers shaping shop in the old pineapple cannery. Oh they were beautiful things. When I went in with my order, I asked if Brewer could make it with Joey's new template. He agreed.

I had been involved in designing boards since my days with Hobie, but that was just basically giving a shaper some specifications and letting him do his thing. I was fascinated with how Joey watched every move Brewer made. He would make him stop so he could check the thickness of the rails and tail, or put a ruler across the bottom to make sure it was flat enough. I watched and learned.

When it was my turn, I put a mask on and stayed right in the shaping room as the dust and foam flew. I didn't say much, but a couple of times Brewer stopped and let me check it out and feel the rails. Man he was a craftsman. Every detail so symmetrical. Perfect rails.

My new board was eight-four, tear-drop gun shape with a flat bottom. I couldn't afford to have anything fancy done with the glass job, so I just ordered it clear. When I came to pick her up, I was surprised that someone had put a big colored drawing of a sun on the deck. In the center of the sun was the word Everlasting. I was stoked, and from then on that board was known as Everlasting.

And what a board. A magic board. From the first time I rode her, it was like nothing I'd ever experienced. My surfing took on a whole new dimension. I was no longer Peter Cole, or Phil Edwards or even Joey Cabell, they all just went flying out the door. I think for the first time in my surfing, I was finally original. Everlasting unlocked something inside that was almost scary. Part speed racer, a little crouching tiger, and at times a screaming banshee. It was like Everlasting was part of my body and all I had to do to control her was think.

As February turned into March, the west swells began to hit The Bay. With the help of Everlasting, I was starting to learn a lot about the bay. The more west the swell direction, the more hollow the waves. West is the best. We got day after day of consistent 10-

foot surf. Jock and Jeff would come from the other side of the island and we had some great jam sessions. Everyone just pushing each other to do more. How far could we go?

With each new swell, there would be five or six more guys trying out the mini-gun thing. Veteran older guys and rookie young guys sharing a common experience of something new. Learning the ropes, and getting in on the new era. One by one, they would all get it, and all know there would be no going back.

I remember driving down Front Street in Lahaina and seeing trash can after trash can filled with scrapped fiber glass. Long boards were stripped and reshaped. Then the day came when there were more guys with mini guns out at Honolua than on long boards. The end of an era. Soon, the long boards were all but extinct, like the dinosaurs.

I saw it happen on Maui, but it was happening in other places too. The North Shore, the mainland, and probably in Australia as well. It was like that scene from the movie "2001" where the apes find the monolith and it changes them forever. Or, like "Close Encounters of the Third Kind," where people see a UFO and then start making drawings and sculptures of the same mountain. We were all suddenly taken over by a power greater than the sum of us. A giant collective mind, spinning off creations to ride waves. Okay, it was the 60s, I had to go there.

While all this was going on, I had managed to enroll myself at Maui Community College. I took English, psychology and a course in celestial navigation. No kidding, the psychology teacher, Mr. Fredrickson, taught a three-unit course in celestial navigation, and it was the class to take. Never mind you needed to have trigonometry to understand it. Actually, Mr. Fredrickson was one of those off-beat professors who just liked to engage in lively conversations with his class. Mostly about sailing the south seas and searching for ancient ship wrecks. I learned a lot about life in that class, and almost nothing about celestial navigation.

There were five or six of us who took classes at MCC. We would car pool over in the morning, attend class and then make it back in time for an afternoon surf. Sometimes we would take boards and surf Pakukalu before school and then show up in class wearing wet trunks and sandals. The classes were much easier than

Orange Coast, so I didn't have to study much. My grades were okay, nothing to write home about.

Really, all I ever thought about was surfing Honolua Bay. What a magical spot. Watching those sets come out of the channel and wrap into the bay was a shear delight. I'd never seen anything so perfect. Once you learned the line up, it was almost like a machine. I learned about lining up by using both the outside points and certain rocks on the beach for reference. There were also certain rock swirls to watch for as the waves approached. A couple of yards too far to the right or left of the rock swirl and you were in for trouble.

At first, I had a little trouble with the take off. A natural tendency is to paddle to the left as a set wraps in. That way you are sort of heading for the channel and setting yourself up to take off on the shoulder. The reality is the shoulder sort of wraps into the peak and jacks up to be steeper than the heart of the peak. I think the shoulder take off at Honolua is every bit as steep as the take off at Sunset. Maybe not.

Once your in, it's a straight drop to the bottom. A thousand-mile-an-hour flight down the elevator shaft. When you hit a bit of flat water, an easy lean in and you're off down the wall at Mac 10.

While everyone danced to a different beat, we all shared a common strategy. Go as hard as you could to the bottom, then go as straight back up the wave as possible. You would repeat that move as many times as possible before the inside line up forced you to stretch out the pattern. Then it was a race to the bowl using middle-of-the-board turns to maximize speed. The secret of making the Honolua bowl was to stay high as long as possible then drop down in front of it and make a big turn around it. Like a ride on a roller coaster. The best roller coaster in the world.

Oh those were the days. We were totally reinventing the sport. Doing things we never imagined just months before. A whole new way to surf. Somebody like Hackman would come in with a new little move, and then we would all be trying to add it in. Jeff Hackman, for my money, was an artist and the waves his canvas. Fluid grace. Watching Jeff ride The Bay was like watching a perfectly choreographed dancer, Fred Astair or Gene Kelly. He rode each wave like he had already ridden it, and was just doing it the second time for the final take.

If Jeff epitomized an art form that seemed almost too perfect, as in you could see what was going to happen next and it was going to be perfect, then Jock Sutherland epitomized pure spontaneity. Jeff played classical. Jock was a jazz man. Jock rode mostly left foot forward at The Bay. He was a switch foot you know, could ride all four ways, and rip it all four ways. Jocko was the one with the strangest moves. He reminded me of some kind of bird flying from branch to branch in a big tree. Rarely repeating the same move twice. Innovation in motion. Tube rides? Oh he could get in the barrel.

There were a lot of guys driving the bus in those days. Leslie Potts, Jackie Baxter, Paul McKinney, Gary Chapman just to name a few. The best part of it was that they were all doing it for each other. There were few photographers on the beach, no movie cameras rolling, no contests. It was just about riding the wave to the best of your ability and seeing how much further you could take it.

Soul surfing had taken on a new perspective in the winter and spring of 1968. Now, we were all really living it. That is, living to surf. Living to commune with a very special force of nature. I've described Honolua like a machine, but really each and every wave seemed to have its own personality. A living thing, that came from life's source. You picked it, or it picked you, and you danced in time. Sometimes in perfect union, other times in a fierce battle for survival. At the end of each day, you took home impressions of elation, triumph, defeat and sometimes fear. We were the workers at a factory called Honolua Bay, and the pay was good. Very good.

Legends Visit the Bay
As spring approached, the legendary Reynolds Yater made his annual pilgrimage to The Bay. He had been coming over for years to surf the clean west swells of spring. He had a friend from Santa Barbara, Burt Smith, who had been living on Maui since the mid-1960s. Yater arrived that year with a beautiful long board shaped especially for the bay. It was, of course, a master piece of crafts-manship, in the Hynson Model spectrum of design. Perfect for past years, but not this year.

Mr. Class — Jeff Hackman had the Bay so wired he looked like he had everything choreographed. Is surfing an art form? You tell me. (Photo by Dick Graham)

I remember seeing him ride the Bay on the first day, sitting outside and picking up the set waves. Smooth turns, clean trims down the line, he was everything I had ever heard about him. But, in this new arena, that was all old hat. He knew it too. I remember seeing him catch a wave and ride it to the inside, and then sit in the channel watching for a long time. Analyzing what was going on, and getting ideas of his own.

A day or so later, out comes Yater on a small mini-gun. He had stripped his longboard and re-shaped it. Wow, that was something. An old master had seen the light and made no qualms about jumping right in. And he did well too. I noticed a big smile on his face as he learned to surf all over again, experiencing the thrill of working the board through sections and reinventing himself along the way.

Another of the older generation who became infatuated with the movement was Carter Pyle. He was a dear friend of Joe Quigg and his body surfing buddy from the Wedge. Carter was a true water-man, who had bailed out of Newport in the mid-1960s. He had been a very successful sail boat designer. He designed the Kite and the Lido 14 and was a pioneer in building the first cats. He built the first P-Cat. His expertise in blending shapes and surfaces to create speed was of infinite interest to those of us who were lucky enough to know him.

One day Carter stopped a couple of us on the street and told us a great story. Phil Edwards had come over for a visit and stayed with him in Lahaina. Edwards and Carter went back a long ways and were connected by their interest in catamarans. Carter said that he had taken Phil out to the Bay and had sat up on the cliff watching the surf for a couple of hours. According to Carter, Phil had just been amazed at what the guys were doing.

It was good to hear, although a little strange too. The way Carter told it, Phil was almost sad to see the change in surfing. Like the end of an era had come. The infidels had taken over the city! The king is dead. Long live the king. It happens to us all though. Change in life is inevitable.

Seasons Change
As the winter of 1968 came to a close, evidence of what had happened was everywhere. Trash cans full of stripped fiberglass, the high-pitched whine of planers, the smell of resin in the air. The stoke of surfing had attained new heights. The tools we used to ride our waves were all new. The rules had been changed, the limitations removed. Like The Steve Miller Band's album, it was a Brave New World. Okay, Aldous Huxley said that first. Speaking of Aldous Huxley, his grandson was one of the guys there on the new frontier. Cremin Huxley. What a great guy and a good surfer, too.

How far would it go? How short could we go? What kind of designs were going to take us to the next level. Visions of 360s, barrel rolls, flying roller coasters were no longer pipe dreams. We all had experienced the best surfing year of our lives and wanted more.

Late that spring, Larry Strada and Buddy Boy formed a surf company to build boards. They called it Lahaina Surfing Designs A.K.A. LSD Surfboards. And, the first couple of boards lived up to the acronym. They were radical creations with god-awful psychedelic finishes. Still, Strada was coming into his own as a shaper. He had the craft and Buddy Boy gave him the opportunity to apply it.

They asked me if I wanted to surf one of their creations and I agreed. It would mean giving up Everlasting, but at the time it seemed like the thing to do. I knew I could ride a shorter board, and I wanted to stay ahead of the curve. So I signed on.

I sold Everlasting for $100. I had ridden her most of the winter and there was not a ding in the board. I'm still proud of that! She got passed around to a couple of guys and was broken in half at the Bay on a late spring swell. Someone put her back together again and she resurfaced briefly the following summer, but she was never the same.

Moon Beam

My next board was a complete aberration. Strada and I had dreamed up an absurd design that featured two diagonally placed concave spots in the tail. Our theory was to utilize these little tear-drop shaped channels to increase speed from the turns. We used a spear-shaped pin-tail outline with a narrow tail. It was 7-6 and about three and a half inches thick. Strada was a bit of an extremist at the time, accentuating every detail to the max. If someone asked for a pointed nose, he got a pointed nose. If someone (me) asked for floatation, he got it.

Buddy Boy did his thing with the glass job. It was bright yellow and the tear drops on the bottom were a dark green. It had some other stripes and stuff, and in all, she was a bit over the top. We christened her "Moon Beam."

The day Moon Beam came out of the glass shop, was one of those special days when anything can happen. Like a sneak swell might jump up out of the blue and catch everyone by surprise. Tom Gaglia, Larry and I picked up the board and just naturally went in search of surf. It was late spring and the bay had been flat for a week. Still we took a ride out in the country just hoping to find some wind swell waves.

West swells in the islands, especially Maui, are sneaky. Sometimes they don't show any indication, until you get close to the Bay. North swells come all the way down the coast into Lahaina and are a dead give away. On this day, we didn't notice much of anything in the way of indicators until we were almost to the bay.

Strada saw a wave break off some obscure reef and started to get excited.

Sure enough when we pulled into the Honolua lookout spot, a set came in out of nowhere and broke in front of the cave. Not a soul around except us three! Oh man, we made a mad scramble out to the point. Now, because of our shorter boards, the parking spot at the bay was right out on the point. We parked and watched as another set came out of the west. Not big, but big enough to break outside, which meant it was at least six feet.

We thought it was destiny. Here we were with this new experimental channel-bottomed spaceship about to make history. I was the test pilot. Chuck Yeager in the flesh ready to break the sound barrier. So we paddle outside and sit out there for a good 10 minutes with nothing happening. Then a set comes in. It stacks up outside and we all had to scratch to get out far enough.

With their longer boards, Strada and Gaglia caught the first two waves of the set. Both were a solid eight feet. I come over the top of the next one, still paddling with all my strength, and I see this perfect 10-footer. At first I thought I'd better not take it, I should wait for a smaller wave and get used to the board. In fact, there was a chance I could still get caught inside!

Then as I get closer to this absolutely flawless wave, I know I've got to go. I turn around and stroke. It was a late take off, so there was no problem catching the wave. I just needed to get to my feet and get down the face. The wave swept me up and up and finally, I felt the Moon Beam catch the wave. I jump up and try to drive her down the face, which is what I'd been doing all winter long with good old Everlasting.

I noticed the difference immediately. I wasn't going Mac 10, I was going very slow. I managed to get in a turn and then I'm staring down this huge lime green wall. I press in for speed, but there's nothing. It was like being in a car and running out of gas on the freeway. And my car, in this case, was slower than a Model T Ford! For a split second I was suspended in this huge green room. I froze in place, hoping that if I could just stay in the right place I could make it out. I tried to trim the board, but old Moon Beam had no trim. She was a little tug boat about to be crunched in a meat grinder.

Oh yeah, I ate it. Big time. The wave exploded on me and I went down, over, and over again. I think Moon Beam disintegrated on impact, but I'm not sure. She ended up in at least three pieces. I swam in and just sat on the rocks. It was very disheartening. But, that night listening to Strada and Gaglia describe my ride, we all had a good laugh. So much for Chuck Yeager.

Summertime Blues in Lahaina
Strada promised to build me another board. A more conventional design. In the mean time, I was out of the line up at The Bay. The season was about at its end anyway. And, with its end, a migration of sorts began. A lot guys packed up and moved back to the mainland to get summer jobs, others moved to Oahu. I still had my job at the Captain's Chart House, and was also driving tourist vans for the Pineapple Hill restaurant.

Gaglia and I had been living in a studio apartment above a garage in Lahaina. What a place it was. It belonged to a lady named Annie who ran a gambling operation in the garage. There were card games every night. Most of the players were Filipinos, who worked in the cane and pineapple fields. Our apartment was clean, close to town and cheap, but the down side was listening to the card game going on all night. And then there were the crabs. Yeah, those kind of crabs. The bathroom was downstairs in the garage and was used by all the card players. We had to keep a full supply of A200, a strong medicine that killed crabs, and use it every time we took a shower. It was pretty rough.

I relocated to a place on the south side of town living with Mark Monroe and Bob Crozier, both from Ocean Beach. As spring time turned to summer, Strada and Buddy Boy moved their surfboard operations to the North Shore. I was still without a board, but I could borrow boards here and there and surf the Harbor.

One day, on a lark, I bought an old board off of a local for $10 and stripped it down. Monroe had set up a surfboard rack in the back yard to fix dings and such, and I proceeded to strip the board and then try to shape it myself. I'd been around shaping rooms enough to know the basics and I had the tool of choice: the Sureform.

I borrowed a template from the big Surf House in town. I only had enough foam for about a seven foot board, so I drew out a little tear drop with a radical tail. Never mind that it was summer and I really didn't need that kind of board. I thought it was cool. I cut it out and did this little shaping dance. You know, walking around the board on the rack and picking it up by the tail. Sighting down the rail line, flipping it over and over, sanding.

It was fun. But oh boy was that one crude shape when I got done. Because of some of the mistakes and do-overs, the board came out about six foot, instead of seven foot. It was pretty bad. Still, I had it glassed and finished it. It was too small for me to ride, and I knew it. So I gave it away to some little kid at the Harbor. I had failed to solve my board problem, but I had opened the door to building my own designs. Hey, I was Joe Quigg! Mike Marshall, Dick Brewer!...Well, not quite.

Eventually, I got a letter from Strada saying my new board would be done in a week. I arranged to fly over to Oahu and pick it up. It was June, and the North Shore was almost deserted. Strada and Buddy Boy were living with Mike Diffenderfer at The Pipeline House. That was a famous house in those days. It had a big porch that looked right out at the Pipeline. What a great place. I think they paid about $250 a month rent, which was outrageous, but doable with four or five guys.

The board Strada had built me was more conventional, but it had an edge to it. It was a light green, seven six, flat bottom, pin tail, pointed nose and thin, really thin. I christened it at Laneakea, in wind surf. Right from the get go I knew two things: one, it was hard to paddle, and two, once I caught a wave it was an unforgiving little sucker. Oh it went fast, but if you weren't in just the right spot it would catch one of its razor-like rails and throw you for a loop.

I took it back to Maui, but I wasn't altogether happy with it. I don't mean to knock Strada, he went on to prove himself as a master shaper. But these were the early days, the experimental days, when we didn't really know what was going to work and what wasn't. The green board had some good qualities, and some bad qualities. It flew like a rocket and you could slice a nice cutback with it. On the other hand, she was a little unforgiving. You had to stay at maximum concentration at all times to make it work. I've found that in surfing, and life, a little cushion is a good thing. Nobody's perfect!

Dancing with Lady Mala
Summer on Maui can be heaven or hell. It can go flat as a lake for a month, then a south swell hits and there's so much good surf, you can't possibly ride it all. The summer of 1968 started out pretty flat, with just a couple of swells rolling through. Mala Wharf got about four feet a couple of times in June, and there were some five and six-foot days in town at Shark Pit and The Breakwall. All and all, it wasn't bad. Then in early July, a big south straight from New Zealand came charging out of the South Pacific.

I remember seeing the Harbor just cranking at about eight foot. I saw Tom Gaglia ride a huge wave all the way into the channel at the Harbor entrance. Boats going in and out of the Harbor had to time the sets. It was hairy. Mala Wharf was going off at six to eight feet. What a perfect wave. It was so hard to get out that some guys were paddling out from the north side of the wharf and paddling around it. I remember getting some screaming lefts in the morning on the green board.

I also remember doing the reef dance on some of the sharpest coral in the western hemisphere when I lost my board. Staying on your board was a priority in those days. No jumping off and letting the leash do the work. You either pulled out over the top, or straightened off. Mala was a lot of work, but oh so worth it.

It's one of those places that kind of sneaks up on you. I remember sitting outside on that morning and watching the swells hit the reefs to the south. We could see Breakwall go off and then the Harbor and then the big walls out in front of town. Then, they would be there, coming out of the blue. Big swells moving gracefully out of the deep water like a hula dancer. Beckoning you to ride with a come hither attraction. So pretty, so nice, so smooth. The take off was easy, almost like a mainland-type wave. You could get in and set up, maybe even fade right a little and then turn down the line. Duck under the first big section, and out on to a nice forgiving shoulder. Big cut back, and then turn off the bottom.

Then things change. The Lady Mala gets an attitude. Like a song that changes tempo, the inside lines up like the Great Wall of China. It's an all out race for the wharf. If you win, you get to paddle back out. If you lose, it's a ride in the soup to the beach, or worse, a swim in over a bed of spikes.

Needless to say, in those days, we only surfed Mala at high tide. A cut up foot in Lahaina was like a death sentence. Not in the literal sense, but with staff infection everywhere, you had to stay out of the water. Or risk getting a mean case of some of the ugliest sores on earth.

New Directions in Speed Surfing
We had a great morning surf at Mala and then the tide dropped. A couple of us went back to the Harbor and just sort of hung around. The Breakwall and Harbor were going off, and the tide wasn't too low. We were thinking about going out, but then somebody got an idea. Why not drive down and check out Malia. If it wasn't happening, we could come back and get Mala again in the evening when the tide had come back in. A good plan that got better.

Dave Rullo had come back to Maui and was one of our crew. Dave, Tom and I loaded our boards up and set course for Malia Bay. I had heard a lot of stories about Malia, but it wasn't a real famous break outside of Maui. I'd never seen any pictures of it in magazines. According to the talk, this was a place that only broke on big south swells. It was a long right reef break that was incredibly fast. Almost too fast to make, especially on a long board.

Gaglia had ridden it on a long board and said that you had to take off on a shoulder and just race for the channel. He said that the wave peels perfectly for a good 200 yards before it gets to you, but it's so fast there's no way to ride that part of it. You basically were riding the inside of a very long, screaming right. Oh, and the bottom was covered with purple vanna sea urchins. If you bounced and got stuck, someone had to pee on you to kill the poison.

Boy, all that sounded really good. We took our time driving down the coast and around the Pali. The Haleakala Crater was a beautiful sight rising 10,000 feet out of the windblown Pacific. Did I mention the wind? It blows hard at Malia. Straight off shore about a million miles an hour. It's a result of the trade winds blowing between Haleakala and the West Maui Mountains of the Moon, which are about 4,000 feet. You get the picture? A giant wind tunnel.

I was thinking that if these waves were like Gaglia had been describing, then we might have a chance of making some of them from further out. After all, we had much different equipment and surfing had changed. This kind of wave was what the new style of surfing was all about. And we had the sticks. I had the Green Hornet (my name for the Strada), Gaglia had an eight-six Brewer gun, and Rullo had my old Everlasting board, which had been put back together after being broken in half. All were speed crafts, and ready for the challenge.

As the road took us around the Pali and into the bay, we could see spray blowing off the waves. Malia has a small boat harbor, with a jetty that protects it from the waves. I could see the backs of waves breaking just out side of the Jetty and then into the bay. Butterfly time.

It's rare in life when things or places turn out to be exactly as they have been described. This was one of those times. When we got there, I stared in disbelief as perfect six-foot walls peeled for hundreds of yards with not one drop of water out of place. The most perfect waves I had ever seen. These were waves like we used to draw on our notebooks in school. You couldn't draw a more perfect wave. And there was nobody out!

We waxed up our boards looking at each other like "Is this really happening." There was an easy paddle out a channel, but once outside you had to turn a corner and paddle up the break toward the jetty. It was hard lining up, and we almost got caught inside when the first set came through. Gaglia cautioned us not to paddle too far up the line. Still we were already much further up than he had ever been.

Oh yeah, and he'd never seen it this big before. He had ridden it about three or four feet. He had said a three-foot wave there felt like a six foot wave anywhere else. On this day, the waves were already well over six feet.

The take off was like nothing I'd ever experienced. The wave started just outside of the jetty breakwall. Not really a peak, just a big wall that pitched over and then just peeled down toward us. The sound really got me. It was so loud and the volume rose to more intense levels as it came at you. It roared like something from hell, and it looked like something from hell. A moving explosion.

I instinctively knew not to watch the wave breaking at me when I paddled. Instead, once I thought I was in a good position, I just looked down the shoulder to my right. That way I could judge whether or not I was going to catch the wave, and not be freaked out by what it looked like coming after me. That was a trick I had learned back at Makaha, don't watch the wave when you're caught inside. Watching it just freaks you out and burns up brain cells, and oxygen.

Getting in those fast Malia waves was rough on the Green Hornet. She was a lowrider. Paper thin and as I've said, not much of a paddler. I remember taking off on an angle and jumping up as soon as I caught the wave. This was not bottom turn vertical surfing. This was cut right and drive. I think the first couple of rides were all of a second long, ending in either a prone out or massive explosion. Getting hit with the lip was like somebody handing you a stick of dynamite. I felt like Wiley Coyote in the Road Runner cartoons. Beep beep, there goes the wave flying by me and I'm toast again.

I never got comfortable on the first go out. It was a different wave altogether. Faster, meaner, more unforgiving than any wave I had ridden. Rullo and Gaglia were getting some good rides on their longer boards. On my second go out, I borrowed Tom's Brewer. The floatation alone made a big difference. And, the bits of experience on my first go out helped get me in better positions. That was the deal: positioning. On the take off, on the wave, throughout the ride you had to think ahead. Any wrong move would be punished.

As the mid-day sun turned to afternoon, guys from Lahaina and other parts of the island started showing up. Also, Buddy Boy and Strada came over from Oahu. Hey, Buddy Boy knew his stuff. When he saw a big south swell had hit town, he and Larry jumped a plane over and headed straight for Malia.

There were probably 10 guys out on my second go-out. Actually, in situations like that, I welcomed the company. A few guys bobbing around in the line-up provides perspective. The show was on. Buddy Boy, with his impeccable ability to judge waves, was phenomenal. Gliding at the speed of sound down long picture perfect lines. Rullo, the style master doing his best Buddy Boy moves. Strada using every bit of his six-foot frame to power down the line.

The waves were a solid six to eight feet. Not big compared to what we'd been riding all winter. But every bit as challenging as anything I'd seen since big Hanalei. Every wave was a race for survival. The new style of surfing was being put to the test. Turn hard, and then turn harder, see how far a turn could put you down the line.

The cool part about Malia was that when you did finally win the race, the wave slowed down and you could actually hit a cutback. Oh that felt good. After running for your life, you finally had control back. A couple of nice cutbacks and then "Screw this, I want more speed!" Can you imagine pulling out of a perfect four or five-foot Malibu-type wave with 50 yards still in front of you? That's how good the outside ride was when you made one.

What a day. One of the best I can remember in all my days of surfing. It was the biggest I ever got to ride Malia. Hey, I'm not sure if I would have ever wanted to see it much bigger. That day also brought about visions of surfboards that would go faster. The faster the better. Flat planing-surfaces, like the Brewers, were proven to be the best tool. Outline shapes, like spears, were also on the agenda for things to come.

New Blanks, New Boards

As the summer went on, the action was mostly at The Harbor. It was a good wave and broke on any swell. In the summertime, it featured a peak with a right and a left. The left lined up for blocks on a good swell. The right offered a nice tight, sometimes tubular section and then cutback city. Lots of fun. There was a Hawaiian guy named George Opello that was the king. He was regular foot and had this one move that he did over and over. Hard bottom turn, then come flying off the lip. He never missed it and nobody could do it as well.

Taking Shape at the Surf House

The guys who stayed at the Surf House—Less Potts, Mike Debose, Steve Galese—remodeled their shop and it was the best in town. You could rent the shaping room, or have someone shape you a board. Then buy the materials and glass it yourself, or have somebody there glass it. Blanks were still hard to come by.

Actually the blank makers, Clark and Walker, were hard pressed get some new molds into action. They were still selling the long board blanks, but the short board had caught on in California, too. The demand from shapers was for smaller blanks.

A couple of us got together, pooled our money, and arranged to buy some blanks and have them shipped over. Clark had come up with a good mold, but was still working on getting the formula right. We found out we could buy reject blanks with stringers for around fifteen bucks. We bought about twenty and had them shipped by container right to Kahului.

We sold them for $25 and made our money back and had some blanks for ourselves. Everybody was happy. It sort of stimulated the economy at the Surf House too. The excitement of building new boards was in the air again.

I decided to shape my own board. I'd been watching Leslie Potts shape, and I'd seen some of the greatest of the era (Quigg, Marshall, Edwards, Brewer, Jones). I knew what it looked like to shape a great board. I think I borrowed Potts' planer. Gaglia and I, with the help of Carter Pyle, came up with our own template. Carter showed us how to use battens from sails to draw the curves on the plywood. We just plugged in numbers, measured, pounded in some nails and then curved the batten around the nails.

Armed with my own fresh template and a good blank, I was set. There was something magic about being in the shaping room. The talk of waves and shapes and the natural curves of nature. Foam dust particles suspended in the neon light. Dust covered faces wearing surgical masks. It was like an operating room and we were all doctors discussing how to work on our latest creation.

With Hendrix and Cream blasting from the upstairs Surf House, we were in our element.

Round-Tail V-Bottoms

Over the summer, a new design had been making the rounds of discussion. Actually, an element that turned into a design. It was the v-bottom tail. The Aussies had brought "V" into play in "67, but they used long V panels. Now, we were hearing about a flat bottom, transitioning to a V-tail. The outline could be a square tail or a slightly rounded square.

In those days, no one had a telephone, so word traveled by messenger. The coconut wireless. A guy like Sammy Hawk, or Owl would show up from the North Shore for a couple of days and give us the run down on what was going on. Cabel was doing this, Brewer was doing that. Bunker Sprekles was standing up on a belly board. It was all verbal. An oral history. As the Hawaiians say "We talk story bra." And the word spread.

I had two blanks, so I decided to shape one as a flat-bottomed pin tail and the other as a round-tail V-bottom. Both I believe were seven-eleven, about twenty and a half wide. With the help of Leslie Potts, and Tom Gaglia I shaped the pin tail into a fairly reasonable fact-simile of a surfboard. Sure the rails were slightly different and the outline of the nose never did quite look right, but it had a nose and a tail and was made of foam and fiberglass!

Gaglia had picked right up on shaping. His boards were immediately symmetrical, as were those made by Potts. Of course, Potts had been shaping almost a year by then. All the boards had distinctive looks. Very individualistic, like the guys who made them.

There were a bunch of guys on Maui by then. They came from all over, Huntington, Newport, Ocean Beach (San Diego), and South Bay. Guys hung in groups, usually because of a common residence. The standard dress for most was a T-shirt, trunks or shorts and flip flops. No hats, no cool sun glasses, no tattoos. Girls with names like Sunshine, Bambi and Flower would cut our hair and make us trunks and shorts. All good.

It was like we were all part of a tribe, or cult, or whatever. Not that anyone gave much thought about that. We just all happened to be traveling in the same direction through time. We were island surfers. And, I'm proud to say, an elite group of individuals at the top of the game.

There were other groups, of course. Like the Black Coral Divers. Oh man, you want to talk about individuals? Those guys were so radical. Like sea-going bikers, or maybe closer to pirates. They didn't rob anybody. They didn't have to. They made a ton of money doing what no sane person would ever do. Dive 200 feet down and collect the precious black coral.

The surf crew and the divers got along for the most part. In fact, Harold Bloomfield, the unofficial leader of the black coral divers, eventually bought the surf house and rented it out to some of the surf crew. Bloomfield had a big plantation house out at Pineapple Hill, which is now the Kapalua Resort. Every couple of months he would throw a big luau and invite a bunch of us. The rules were you brought a case of Primo Beer. Primo. No other beer allowed. And every guest had to bring a case.

That could be a hassle, because you'd walk into the market to buy beer and they'd be out of Primo. The guy would look at you and say "Harold must be giving da kine party." And it was "da kine" all right.

The food was always traditional Hawaiian. Kalua pig roasted for 24 hours in a pit, lomi lomi salmon, raw opiie, poi, the whole she-bang. You'd roll in with your case of Primo, chuck it in these huge buckets of ice, and grab a plate. You had to. These were the rules. And you best follow the rules at a black coral diver party, because they were far from us mellow surfer types. Oh yeah, there were times when somebody would get out of line, and they would be gone, only to show up a couple of days later with a couple of shiners and a tooth knocked out.

But, if you got into the groove with the black coral guys, they were pretty cool. The plantation house had a huge grass yard decorated with torches and palm fronds. Always a big bon fire and plenty of picnic tables. Parties would rage until the wee hours with the black coral guys all playing conga drums and bongos. The next morning, like clock work, they would all be chugging out of the harbor at 6 a.m. in their dive boats like there was nothing to it.

And we would be checking the surf or going to shape boards. No problem. Like I've said, the surf house shop had big speakers that were plugged into the stereo upstairs, so whatever was blasting up there, was blasting in the shaping room. Mostly Jimi Hendrix, but then there were runs on The Beatles, Moody Blues and Rolling Stones.

I shaped a round tail board and it actually came out better than the pin tail, maybe because I shaped the pin tail first and had gained a lot of experience. Oh yeah, master shaper in motion. Those boards were, well, rather crude, but I was proud. And I'll tell you this, the process of designing and crafting a shape was so inspirational. It made you feel like an artist, or in my case maybe like a mad scientist, Frankenstein comes to mind!

We cranked out a bunch of boards during the end of the summer. All in preparation for The Bay. Septembers are long in Lahaina. Long and hot. Waiting for that first sign of a northern swell. Watching the Lahaina Harbor for any sign that there might be a swell on the way. Driving out to The Bay, just for the sake of driving. Then one day it happens and the whole town goes nuts.

Broken Arrows
The first swell of fall 1968 was a strong North. It came up over night, and word spread quickly through town in the early morning. I remember taking both boards and trying to decide which one to ride first. When I saw the waves were pushing ten feet, I went with the pin tail. It was a conservative choice. Hey, I'd never ridden a V-bottom and wasn't about to try and figure it out on waves like those.

Honolua is a little more forgiving on a North swell, that is, it's not quite so sneaky. You can see the sets coming from around the corner and it gives everybody time to jockey for position and get outside far enough not to get caught inside. Getting caught inside, out in front of the cave, was a fatal error in those days.

I remember riding a couple of waves, and having a great time. Everybody was smiling. First swell of the year, and we all had new boards. Great stuff. The swell was strong, almost like a mid-winter swell. George Opello was ripping on a new board Potts had made him from one of our blanks. Then on one wave he makes this incredibly hard bottom turn and the board breaks in half right under him. Bummer.

Another guy lost his new board and it broke in half like a tooth pick after hitting the rocks. I got a set wave on my pin and was doing my best roller derby turns to make the inside when I knew I wasn't going to make the long peeling section. No big deal, I'd just straighten out and go to the old prone position. I make the move and the wave comes crashing down on me and the next thing I know, I'm riding a belly board. Yep, the pin tail snapped in half like a twig with me still holding on to the nose.

It took us a while to figure it out, but by the end of the day, with more than half of the new fleet of boards in pieces, the verdict was in. The reject blanks and light-weight glass jobs were not strong enough for winter surf. We were bummed. I remember Potts smiling and telling George Opello "Hey they're just like paper dresses...they only last so long!" I'm not sure George felt that way.

My round tail, made it through the day. Maybe because I was a little more careful with it. Maybe because I was making more waves. From the first wave, I felt the difference in performance. That little touch of V in the tail opened up new directions. It was like the board gave you more access to the wave's energy. I was coming off the bottom quicker and at a greater vertical angle. That put me up higher in the wave much faster than the conventional flat bottomed pin tail. Then a little move to the outside and down you go. Very fast and easy. It was definitely another breakthrough in surfboard design. Stoked again.

Back to the Drawing Boards
Over the next couple of weeks we managed to order some more blanks from Clark. On the advice of Joey Cabell, we ordered a special new mold and had quarter-inch spruce stringers put in for added strength. I had made a trip over to the North Shore to see Joey and get the blank thing going. I didn't take a board, but knew I could borrow one if the surf was good.

I planned to stay for one night. Flew over in the morning, rented a junker in Honolulu and drove out to the North Shore. I spent the first day hanging out at Sunset and visiting some shaping rooms. I saw Mike Diffendiffer and Strada's shaping rooms. I was very much on a fact-finding mission, checking out how they had their rooms set up, what kind of templates they were using. Diff was linving in "The White House," which was right in front of the rights at Pipeline. Strada and Rullo had moved into a classic house in Haleiwa at Seagull lake. They built a great shop there complete with shaping rooms and glassing room.

Rullo and Strada formed a new surfboard company called Ollur Adarts. Their names spelled backwards. Strada was turning out some great boards, and like always he was experimenting. He shaped Rullo a nice mini-gun with a little V in the bottom. While the trend at the time was the pin-tail, Rullo's board had a small square tail. Rullo was tearing up Sunset on it.

There was no surf to speak of during the trip and it rained both days. Still I had fun and got to see a lot of very cutting edge surf-boards. When I returned to Maui, I had a design in mind for my next board. When the blanks arrived about two weeks later I jumped right in the surf house shaping room and cranked out a board.

I put some pretty heavy V in the tail that went up almost a third of the board. From there it was as flat as I could get it, and a little belly in the nose. The blank Joey had recommended was great. Nice kick in the nose and it was very uniform, which made it easier to shape. The good blank made a big difference in the outcome. Somehow the rails had actually matched and the outline was damn near symmetrical!

Gaglia and I had moved into a cane house in Honokawi. Jackie Baxter had been living there and we kind of inherited it when Jackie went back to the mainland for the summer. Cane houses were made for sugar cane workers and consisted of clapboard style cottages built on stilts. They usually had nice front porches, two or three bedrooms and they came with or without electricity, and indoor plumbing depending on their location.

This one had electricity and a bathroom out back that had hot water. It was right on the main thoroughfare that led to The Bay so everybody going to and from Honolua had to drive right by. It was a nice set up, and we lived there with several other guys. Sort of that revolving door thing with Gaglia and me as the permanent residents.

It was probably early December when my new board was done. The Beatles had just released The White Album and we were blasting it over the stereo at the Surf House. I named my new board Julia, for a song on the album, and for a high school girlfriend.

Power Surfing — Jackie Baxter was always a power surfer and when he got on a short board, well he pushed the envelope. He had a slashing style that was all his own. (Photo by Richard Graham)

Membership in the Tribe

What a great winter. The surf came up in December and stayed up through the end of January. The Bay was eight, ten and twelve feet consistently and man did we get some waves. Gray days, howling tradewinds and plenty of juice. The round tail V-bottoms were the board du jour and they took us all to new plateaus.

I can remember getting rides and thinking to myself "I'm the luckiest person in the world right now!" I thought about my parents and my girlfriend, Ellen, and what it would be like for them if I could take them for a ride and let them see what I was seeing. It was like jumping off a two-story building and having the ability to fly in almost any direction. Or it was like driving a high-powered sports car and putting your foot down on the gas. And it was much more. An intimate interaction with each wave, the exhilaration and excitement of pushing the boundaries. The joy of doing something few people in the world had a chance to do.

We were part of a developing sub-culture, like a tribe of nomadic hunters. The tribe was the tribe of Island surfers. To become a member of the tribe you needed to prove yourself as a warrior. That meant riding what ever came through, within reason of course. Everybody has their limits and an instinct for survival. Some warriors relied on sheer nerve. Some used power and strength. Some used their cunning and wit. All endeavored for respect within the tribe.

The tribe had various bands, the North Shore band, the Kauai band, the Maui band. Within the Island bands were cliques of guys who hung together. Small groups who usually hailed from the same area. The Huntington guys, the La Jolla guys, Newport guys and so on. And, like the old west, there were guys who rode together, sidekicks.

Jeff Hackman and Jock Sutherland were such a pair. And, if I may string this metaphor one more step, two of the top gun slingers in the west! They would come down the hill from Kula and stop by our house in Honokawi on their way to and from the bay. What a pair, they both had so much energy in and out of the water. Without exception, every time those two paddled out, everyone's level of surfing went up a notch. They would establish the bar, and we all tried to reach it.

The Bay had crowds even then. More so on the six to eight-foot days than on the ten to twelve-foot days. There was a core group who rode the place like an eight-to-five job. The regulars. Through the winter guys would come from the mainland and try to leave their mark. Some would stay, others would go back home with stories to tell their kids. I remember a group that came over from the South Bay. Drew Harrison, Mike Purpose, Charlie Quiznell, and Steve Slickenmeyer among them. They all paddled out on the first day with really bad imitations of mini guns from who knows where. I saw their eyes bulging out watching the likes of Jock and Jeff riding waves like they had never seen. Doing things they had never seen. Drew and Purpose were at the top of the game in mainland contests, but at The Bay, they were just trying to survive. This was a whole different game.

We all did a lot of island hopping in those days, switching bands as one would progress. I remained tried and true to Maui, although I would go over to the North Shore from time to time. I'll be the first to admit, I don't think I could have made the grade as a true North Shore guy. The place has always intimidated the hell out of me. I went over just to stay close to the action, to see what was going on and who was doing what.

I made a trip over in January of 1969 to visit Strada and Rullo, or should I say Ollur and Adarts. They were sidekicks who had established themselves as innovators. Strada was the craftsman and designer. He shaped, sanded and glossed the boards. Rullo was the glasser and chief test pilot. Which leads to a classic North Shore story.

The Hydro-Fin
Since the transition to short boards, everyone was always trying to push the envelope in design. Herbie Fletcher was shaping reverse tear-drops, a guy named Vinnie Bryant was riding these belly-board like creations with square rails! So Rullo and Strada came up with the ultimate creation: The Fin. Actually, it was a little board that was shaped like a fin. Strada had glued three or four blanks together to make a board that was almost four-feet thick!

It was all of six feet long, with a flowing tear-drop outline. The bottom was this sculptured fin-like shape. The idea was instead of riding a board, you would ride a fin. Okay, you have to remember it was the sixties, and thinking was...well you know.

So Strada creates this very masterful craft that was going to put Ollur Adarts on the map. Just to make it all more dramatic, they made it all black. As the story goes, the surf comes up just as the Fin was finished. Rullo paddles it out at ten-plus Lanikea. According to Rullo, after he made some adjustments it actually paddled him pretty good. He makes it outside, which is no small accomplishment at ten-foot Lanikea. So, when a set comes through the guys in the line-up give him a great wave. He strokes, but the board begins to stall as the wave picks him up. Totally committed, he paddles faster. He feels the wave taking the board and he stands up.

I wasn't there to actually see it, but I've heard the story enough times I can visualize it. Rullo makes it to his feet just at the wave starts pitching out. The Fin starts careening down the face, pushing water like a New York tugboat, then it just makes a 90 degree turn to the left. Rullo goes airborne and the rest is history. Bad wipe-out. Very bad.

He tells a funny story of swimming in and seeing this thing floating upside down, looking like some sort of killer whale. Not to be discouraged, he actually went back out and caught another wave. Oh yeah, same exact result. The Fin was finished!

A King Evolves

That was the talk of the town when I went over that winter. That and stories about a guy who was reinventing the art of riding the tube. I was cruising the North Shore with Cabell and the surf was up. Sunset was ten to twelve, but crowded. We decide to head down to the Pipeline and see what was up. I remember it was a gray rainy day, and I wasn't all that stoked. Yeah, I was a little scared, too.

When we walked out on the beach at Pipeline it was littered with onlookers and photographers. I saw solid ten-foot lefts and a bunch of guys in the line up. I knew right off I wasn't going out, but I did want to see some action. And boy did I.

A set came in and I see this guy taking off way back. A smooth looking goofy-foot drops in, drives to the bottom and just cranks this turn. I mean, he was so far over he looked like a water skier dragging his shoulder. He jets up to the middle of the wave and then disappears in the tube. I'm thinking he's history. The wave breaks and he's gone from sight for three or four seconds, then he comes flying out of the tube with the famous Pipeline spit. The guy straightens up, and ever so casually puts his arms in the air as he pulls out.

A rash of questions go through my brain. How big was the board? How did he get so much speed? Who is that guy? I turn to Joey and, of course, he knows. Gerry Lopez on a seven-six Brewer. Oh man, not the same Gerry Lopez from Kauai. Yep the very same, although he had gone through a total metamorphous from smooth, casual long board surfer to radical, jet pilot, speedster. And, yes, master of the tube. What a difference a board makes!

I came back from the North Shore with a lot of good ideas for boards. The winter was in full swing and I was ready to make a new board. Unfortunately, I couldn't afford a new blank. I ended up buying an old tanker, and stripping it down. It was a big thick board with three redwood stringers. The best I could do at the time.

After seeing Gerry at Pipeline, and watching Joey and the guys at Sunset, I wanted more speed out of my board. Rails had been getting sharper with more of a down turn since about the second phase of the mini gun. In fact, some shapers had been turning the rails all the way down in the last two feet of the board. There was a lot of talk about harder rails, and flat bottoms. Still there were those who argued that there were no flat surfaces nor 90-degree angles in nature. They said surfboards should be naturally flowing shapes like the porpoise.

All I knew is I wanted to go fast. So I set out with a plan of shaping a very pointed and drawn outline shape. The blank was a problem from the start. I had never shaped a blank with three stringers and trying to get the outline right was hard. And, every time I used the sanding block, the stringers would remain high. I got real familiar with the hand plane.

It was early evening when I started shaping that board and late night when I got done. In the end, everything in the board came out as a compromise. It was like the blank just did what it wanted. At one point I was so frustrated that I thought I would just shape something really radical and not worry about it. Shape something absurd and then throw it in the trash can. Eventually, a board came to life out of it. A rather crude and misguided board. I named her Margaret, after a Beatles song that had been playing all night.

It was, well...a one of a kind board. I had turned the right rail all the way down about half way up the board and left the left rail soft. Margaret was a Honolua special. Forget about going backside. This was a one-way ticket, a ride on the wild side.

I had her glassed and ended up riding her for more than a month. No, the right rail theory didn't really work. It caught so many edges, Margaret almost self destructed. Mean-while, guys like Jeff and Jock were getting better and better on their precision made Brewers.

More guys joined the tribe and started ripping the bay. Gary Chapman had moved from the North Shore, and Steve Dabney came over from the mainland. Both were hot surfers and immediately fit in the line-up. Dabney had a girlfriend named Shirley who surfed, one of only three that attempted to ride the Bay in those days. She had more guts than skill, but she would paddle out at six to eight foot and do her best.

The Queen of Honolua
Of course, there was one girl in the line-up that did more than just show up. Eleanor Johnson. She had grown up in Kailua and surfed since she was a little girl. She rode long boards better than a lot of guys and when we moved to the short board she was right there. On Maui, she was something of a legend. The only girl who could really ride the Bay.

I had heard about her before I got to Maui, and she was everything that I heard. A strong, tanned beauty, who took no shit from anyone. She lived in Lahaina and had a classic poi dog named "My Dog." Eleanor was one of a kind. I admit, I had a crush on her for awhile. But, she went for older guys. She lived with Bruce Jones for awhile, and then ended up marrying a guy named Bill Johnson. Classic lady, way ahead of her time.

As winter turned to spring, surfing at the Bay continued to evolve. Chapman and Potts were taking off further back in the peak and powering around sections. Dabney was like some kind of human humming bird, ripping the waves and staying out for half a day at a time. Neal Norris was ripping with a unique style straight out of the Wind-an-Sea mode. Pat Cosgrove and Paul McKinney shined when the waves got over ten feet. And there were more. All riding just for the fun of it. Soul surfing with only ear-to-ear smiles as a reward.

Tom Gaglia emerged as a shaper. His boards were always very well crafted and he started shaping for other guys and actually got paid! Although my shaping wasn't quite up to par, we decided to form our own surfboard company. We called it Downhome Surfboards, because our place out in Honokawai was such a down-home sort of spread.

Downhome Lahaina

We bought some blanks and set up a deal to use the Surf House shaping and glassing rooms. Tom shaped and glassed. I shaped and sanded. Hey, no one else wanted to be the sander, and I actually made some money doing it. My shaping improved some, and I actually turned out a couple of pretty good boards. I even shaped a board for Jock. Yep there was a month or so in the spring of 1968, when I could say I had one of the best riders in the world riding my board. It did wonders for my popularity as a shaper. Guys were actually paying me to shape boards! Jock, of course, could ride anything and make it look good. It was just pure luck that he picked me to shape him a board.

Oh those were fun days. Waking up early and checking the surf, then going over to the Lahaina Bakery for breakfast. Helen, the lady who owned the Bakery, had moved it from its original location on Front Street to a place that was right in front of the Surf House. We would work in the morning and then take coffee breaks at the Bakery. In the afternoon, we would punch the clock at the Bay. It was a great life.

When the winter finally came to an end, there was the typical exodus for the mainland. Guys could make more money on the mainland and, of course, there was always going back to mom's and the full refrigerator. I never went that route though. I liked living in the islands and thought I'd never go back to Newport. I was a kamaina! That's a mainlander who moves permanently to Hawaii.

With winter's end also came the end of school at Maui Community College. I had done pretty well there, actually maintaining a 3.2 GPA. But, the curriculum was somewhat less than demanding. Being out of school, meant being available for the draft, and I had to register. I needed a position in the Maui National Guard.

The Draft

As it turned out, a couple of positions did become available. The only problem was I was third on the list. John Geyer and Pat Huggins, both from Newport, were ahead of me. They got accepted and were shipped to Fort Ord for training. Then I got my draft notice! Just like that. I was devastated. My perfect life on Maui was going to be shattered.

Viet Nam was like some nightmare that you couldn't shake. People everywhere were protesting the war. Well, not everywhere. In Hawaii, many of the locals felt it was their duty to join the service and do whatever they were told. I had been ready to join the National Guard, and serve that way, but go to Viet Nam? No way. I, like most of my contemporaries felt that if the United States was attacked, or threatened by China or Russia, I would be right there in the fight. But, why were we fighting in Viet Nam? There was no good reason. So what if Viet Nam wanted to be a communist nation. Was that really going to threaten our way of life? And if it did, then why the hell not go in there full-force and blow the shit of them? There were no good answers.

After getting my draft notice, I decided to go back home and visit my parents. I flew back to California and took a bus to my parent's house. I was only there for a week, but during that week I had a chance to get together with some old friends, all of whom felt the same way I did about going to Viet Nam. So, I talked to my parents. I told them my feelings and they were supportive, in a way. They agreed that the war was not being handled properly. In the end, I told them I was going to be a consciences objector. I think my mom was glad.

When my day came to report to the draft board, I had a plan all worked out. Guys were doing all kinds of things to get out. But, after talking to someone who had just been rejected, I found out that if you just went in and played crazy, they might reject you. In Hawaii, there were all kinds of guys who were ready to go. So a bad apple was easier to reject.

I went in stone sober and just got into this state of mind. I scribbled on all the exams, and when it came time for the blood test, I passed out and fell off this little stage. That was no act. I had been fasting for a day or so, and I have always been scared of needles. So I go out like a light, and end up in the infirmary. From there, I go to the shrink, and in the end they tell me to follow this white line on the floor and sign some papers at the door. Uncle Sam had decided I wasn't Army material.

Looking back, I have very mixed feelings about that. I feel guilty for not standing up and going. I don't like to talk about it. I am ashamed. But, at the same time I still feel that Viet-Nam was a lousy war, and that thousands of guys died for no reason. No one came back unscathed. I did what I thought was right at the time, and I have to live with it.

The biggest irony of the whole thing was that right after I got my "1Y" papers keeping me out of the draft, they called up the Maui National Guard to go to Viet Nam! Yep, all those guys who had it made in the Guard, were going to Viet Nam.

Actually, there's quite a story about how some of them got out of it, but I wasn't there. I do know that many of them were never the same again. It was a bad deal.

The Steve Miller Experience
My life went back to some normalcy, and I had one other very memorable experience in that summer. I had taken a new job at The Lahaina Broiler, a restaurant right on the water in Lahaina. It was a beautiful place built under a sprawling Keavi tree with an open Lanai and a million-dollar view. To the north the point marking the tradewind line is called the Lahaina Rhodes. The point was also the outside of Mala Wharf's reef. To the south was the Lahaina Harbor and a classic old whaling vessel called The Carthiginian. Long green walls would break out in front and then roll in to splash up on the rocks in front of the restaurant. The smell of the sea, mixed with the fresh grilled fish and steaks created a magic atmosphere.

I took the job in early summer, and split my time between night-time bus boy and day waiter. The day waiter part of the gig was best, work wise. I could surf early in the morning and then go to work, make some money, eat good, and then had the afternoon off for jaunts down to Shark Pit or the Harbor. Most days we had two waiters on the floor and a bus boy. I worked a lot with a girl named Jo May, who was a stone knock out. She had a smile and body that wouldn't quit. Kill Bod, we used to say, because a body like that could be lethal.

The second love of my life next to surfing has always been music. I had been playing guitar since I was about 13. Surf music, rock and roll and blues. In fact, I had become something of a blues aficiona-

Breakfast Constitutional — The Pioneer Inn was a great place to meet for breakfast. Of course, the talk was surfing and design. Many a new board was drawn up on a napkin. In this picture, it looks as if I'm getting ready to go to The Broiler for work after a quick cup with the boys. Life was good! (Photo by Dick Graham)

do. My days with Oakie in Newport had given me access to a vast library of blues. And I had done my homework. I knew all the players in all of Muddy Waters bands, and Howlin Wolf, Little Walter and Junior Wells were like old friends. I could listen to a 20-year old blues record and tell you who was playing guitar, bass and piano. I just loved the stuff, and worked hard trying to play it.

Of course, I was into the contemporary stuff, too. Hey, we're talking a great musical period here. Jimi Hendrix, Santana, Quicksilver Messenger Service, not to mention the Stones and the Beatles. Music was on a parallel course with surfing, or vice versa according to your perspective. It was 1968, the whole world was going through a metamorphose of sorts.

Having the job at the Broiler gave me the where-with-all to do some things from a musical perspective. I had an electric guitar and amp, which I played with anybody who would jam. A couple of us got together and formed a little band to play parties. Pia and Noah Alluli, were Hawaiian guys from Kailua who had a great house out in the Honokawai, which was on the way to the Bay and just country then. Pia played bass and Noah was a drummer. Together with a guitar player named Rod Stair, we had some great jams. We practiced out at the country house and played as loud as we wanted with no complaints. Great fun. A surf in the morning and then jam in the afternoon. Good stuff.

I had flown over to Honolulu a couple of times to see groups. I saw Jimi Hendrix, Vanilla Fudge and Creedence Clearwater Revival. Then one of my favorites came to town and I knew I had to go. The Steve Miller Band. I had loved their first two albums, and I knew that Miller had a great reputation as a pure blues player in addition to his talent as a rocker. I could name every guy in the band. Boz Skaggs, Lonnie Turner, Tim Davis, okay I forget the keyboard player's name now, but I knew it then.

The Steve Miller Band was scheduled to play on Friday night at the HIC in Honolulu. The trouble was, I had been scheduled to work Friday and Saturday lunch at the Broiler. So naturally, I figured out a way. I flew over Friday after my lunch shift and flew back the next morning in time for my next shift. I arranged to stay in town (Honolulu).

So off I went Friday. I had to take the bus from the airport to town, but I arrived in time to see the last part of the opening band. Then there was a long wait for the Steve Miller Band. Like about an hour. People were chanting and getting kind of rowdy by the time they came on. Then, much to my surprise, the band came on stage as a three-piece. No keyboards, no Boz Skaggs on guitar. Just Miller, Bassist Lonnie Turner, and drummer Tim Davis.

It was hot and muggy inside the HIC and you could see sweat running down Miller's face from the first song. They had a couple of sound problems at first, but then got into it. He had just written the song "Living in the USA," and they did it really well. They went on to play a bunch of songs no one had really heard of, all of which would become hits later. But, the crowd was there to see the stuff they had done on the first two albums, and they were disappointed. I enjoyed it because I knew what they were doing was awesome. Miller's guitar was filling out the songs in a way that few three-piece bands could match. I recognized his expertise and reveled in watching him play.

My guitar buddy Rod had made the trip, and invited me to stay at some friends of his in town. Rod wasn't a surfer. He fancied himself a guitar player from San Francisco, actually, I think he was from Laguna and had only lived in San Francisco a couple of months. He did know people in the music business though. In fact, he knew the guys who had put on the HIC concert that night.

I guess the reviews of Steve Miller were not that good, and we read in the morning paper that the next two nights had been cancelled. They blamed it on an equipment problem or something. Rod and I caught an early flight back to Maui and I had plenty of time to get to work. It would be a busy day because it was the weekend of the annual Lahaina Whaling Spree, which was sort of a Hawaiian style Fat Tuesday. It was drinking and partying to the max, with lots of entertainment. In fact, our little band was scheduled to play at a concert down at the Banyan Tree on Sunday.

That day Jo May and I and a couple of others had the floor at The Broiler. We opened at 11:30 and served lunch until 2:30. Jo May and I had adjoining sections of the restaurant, both with water-front tables. We were setting up our tables about 11:15, when in comes Rod, and two other guys. One guy is very cool with an afro hair style and bell bottoms, the other guy has a tank top and bun huggers! I'm serious, bun huggers.

Rod kind of pulls me over to the side and says, "You know who that is?" I don't. He tells me to take a closer look. I do, and I realize, it's Steve Miller. I couldn't believe it. Rod's friend, the guy who put on the concert, had brought the Miller Band over to Maui for the weekend just to kick back and get some rest. I guess they had an intense touring schedule, and wanted the break in Hawaii. Hey, no better place than Lahaina, and on Whaling Spree Weekend!

Rod introduced me to the producer guy, Mike, and Steve Miller. I promptly escorted them to a table in my section. I took their order as soon as the kitchen opened and then the place started filling up. The producer guy was drinking iced tea, Miller had a Mai Tai, and then went into a string of beers. As time allowed, I would drop by the table and freshen up their water, take away empties, that sort of thing. Rod had lunch with them and left.

The sight of Jo May had definitely caught Miller's attention, so I introduced her. Producer Mike left soon after Rod, but Miller stayed drinking Primo Beer and enjoying the view. As the lunch crowd slowed, I got more of a chance to talk to him. So I sort of made some small talk, and then we started talking about the blues. I kept pulling names out of the hat about guys who I thought had influenced him. He just smiled and nodded. I picked up right away that he was a good guy, not some rock star with an over inflated ego. Just a guy who loved to play music.

As the afternoon went on, Jo May had joined us in a couple of conversations. We all had a good time talking about music and all kind of things. He stayed the whole shift and even sat there while we were breaking down. I could tell he didn't get a chance to just relax and talk with regular people. When we were all done, he asked if we'd take him out and show him the town.

I was driving this old International Travel-All at the time. It was a dirty yellow, and had all kinds of body rot. I was embarrassed, but he thought it was cool. We all piled in the front seat and I took him for a mini tour of town. We also went to my place, so I could change out of my Broiler uniform and to Jo May's for the same reason. She came out in this very tight, very short shift that, well, let's just say it did her justice.

On the way through town, we passed by The Whale's Tale. Sounds of live music poured out the door and Miller's eyes lit up. He asked if the band might let him sit in. I knew the band. They were from the North Shore and came over to Maui a couple of times before. The lead guitar was this guy named Dale. Being part of the musicians circle in Lahaina, I had met Dale on several occasions. Of course, he would never give me the time of day. He was a pretty good guitar player though, I'll give him that.

We took Miller to his room at The Travel Lodge to get his guitar. It was classic, he didn't even think of changing out of his bun huggers. He just went in picked up his ax and got back in the car. I'll never forget the looks on people's faces when we came into the Whales Tale. The band was cranking and everyone was throwing down beers at the bar. Here we come, a knock-out chick and a guy wearing bun huggers carrying a Les Paul case.

The first guy I see is my friend Bubby Hill, who was a regular at The Bay and in our guitar world. Bubby gave the guy in the bun huggers a rare glance and then gave me a look like "what the hell?" I smiled and whispered in his ear "Watch this!" I left Miller and Jo May at the bar with Bubby and made my way through the crowd to the bandstand. At the end of a song, I motioned to Dale. He gave me a demeaning sort of look but came over. I asked him if

Steve Miller could sit in with them. He gave me a look like I was crazy. But I told him it was for real, and that Steve Miller was at the bar with his guitar.

All of the sudden, I saw Dale get sort of nervous. It was a different look for him to say the least. Sure enough though, he said okay. Miller took the stage, plugged into an amp and just started ripping some old blues tunes. Dale's band backed him up with Dale playing some good rhythm. The music was intense pulsating blues rock, with Miller ad-libbing vocals and playing some kick-ass leads. And in bun huggers too!

Then it got even better. Tim Davis, Miller's drummer, had been walking by and heard the music. He knew the sound. Next thing you know, Tim Davis is playing drums and the music takes on a new dimension.

Word spreads fast on the coconut wireless, and before we knew it the place was so packed that people were standing out in the street to listen. Everyone was getting squished inside. It was wild. Chicks were taking off their tops and the dancing was, well, I'm not really sure it was dancing.

So the cops come, then the fire department and they shut the whole place down. Just like that. Everyone was bummed, but it wasn't nasty. No riot here. Not on Maui, people were much too mellow for that. Anyway, Pia and Noah were there and when the place shut down, Pia jumps up on stage and says "Party in the country."

It was about 4:30 or so on a warm afternoon. Great time for a party. We told Dale to bring his band, and both Miller and Davis said they would come. Jo May knew where the house was, so she stayed with Miller and said she would bring him out. The rest of us packed up the band's equipment and headed out for the country.

What a night that turned out to be. We got out there and set up a makeshift stage. Our band played first, knocking out about an hour's worth of funky stuff. Then Dale's band took over. People from all over the island were showing up. And everyone was asking "Where's Steve Miller?"

It was probably after eight o'clock when our band was doing a second set. We were thrashing away up there when I remember the room sort of going silent and people stopped dancing. We stopped playing and I look out to see the crowd split like the Red Sea. The man had arrived. Steve Miller strolled through the room wearing shorts and a T-shirt, Les Paul in one hand, a glowing Jo May in the other.

He walked right up and plugged in. I didn't know what to do. In fact, my guitar was so out of tune that the whole band winced when I tried an E chord. Miller was cool and helped me tune. Actually gave me a little tuning lesson that I've never forgotten. Anyway, we tune up and launch into a little blues shuffle in the key of A, it was one of the only tunes our band could do well. I don't remember much except Steve Miller smiling and playing lightening-fast melodic leads. I declined a solo when he looked at me. I was so nervous, I could hardly play.

So after the one song, I spy Dale out in the audience and make him come in and take over. Which, he had no problem with. The rest of Dale's band took the stage and the jam was on. It was a grand jam and lasted for more than an hour. Then Miller and Jo May disappeared into the night and the party wound down.

The next day, Miller came down to the Banyon Tree and jammed again. That was an outdoor concert of sorts and he brought his bass player and drummer and they did the same set they had done in Honolulu. It was great and everyone got to see the Steve Miller Band for free. Hey, Maui no ka oui!

Surfing and music went hand in hand to me in those days. It was like when I listened to a guy take a solo, I visualized a wave and riding down the line. The wave was the band, the lead solo. The wave could be a jazz wave or a slow blues, it didn't matter. The surfer got to play the solo and do his best riffs to the rhythms of the ocean. Harmony.

Long Hot Summer
The Lahaina summers can be long and hot. Okay, they are long and hot, and sometimes flat as a lake. Oh, there's usually always a

little wind swell somewhere, but no real surf to speak of. I remember a month of no surf. We spent our days making boards and dreaming of ten-foot days at the Bay. In the afternoons we would go out at the harbor just to get wet. The surf would be so small, it was hard to even catch the waves.

Still, we would go out and try new things. One day, I think it was Bubby Hill who got the idea, we all started surfing goofy-foot. Unless you were already a goofy-foot, then you surfed regular-foot. It made it more fun. It was like learning to surf all over again. And, it put a little bit of competitive spirit back in the water with everybody trying to out-do the other. I don't know if it ever helped our progression in surfing, but it passed the time.

The streets in Lahaina in summer time got so hot you could feel the heat through your flip flops. Still, the town was crowded with tourists and more and more people would arrive from the mainland to catch the spirit of Lahaina. Hippies from San Francisco arrived and added a different sort of element to the mix. Good and bad, of course. I remember one guy who went by the name of Tarkin. He was tall and skinny with hair that went down to his waist. He was that sort of cosmic guru type who had all kinds of advice. Everything from how to cure staff infection to a better love life through herbal remedies. Oh yeah, lots of herbal remedies.

Tarkin would come over to the surf house and get everybody meditating and chanting. The thing then was to ooommmm. You know everybody sits around in lotus positions chanting ooooommmmmmm. Maybe it's Aum, I don't know, I just remember listening to Ravi Shankar and waiting for somebody to start levitating.

When Dogs Run Free

There was this sandwich shack across from the Broiler called Charlie's Juice Stand. The crew would gather there and drink carrot juice and smoothies and eat avocado sandwiches with sprouts. We were very organic, of course.

Charlie's was named after a dog. Yep. Charlie was a Great Dane with Dalmatian-like markings. Dogs ran free then, just like the Bob Dylan song. I swear Dylan may have written that song about Maui. The dogs hung out in packs, just like us. Charlie had is own little band of poi dogs and scrappers. They'd clean up bread crumbs and anything you would toss at them around the juice stand.

That was on the north end of Lahaina. The south end was ruled by this mean pack of dogs that consisted of poi dogs, pit bulls and a huge alpha male that was some kind of Japanese fighting dog. His name was Nocta or something and he was bad ass. You didn't even want to look at him out of fear of him going mad-dog on you. He was owned by Harold Bloomfield and he was always out in front of the dive shop with his little pack.

For the most part, the Charlie pack stayed up by the juice stand and Nocta ruled the area by the dive shop. But, every once in a while one of the bands would stray into the other's territory and all hell would break lose. The worst of those scraps was one hot summer day when Charlie and Nocta went at it. Oh man what a fight.

I remember kicking back at the juice stand with a smoothy when I noticed some people running down the street toward the dive shop. Naturally, a few of us there kind of fell in to see what was happening. The next minute we are in a crowd of people marching down Front Street. I overheard some of the talk: "Charlie and Bloomfield's dog are going at it...no one can break them up. Cops are on the way."

I arrived to peer over shoulders at a sight I'd just as soon forget. Two big, aggressive animals just going at it with all the hate in the world reflecting in their eyes. They went at it like mad roosters, or cats, or I don't know what. But, it was fast and furious and fur was flying. Bad stuff.

Everyone just stood back and stayed out of the way. No one, not even Bloomfield, could stop them. And he tried. It was bitter, and bloody, and it went on for the better part of an hour. The cops came and just let them go. They were trying to get the dog catcher from the other side of the island to come over with a tranquilizer gun. Good luck. Finally, after what seemed an eternity, they both just looked at each other and limped off in opposite directions. It was a draw.

Things changed after that. The town almost took up sides about the whole deal. The surfers and hippies were aligned with Charlie. The black coral divers and a contingent of locals were with Nocta.

There was bad blood for awhile and there were a few of us who would avoid the dive shop portion of Front Street. All because of a pack of dogs.

It was if Lahaina itself was changing. More people, more friction, a clash in cultures with a new reality settling in. By the end of summer, I had moved in with Jamie MacGlophlin. He had a house on the north side of town. It was a nice new track house with plenty of room. Jamie rented rooms to Gary Chapman, Bruce Page, Larry Miller and me. It was an all Newport crew, and we had some great times there. Gary and Jamie had set up a glass shop down at Huxley's house, which was a cool place to hang out. It was an all South Bay house with Huxley, Billy Ray James and David "Sculley" Souder. Later that year Charlie Quiznell and Steve Slickenmeyer moved in and basically rewrote the book on how to go backside at Honolua.

As fall approached, the town started buzzing with planers working over new boards for the bay. I was making boards for a small group of guys, mostly Newport guys and locals. Tom Gaglia and I had built a shaping room in an abandoned house up on Lahaina Luna Road. We tapped into some power at a friend's house next door. It was a great room, with nice racks and side lights. Tom's boards were getting better and better, and mine were sort of improving. With the help of Carter Pyle, we made some great templates with beautiful flowing curves.

I shaped myself a board with one of the new templates and it came out really good. The outcome of my endeavors with the planer were mostly dictated by the blank. I remember having a really bad blank over the summer and ended up shaping a board that was so bad, we named it the Mutant. It was like 14-inches wide. A complete mistake from beginning to end. We ended up nailing it to the shaping room wall for decoration!

My new board actually came out nice. It was seven-eleven with a nose reminiscent of Everlasting and a nice tear-drop shape with a continuous curve in the outline shape. The bottom was as flat as I could get it. The rails were turned down, but soft, and the tail was round. I incorporated long V panels in the bottom.

Jamie glassed the board and Chapman, who was the glosser, put this very cool tear drop swoosh on the deck. Ever since I had

Everlasting, I liked to have something on the deck to focus on. Chapman did a great job of designing a sort of mantra-like shape using dark purple pigment.

It was probably early December when she was done. The Beatles had just released The Abby Road and we were blasting it over the stereo at Jamie's and Huxley's house. That was our surf music and our anthem for the times.

Chappy and the Wet Seal — There were only a few girls surfing the Bay in those days. One was The Wet Seal, whose real name was Diane (Can't remember her last name, sorry). She was a beaut, and we all looked after her. Here she is with Gary Chapman with outside point Honolua in the background..........

Bring on the Bay

1969 will go down in history as one of the greatest winters ever. The surf came up in December and stayed up through the end of March. The Bay was eight, ten and twelve feet consistently and man did we get some waves. Cranking north swells, rides from the outside point all the way through the bowl. The round tail V-bottoms were still the ride and served us all well.

There were a least a dozen guys who could surf The Bay at the same level. By that I mean really ride it. Dabney, Chapman, Potts, Buddy Boy, Paul McKinney all come to mind. Jamie MacGlophlin had always been the best at going backside. That was until a couple South Bay guys with funny last names showed up. Quizznell and Slickenmeyer, were a pair to draw to at Honolua Bay. Real gun slingers who went backside with a flare. Their styles were very different, but the result was the same. Damn good surfing. I can't tell you which one was better. They both rode deep and seemed always on the edge of disaster. It was just beautiful to watch.

For me, that was one of the thrills of the Bay. Just watching. After a good two-hour surf, it felt so good to find a nice warm rock in the sun, out of the wind, and just watch guys rip.

That winter, a swell came out of the Aleutians like no other anyone could remember. The North Shore turned into one big long stretch of whitewater with waves breaking over Kam Highway. There were cloud-breaks outside of the cloud-breaks and only one place to be. Honolua Bay was on fire. For about a week, the waves were never under 10-feet, with one day actually too big for the Bay.

It started with a bang. We woke up in Lahaina to the sounds of roaring surf out of the north west. It was so big that the entire West side was like one big point-break right. The Harbor was eight-to-ten feet and closing out the channel. When we got out to the Bay, it was unrecognizable. There was no Bay. It was all white-water, with one huge peak breaking far outside of the dead center of the bay. No way to surf it. At least not for me.

Actually, some guys did try and go out later in the day. Mike McClellan, Leslie Pots and Craig "Owl" Chapman. They all paddled out to the peak, but no one got any good waves. On some sets, the waves were so big that they sucked all the water out of the bay and you could see the reef in front of the cave. It was at least 20 feet.

For our part, we watched for awhile and then went in search of something to ride. We ended up on the south end of Lahaina where the waves had rapped in to form a nice, eight-foot right that just peeled down the beach. I remember spending a gray afternoon riding an unknown, and un-surfed reef. Never saw it come close to breaking again.

Precious Moments — You know that commercial where it says "life doesn't get any better than this?" For me, this was one of those moments. Riding high, good board under my feet, coming into the bowl. If I could only turn back time ... (Photo by Dick Graham)

Honolua at Perfection

The next day, the weather switched from gray and rainy, to perfect tradewinds and sun. The swell had died overnight and switched to more west. I shouldn't say died. When we got to the bay, it was all of 15-feet and just perfect.

There were guys in the water. A lot of guys, actually. A whole contingent of North Shore guys had made the trip over, and just about everyone on the island was there. Still, there were plenty of waves if you knew what you were doing.

I had learned a lot about The Bay and knew a couple of its secrets. That helped, especially on a west swell, where the waves were harder to see coming. I knew where to look for signs of a set coming. Not like on north swells where waves stuck out like sore thumbs coming around the corner and everyone got the word at the same time. West swells are sneaky. They look like they are actually coming from the channel between Molokai and Lanai. The secret is that you have to look toward town to get a tip on a set. And then you have to move fast to get into position.

A west swell appears more as a peak than a line. Instincts tell you to paddle for the channel and take off on the shoulder of the peak, and that's what most guys did. That west-side shoulder, however, gets real steep real fast, and it is an instant elevator shaft for those getting in late. Back then, without leashes, when you got wiped out in the peak of a west swell, your board went straight toward the cave. A swim to the cave was like running a gauntlet. You had to get in and out between waves. The bottom was sharp coral and rocks and it almost always meant a brush with blood, or worse, a broken board.

Some guys didn't even try to get their boards back. And, if someone else did go in and get it, they would have salvage rights. Tough luck. I think Paul McKinny claimed more than one of his boards that way. Bay rules.

I think Buddy Boy was the one who showed me the ropes on a big west swell. The trick was when a set came in, you paddled for the point, instead of the channel. Mind you, that is easier said than done. When a huge set is bearing down on the line up, it goes against everything in your psyche to paddle directly into it. Getting caught inside was a sure life-and-death experience. Oh, you would survive, but it wouldn't be easy. Honolua can be as wicked a lady as any in the islands.

The plan, if you had the cajones to pull it off, was to paddle directly into the approaching peak. What happens is the peak, as it builds on the reef, shifts toward the channel causing the shoulder to bowl. This leaves a little saddle on the right side of the peak, which provides the opportunity to either paddle over the saddle, or turn around and take off. Good wave judgement here is imperative.

If you time it right, you can get into the wave early from the back door and drive down hard to the bottom of the peak. A big, swooping bottom-turn and you come flying into the first bowl-like section. If you make it, your set. If you have to straighten off, well, you're pretty much screwed.

I remember listening to Brewer talk about what to do when you straighten off on a huge wave. It was a simple strategy, really, and it worked. You prone out then slide back on the board so that both your legs are dragging from behind the board in a wishbone-like position. This gives you the stability for the impact and you can sort of control your own drag. Of course, if the wave is big enough, it sucks you up into the soup and then, more than likely, you go endo. If you can hold on and maintain your body attitude without getting stuck in the balls with the tail, you can actually do a complete flip and then come shooting out in the soup again. Brewer told us stories about Buzzy Trent going endo twice on big waves at Waimea and making it.

So, the deal on a big west swell at Honolua is to roll the dice and go for the back door. Actually, if you're lucky and do it right, it is a pretty safe move and sets you up for a great ride. The biggest problem with that move back then was making sure the guys scratching for the shoulder knew you were coming. Oh yeah, there was a lot of yelling going on. The last thing you needed was for some guy to be dropping in on you from the shoulder.

Notoriety Doesn't Come Cheap
Now, over the years I've been lucky enough to get my picture in a couple of magazines. But, of all (not that many really) the photos that gained me notoriety, none is more remembered by my contemporaries than a sequence shot taken on that swell of 1969 at Honolua. It was a sequence of me executing the back door move.

It must have been late morning when a big set poured out of the channel and sent us all scratching for the horizon. I broke off from the pack and headed for the point. I could tell there were four or five big waves in the set, so I paddled over the saddle of the first two. I could hear guys inside of me yelling and scrambling for position and I wanted them to clear out a little before I took a wave.

I come over the saddle of the third wave and see this magnificent twelve-plus beauty rolling over the outside reef. What a wave! A huge, blue green pyramid, and I was in the perfect spot for a back-door glide in. Time stopped. I wasn't thinking of anything else going on around me, just that I had the position and I was going. I turned around and stroked in easily from the saddle. It wasn't until I caught it and was looking down the line that I became aware of a couple of guys turning around to take off in front of me.

Yep, that was one of the problems with the backdoor move. The guys on shoulder might think you weren't going to make it. And, rather than see a good wave go by, they just might take off in front of you. That's when you had to do your best hoot, or yell, or scream some expletive just to let them know you were coming down!

Well, here I am dropping in when I realize there's a guy on the other side of the peak stroking in. I yell, but he doesn't hear me. The sequence, which appeared in Surfing Magazine, shows me catching the wave and dropping in. Then, a guy catches the wave right in the peak and drops in front of me. None other than my good bro Leslie Potts!

Now Les was no novice at the Bay and if anyone could take the drop in the peak, it was him. He knew what to do. He knew to make the drop you had to drive straight down to the bottom, go out in front of the coming explosion and pull off a huge turn. That's exactly what he did.

All I remember was seeing him fly down at me and lay into this turn. His spray knocked me clean off my board and I found myself on my back staring up at this massive killer wave. Oh I ate my lunch alright. I got killed. Smashed. Crunched. Pummeled. Did I leave anything out? It was one of the worst wipeouts ever for me. Over the falls twice, bouncing off the reef both times. Unbelievably, my board didn't break, and some guys saved it from hitting the rocks.

So what happened in the sequence? Well, you turn the page to an absolutely beautiful two-page spread of Leslie Potts getting tubed in a perfect Honolua wave! It was the best picture ever of Leslie, and one of the best of the times.

Did we remain buddies after that? Sure, he claims he never saw me, and I'll take him at his word. Hey there was a chance I may not have made it around that section, and it was a perfect wave. But, I still dream of being in that huge barrel just like Les.

To this day, whenever I run across somebody who was on Maui then, they will bring up that story. And, I don't mind, I just tell them "I would have made it!"

The next three or four days were like heaven. The waves were well over ten feet and absolutely perfect. Dick Graham and Duke Boyd were there from Surfing Magazine taking pictures. Severson was there too, making the movie "Sunshine Sea." What ever happened to that movie? There were a lot of good days at the bay, but none better that I can remember during that swell of 1969.

The Take Off — Yep, there I was in the driver's seat ready for a big turn, and probably yelling at Les... to no avail. (Photo by Richard Graham)

Howdy — Les said he never saw me, and I believe him, there's a lot going on when the wind is howling and you're paddling in a set wave. Les did what he needed to do, drove to the bottom and leaned into a hard turn. I'm thinking, "oh no, I'm right in front of the cave!" Lunch was on the menu! (Photo by Richard Graham)

Down the line — Les Potts in a place I can only dream about. He rocketed all the way down the line in one of the best and longest tubes of the year. Meanwhile, I was doing a little deep sea diving. Such is life! (Photo by Dick Graham)

Big Brown and the Shark Attack

The larger waves inspired me to build a longer gun. Not that my board was too small for the big waves, I just wanted something more comfortable. I ended up shaping myself an eight-eight, which was way long, even for that time. It turned out pretty good. It had a brown bottom and brown rails, with most of the same elements that were in my seven-eleven.

I rode the Bay on it and it was fun, but I could tell it was too much board for the most part. Still, I loved the way it paddled and the feeling it gave me of being safe. I still like those feelings! I had two memorable occasions on the board.

The first was on a Kona wind day at Pakukalu. There was a big north swell, but the whole west side was blown out. We headed for Kahalui, where the wind was howling off shore. Pakukalu could get big. I think I've already described it as a big island-style Cottons Point. By that I mean it was a big left that always seemed to have the ability to pop up a set that was out farther than anyone was sitting.

Cottons does that. You're sitting outside waiting for a wave and out of nowhere comes a huge outside set that catches everybody by surprise. Pakukalu did that and more. It was hard finding the right

189

place to sit, and forget about hanging out on the inside. You would get toasted every time. Did I mention the sharks? Yeah, Pakukalu was famous for them, too. There was a river mouth there that came down from a dairy. Sharks like that sort of deal, plus the water was brown from cane run off, which was even better for them.

On this particular day, the surf was over ten feet. Nice big peaks. I decided to ride the brown gun and it turned out to be a good decision. I could get outside quick and take advantage of those sneaky big sets. I have always liked going backside, something about riding with your back to the wave.

So we were having quite a day of it. There were not too many people out, because it was kind of fierce. Guys come up with a lot of excuses on days like that, if you know what I mean. Anyway, I'm sitting outside with Steve Dabney, Gary Chapman, Jock Sutherland, and a couple of other guys when somebody sees a pair of fins cruising on the outside.

Someone yells "sharks!" I look outside and just catch a glimpse of two dark fins sort of making their way toward us. Just then a set was coming in. The first wave was not big, probably about six to eight feet. Dabney is in position and he turns around for it. I look at him and say "Hey I'm going, too," and he gives me a nod. We both catch it and then proceed to stand up, straighten-off and prone-out. We looked at each other and both knew we were heading in for the same reason. "There were sharks out there!"

It was already late afternoon and we proned our boards right to the beach and scurried up over the rocks to the safety of the parking lot. We were telling everyone about the two fins heading right for the pack and guys were nodding like "Wow, sharks."

There were only a hand full of us out at the time and I fully expected everyone to do what Dabney and I did. That is, get the hell out of the water. But they didn't. Jock and Chapman continued to ride waves and paddle back out. In fact, they were getting some incredible waves, and with two less guys in the line up. They must have rode for another 45 minutes before the sun set and it started getting dark.

When they came in, we asked "What the hell were you guys thinking?" They just laughed at us. Turns out the fins were a big mantaray who just swam by. Oh, we were a laughing stock then. Two pretty good surfers proning out all the way to the beach scared shitless! Oh hell, I'd probably do the same thing again.

Back to Kauai

The other memorable experience on the brown board came on a trip over to Kauai. Joey Cabell had given me a call at The Broiler and invited me over for a couple of days. He had Mike Doyle staying with him and they were both learning to play the guitar. Joey wanted me to come over and bring my guitar and board. I hadn't been back to Kauai since coming to Maui, so I took him up on the invitation.

I took the brown board and a new little seven-six that I'd just finished. You want to talk about luck? I had not even had a chance to ride the new board and was looking forward to getting it out at Hanalei Bowl. But I did better than that.

On the way over to Kahalui Airport, I was driving along the Pali, when I noticed a little whitewater down on the cliff. It was mid - day, and I had arranged to take a one o'clock flight over to Lihue. As I got closer and closer to Malia, I kept seeing whitewater. I decided to check it out. So I pull in the little parking lot and am amazed to see it breaking. There were perfect three-foot waves with not a soul in sight.

I quickly drove to a nearby store and used a pay phone to call Joey. I told him I was going to catch a later flight and would call before I left. With that I went back to Malia and paddled out on my new little board. As it turned out, the waves were a bit inconsistent, but every once in while a good little set came through and I got some waves. Just surfing it alone was an experience I'll never forget. Eventually, a couple of local guys from Kehei paddled out and I left it to them. Good fun.

What an adventure life was then. One day I'm waiting tables at The Broiler, the next day I'm taking all the money I have to my name and catching a plane to Kauai. And, on the way, I get one of the best waves in the world all to myself!

That was quite a trip too. When I called Joey the second time, he said that he and Doyle had decided to go to Honolulu for the night and that they would leave the car in Lihue for me. I could drive out to his place and then pick them up the next day. That was the way it was, I guess we were all kind of free spirits, flowing with whatever happened.

I found Joey's car in the airport parking lot, the same old Ford stationwagon he had when I was there before. I knew where he lived from those days going out there for dinner with Lisa Starr. It was still a long drive out to Hanalei and Haiena. A long, dark drive in an old beat up car. I remember hoping I would make it. For a guy with a lot of money, Joey's ride left a lot to be desired.

There wasn't much out in Haiena in those days. Maybe one store, no restaurants, no hotels or condos, and hardly any lights. I felt like Ikabod Crane finding my way through the enchanted forest. Oh, and the Headless Horseman could appear at any time. Yep, I was a little scared. I don't know of what, but just edgy.

I got to his house, found the key and let myself in. It was a small cottage, but it had electricity, thank goodness. No TV of course. But I had my guitar. Oddly enough and old friend who was living in that area saw the lights on and stopped by. It was Roger Zieger. He kept me company and we played guitar. Just before I went to bed that night, I remember looking up at the ceiling and seeing a centipede. I didn't pay it much attention and just turned off the light.

Sometime in the middle of the night, I was awakened by a searing pain in my neck. Worse than a bee sting, much worse. I went into the bathroom and saw two big welts on my neck. I rushed back into the bedroom, turned on the light and tore the covers off the bed. Sure enough there was that centipede, all set to get me again. I got a knife from the kitchen and cut that sucker up in about a million pieces. Didn't sleep a wink the rest of the night.

Making Music of the Day
The next day, Joey called from the airport and said they were going to catch a ride out. A friend of Doyle's, actually his business partner, was coming with them. His name was John Baker and he, Doyle and Rusty Miller had just started a company that was going to manufacture a specialized wax for surfing. They called the com-

pany Surf Research. They told me all about their new wax, and I didn't say much. After all, what was wrong with regular old paraffin? Surf wax? It would never fly!

Baker had a girl with him, I can't remember her name or if she was a girlfriend or just a friend, but I remember she was pretty. And, she surfed! We spent the afternoon, checking out each other's boards and playing a little guitar. Joey and Doyle had just seen the movie Midnight Cowboy and had purchased the sheet music to the theme song "Echos of my Mind," by Fred Neil. (Yeah, I know Nielson made it a hit, but Fred Neil wrote it.) I helped them figure it out and regretted it the whole rest of the trip.

Talk about two type "A" personalities latching on to something. They both had guitars and man they just banged away at that song like there was no tomorrow. Worse yet, they were trying to sing it! Oh man, it was all about finger nails on the black board. I just did my best to smile, and make conversation with Baker and his girlfriend. We all had dinner at the Rice Mill that night and I enjoyed talking to Baker about the surf business. Still didn't think his product was going to amount to much, but I kept that to myself.

The next day was one of the perfect Hawaiian winter days. Warm sun, slight tradewinds and a nice swell. We surfed Hanalei bowl in the morning and it was great. After lunch at Joey's, we decided to take a look at Cannons before going back to Hanalei. Good thing. It was six to eight feet and perfect. I had only surfed it once before, and had never seen it really go off. Carlos had told me all about it though. A Pipeline type left.

It was all of that. Big spitting tubes, very juicy to say the least. We all went out. Baker and his girlfriend were a little out of their element and mostly stayed in the channel, although John got some waves and I could tell he was really stoked to be in some real island action. It was fun.

Larry Strada and Mike Diffendiffer, who had both moved to Kauai, came out and joined us. What a great session. I remember seeing Strada get this incredible backside tube, but he had to grab a rail when the wave spit him out. I razzed him about it. "Rail grabber!" But I was envious; it was a great ride.

That was a perfect day, followed by another great dinner. Joey, always the great host, cooked fresh Ahi Tuna and rice. Now that was a product that would sell!

A Paddle to Remember
So this story started off about the brown gun I had made and I'm getting to that. Actually, I had ridden it at Cannons and it was safe and comforting, but too long for the waves. I think Diffendiffer brought that to my attention. He was also very discerning about some of its flaws. Hey, he was the master shaper and I knew he was right. It wasn't in the same class as his boards, or Strada's.

The surf went flat overnight, but the next day again fell into that picture perfect category. Joey suggested we take a paddle down the Napali Coast to a secluded beach called Hanakapi'ai that had great body surfing. You could take a trail by land, which was about a two-hour hike, or you could take a two-mile paddle and be there in less than an hour. We went for the latter.

It was Baker and his girl, Doyle, Joey and me. I opted for the brown board, for paddling sake. Anyway, we didn't anticipate any surf. We took a nice leisurely paddle down, checking out the cliffs and the birds. The water was perfectly clear and the white foam of the swells smashing against the black lava cliffs churned stories of ancient Hawaiian legends in my mind.

We arrived at a beautiful valley with a white sand beach. Paradise? You bet. There was a waterfall in the background and thick rainforest. And, sure enough, there was a nice left shore break to body surf. We did some body surfing and then hiked back in the forest to pick some wild fruit. Mostly lilikoi, or passion fruit, and star fruit.

When we got back from the hike, we noticed that the surf had come up a little. In fact, there was a nice little peak forming up in the bay. We all went out and started catching waves. It was very consistent, about three feet, with some four foot sets. Everyone was having fun. I was wishing I had my little board, especially surfing with the likes of Mike Doyle and Joey Cabell.

The surf kept coming in, getting a little bigger with each set. After a while Baker's girlfriend went in to rest. By then, there were some six-foot sets. And it was getting pretty good too. A nice peak with a lined up right. We started really getting into it. It was a beachbreak though, and paddling back out got a little tougher as the waves continued to rise.

Funny thing about Doyle and Cabell. They were both old-school surfers and very competitive. They were doing their best to out-shine each other. In fact, both of them took off in front of each other on several occasions. Can you imagine? We are the only ones out and they are taking off in front of each other! All very friendly though. That was how they grew up. No big deal.

The surf continued to rise and before we knew it there were eight-foot peaks coming through. After a couple of hours, I decided to take a break. I joined Baker and his girl on the beach. Then awhile later, Cabell and Doyle came in. We all stood there remarking on the change in conditions we were witnessing. Joey, said that if we hurried back, we might still have time to get a surf at Hanalei. That sounded good, but getting back appeared to be a problem.

There were ten-foot sets coming in and the peak had turned into a big wall. The body surfing left at the other end of the beach was looking like Waimea Shorebreak. It would be a tough paddle out. There was no way the girl was going to make it, so Baker opted to walk back with her on the trail. That must have been quite a hike carrying boards, but we didn't exactly have a breeze getting back ourselves.

I was debating on whether or not to walk back with Baker, but I guess my ego came into play. Plus I had a good paddling board and was with two of the best water men in surfing. So, I hit the shore-break running right alongside of Joey and Doyle.

We timed our entry for a lull in the sets, but still had to push through some pretty big white water. Somehow, I managed to snake myself out and was relieved when I got outside. I followed in behind Doyle and we started our trek up the coast. We could see huge swells outside, but felt safe in deep blue water. Still, the swells came crashing up against the jagged lava cliffs with tremen-dous power sending sheets of spray hundreds of feet in the air. Fear soaked into my bones.

The wind was swirling too, and the clouds whisked by as if blown by some huge wind machine. I don't mind telling you I was nerv-ous. I asked Doyle if we shouldn't be further out, but he said that we should follow Joey's lead. He knew the terrain better than us. Of course, that was like saying: "Hey just keep following Superman," as he launches off a building.

I was in good paddling shape, but no match of Cabell or Doyle. I will always be grateful for Doyle hanging back with me that day. He could have stayed with Joey, but he hung with me. I have since experienced several other rather tenuous moments with Joey Cabell, both sailing and skiing. He is a good man. The best, but he's not one to cut any slack when danger lurks. When the going gets tough, you better pull your own weight. When you hang with Joey, you damn well better be able to hang!

So we make our way up the coast, careful to stay inside of what was now an outside line of breakers, and the cliffs. The waves were breaking closer to us now, with the big soups dissipating just outside of where we were paddling. It seemed like with each new set, the soup would come a little nearer. Testing us. Imagine this: on the left there is huge whitewater and thunderous waves, on the right gigantic swells crashing into shear cliffs. With each swell, there was huge backwash going out. Oh man, talk about Maytag.

Scared? Oh yeah, shitless by now. Joey was probably a hundred yards in front of us as we approached the beach at the end of the road. Hell, as they say, was breaking loose all around us. I think it must have been like being in some fierce firefight with bombs exploding everywhere at random.

We watched as Cabell seemed to paddle closer to the cliffs. Too close, one big swell and he could get tossed on to the lava rocks. Just then, we hear a huge sound like thunder and we look out to see this giant title-wave like soup coming at us. There was no time to think. Doyle and I turned and paddled like mad out to sea. It was either battle the big soup or get swept into the rocks.

Luckily, the soup backed off a little and we both pushed through it. I came out the other side and looked for Doyle. He was there smiling, like this is fun! Then we both look to the beach and see the soup we just got through smash against the cliffs. It was like an atomic bomb. Water everywhere. Anybody in the vicinity of that was in deep shit. There was no sign of Joey or his board.

We sat there a minute trying to decide what to do. Hanalei was too far. The beach at the end of the road was hard to make out through all the mist and white water, but that was probably our best bet. On Doyle's advice we paddled out further and around this sort of point that marked the beginning of the Napali Coast.

The plan was to position ourselves as best we could in front of the beach and then just get swept in. I was beyond scared now. Fear had given way to pure adrenaline rush. It was literally do or die. We paddled to a spot that looked good and then another set thundered on the outside. I watched as this mammoth wall of soup came at us. Remember that Dick Brewer move? This was the time for it.

We turned our boards toward the beach, slid way back on the tails and prepared for impact. I don't know if I closed my eyes or what, but I took a deep breath and just hung on with a death grip. Too bad leashes hadn't been invented yet, they would have come in mighty handy about then. Anyway, the soup swept me up and sure enough I find myself getting lifted head over heels. A full vertical flip. I managed to hang on though. In a flash, I come rocketing out of the soup heading straight for the beach.

I looked to my right and see Doyle has made it too. We actually exchange looks before the soup hits us again and we both disappear. This time it just swept me up and I used my legs like rudders to guide myself back down. Again I come flying out right beside Doyle. This time we both knew we were going to make it with out losing our boards and there is a moment of joy. We laugh. Then, damn, we look to see what's ahead.

Here were are bouncing along toward the beach captives of an overhead wall of white water and what do you suppose is sticking up about 20 yards in front of us? Oh yeah, a huge exposed reef standing a good three feet out of the water. Instinctively, I slid back on the board and dangled my legs to create drag. It helped a little and I got elevated up in the soup, but the last thing I could do was just pull up on the nose with all my strength as I came crashing into the reef.

Some how, it wasn't too bad. The bottom of the good old brown board would never be the same, but I escaped with only a few minor cuts. Same for Doyle. When the soup finally let us down, we were high and dry on this reef in the middle of the small bay. I remember ambling across the reef and then jumping into the calm protected water inside of the reef. Oh it felt good.

We paddled that last 50 yards or so to the beach and I know I was thinking "hey I'm so glad to be alive!" Doyle just looked like he had the time of his life, no big deal. Then we thought about Joey. Where was he? We looked out on the cliff, thinking he may be out there bleeding.

About then, Joey appears out of the jungle on the other side of road and he's carrying three or four avocados. He walks up and hands us each an avo, and says something like "I knew this tree was going to have some good fruit."

That's it. Nothing was said. We ate those avos like apples, except spitting out the skin. Rare company.

It would be awhile until we learned that Joey had just beat out that huge soup that blasted the cliffs, and that Baker and the girl had one hell of a time on the trail back from Honokopiai. All and all, it was a trip to remember.

Make 'em and Break 'em
I flew back to Maui the next day just in time to make my shift at The Broiler. Oh, I had stories to tell. The Bay continued to go off on a regular basis. There just were no lulls in the swell that year. Rarely was there a day without surf. In town, we continued to crank boards out as fast as the Bay could eat them up. Paper dresses, as Potts would say. Make 'em and break 'em.

March was always a good month at Honolua. That's why a lot of guys made annual trips to Maui in March. Reynolds Yater, Hyson, Diffendiffer and others would come and stay for the whole month. They all came that year, and in a way, set the stage for one of the big changes in surfboard design.

An Agent of Change
As always, Hynson showed up that year with a quiver of new boards. And this time they were really new. By that I mean different. They were spear-like outline shapes, absolutely flat bottoms with the exception of a little V-line roundness in the tail. They also

had the most radical rails anyone had ever seen. They were turned down hard all the way to the nose!

No one had seen such a departure in surfboard design since Vinnie Bryant and Bunker Sprekles had made those square-railed belly-boards. Mind you, they could ride them, but they weren't for the masses. Turned down rails all the way to the nose! And, of course, Hynson being Hynson went out and grand-standed across some beautiful Honolua walls just to show how it was done.

Oh yeah, he went fast alright. And, he was making some incredible waves. His new design was soon the talk of the town.

So there I was one afternoon finishing up at The Broiler and in comes Hynson. He had always been sort of aloof to me. Cursory greetings and smiles, but no real conversation. But this time he was very talkative, and I soon found out that he could be very persuasive. He started telling me about the new "downrailers" and how they would revolutionize surfing. I listened. Then he made an offer. He said that he would shape one just for me, no strings attached. Just give me the board and let me see what I thought. If I didn't like it, I could sell it.

He went right to work on it without asking me anything. Not how long I wanted it, or what the outline. This was all him. The whole board was finished in less than a week.

On the cover — It was always a surprise to me to get a picture in a magazine. I was usually one of the last to find out. This was the cover of the 1969 Surfing Year Book, photo by Ron Dahlquist. I never knew Ron had taken the picture, it was just another day at the factory for me. It means a lot more to me now than it did then. Thanks Ron.

Purple Haze

I picked it up at the Allen Gray's glass shop and was immediately swept away with its look. Seven-eleven, spear-like outline with a rounded pin tail. Flat and turned down like nothing I'd ever seen. Gray had glassed it with a very light purple opaque color. It was one-of-a-kind and a real standout.

I took it out on a north-wind day with about a six-plus swell running at the Bay. Not perfect waves, and especially not perfect to try a new board. Especially a board that looked like the most unforgiving thing I'd ever seen. Still I paddled it out and knew right away that it was a special board. It paddled high in the water and seemed to just cut through the chop like a rocket. And that was just paddling out! I rode a couple of waves and was amazed at how it reacted under my feet. Very responsive, very fast.

I started moving it around on waves, trying little moves that I'd been working on, sort of putting in through a series of tests. It passed them all. Then I got a wave that changed my whole way of thinking. It was maybe about eight-feet, a big wall with little chance of making it through the bowl. I laid into a turn and started running down the line. With each turn, came more speed. I was really flying when I hit the inside section. The bowl was looming up and certain to break long before I would reach it.

In a split second, I decided to pull out the top. I was a little late on that decision though and I had to punch through the lip in order to make it out the back. I cranked a turn off the bottom and set course for the top of the wave. I would be lucky to punch through and would have to hang on to the board for fear of getting sucked back over the falls.

I ducked and punched the lip at full speed. That pointed, turned-down nose split through the wave like a spear. I was still standing as I punched through, which was a victory in itself. Then I felt the board going back over and knew I was going to go over the falls. For some reason I'll never know, I decided to ride her down standing up. So I sort of hop up a little and press down with my weight forward and sure enough I'm riding down the top of the already broken wave.

I bounce down the foam, picking up speed all the way. Enough speed to make it out in front of the soup and make a big bottom turn. From there I could just do a quick cut back and straighten off. I come flying out of the bottom and give it everything I've got for a bottom turn. I set the rail way up by the nose to draw out the projection as far as possible.

The turn seemed to take forever, and I could feel myself riding that rail around like a flat-track motorcycle rider. Oh, it felt good and I hung with it as long as possible. Too long in fact. By the time I was headed down the line again, still in the soup mind you, there was no way I was going to make a cutback and straighten off. So I just set my legs in the old Peter Cole position and prepared to get bombed by the soup. Funny thing was, I was going pretty fast. And the soup got me, but didn't knock me off as expected. In fact the purple board felt stable under my feet. And I was bombing through the soup like a bulldozer.

I actually made it to the shoulder on the other side of the bowl, something I never thought possible. In fact, that whole ride was something I had never even come close to before. Stoked? Oh man, it was a new world.

From there each wave took on new meaning. I was going faster, further, and more vertical than ever before. And, I wasn't the only one. Hynson was loaning out his quiver to Jock and Chapman and Roger Yates and Potts. Soon, the whole town was buzzing about "downrailers."

I named the board Purple Haze, and like the song, it represented a departure in conventional thinking.

The rails were very box-like, turned down hard. The increased volume in the board made it float like a cork. Great outline shape with a accentuated pointed nose, wide point forward of center and nice flowing lines to the tail, which was rounded to a little point. The bottom was flat, except toward the tail, where Hynson had shaped in very soft V panels in front of the fin. Then, instead of ending in a V shape, he flattened it out again and then put a little kick in the very end.

Riding Purple Haze was like driving a finely tuned sports car. It was responsive, extremely fast and it paddled. For some reason, it always reminded me of a nuclear submarine. Something about its lines. What a board.

I rode the Purple Haze for most of the rest of the winter. When the surf began to get smaller in the spring, I went back to shaping my own creations. Downrailers to be sure!

Big Red and Little Green

That spring, Gaglia and I found a great house out in Napili. It was small, but it had two bedrooms and a hot shower. Better yet, it was on a rugged lava point that separated two coves, both with beautiful white sand beaches. We called the house Little Green. A couple of our buddies from school, Tom Powers and Jeff Mene had lived there the previous winter. They passed it on to us when they scored the bigger house right next door. The called it Big Red. Big Red was a large four-bedroom place built on the main highway and they lived there with Moe Learner.

Little Green and Big Red became the epicenter for our growing band of wave riders. Gaglia and I formed instant bonds with Tom Powers ("Zorro"), Jeff Mene ("Loaf"), and Moe Learner. Steve Dabney lived nearby and collectively we all called ourselves "The Raiders." When we loaded the cars with boards and hit The Bay, we were an instant crowd. For awhile there, The Raiders owned the dawn patrol and late evening sessions at The Bay.

Napili was close to Honolua and it was in the country, which meant it was cooler in the summer than Lahaina. The tradewinds blew regularly in Napili and the ocean was clear and blue. What a place it was then, no hotels, no Kapalua golf resort, no endless condominiums. Pineapple Hill was covered with pineapples, and the restaurant at the top overlooked the fields of fruit and the lava-scaped Napili coastline. There was a resort at the foot of the hill called Tea House of the Maui Moon. It must have been built in the late 1950s. It was a quaint little place and it had a restaurant that served great breakfasts.

Breakfast became a big thing with me then. A good breakfast had been part of being a surfboard builder as long as I could remember. Quigg and Marshall had the Snug Harbor in Newport. The North Shore had Meriam's and the Sea View Inn. On Maui it was the Lahaina Bakery or the Pioneer Inn in town. The Tea House was our secret spot.

I loved to get up early and go to one of those spots and drink coffee. Depending on my budget, I would have toast and jam, or maybe two eggs over-medium with hash browns. We avoided most of the regular meats, but if I could afford it, and there weren't too many friends around, I would go for eggs and Portuguese sausage. That was good!

Of course, we were all quasi vegetarians at the time. But things were changing fast. With more people came more social life, and changes in the mostly male dominated soul surf culture.

The house in Napili gave us some sanctuary from the bustling Lahaina life. Still, Gaglia and I both worked at the Broiler and we built our boards in town. As summer came, He went back to the mainland for a couple of months. I stayed at Little Green and worked. That was another of those long hot summers with minimal surf.

When Gaglia returned in late August, he brought back some boards he had made on the coast. One was a radical little six-foot plus board with a round nose and round tail. It had fin boxes, as in three fin boxes. He called it the Rubber Band, and it was an innovation for the times. I'd never heard of three fins.

We went about setting up our own shaping shop and glass shop in the old pineapple cannery. Downhome Surfboards was going to actually have a shop. Gaglia had honed his shaping skills and had some great ideas.

The Hynson down rail design brought with it a new element. Well, old element somewhat revised. That was nose riding. Roger Yates had taken the lead on that toward the end of the previous winter by getting some great nose rides on one of the boards Hynson had left behind. That opened our eyes to what could be done with new board design, and in surfing the new boards on smaller waves.

I made myself a quiver of boards from an eight-eight gun to a seven-six hot-dog board. We gave the gun a classic glass job that had a U.S. Airforce insignia on the bottom. It was a great board. Gaglia shaped a nose rider style hot-dog board that we glassed to look like a tennis shoe. These were our show boards, and they brought us customers.

Downhome was never a major financial success, all our profits went into making new boards. But, we got to build boards and that was what it was all about. When the Bay started breaking again in the fall of 1970, there were a lot of Downhomes in the water.

The level of surfing continued to rise with guys going faster and deeper than ever before. As I've said, it seemed to me that there was never one single standout at the Bay. Everyday there would be a new top dog. One day it was Potts, the next it was Dabney or Yates, or any of a dozen guys. It was like a jam session where anybody could jump out and take the lead. And all the other guys would lay back and enjoy the song.

Designs in Style — Board were changing all over the islands. On Kauai, shapers John "J.A." Allen and Mike Diffenderfer were turning out some spears. From left: Kim Harp with a J.A. Pintail, J.A. with a little round tail, and Tom "Zorro" Powers with a classic Diffenderfer gun.

The Big Change

That's a sort of idealistic view, of course. There was competition. More and more guys were showing up from the North Shore whenever there was a big swell. Somebody even organized a Honolua Bay surf contest. Actually, they had held one in a previous winter. Vinnie Bryant had won on his belly-board creation. But, nobody from Maui paid much attention. That first contest was held on a bad day, and not many of us would have gone out anyway.

But, the second time they tried it, the surf was good. A bunch of guys came over from the North Shore. None of the Maui regulars entered. In fact, we all just surfed as usual and tried to ignore all the hoopla. Rullo was there that day and got some of the best waves. Ask him today and he'll tell you he won it hands down, although he was not an official entry. Actually, Gerry Lopez won the thing. He got some good waves and more importantly wasn't uptight about all of us regulars in the line up. Hey, what were they thinking? We were suppose to give them the best waves at one of the world's best surfing spots for their silly contest?

Gerry was cool about it and just laughed. He positioned himself to get waves just as he would have on a regular day. And he did good! There was one thing that got us all a little uptight though. He and a couple of other guys in the contest were wearing these rubber rope things attached to their boards and ankles! Yep, they had brought leashes.

We scorned them for it. Said it was cheating. Vowed that it would never take hold at Honolua. Oh yeah, but then the next swell there were a whole bunch of other guys out in the water with leashes. Guys like Fat Paul (North Shore guy) were taking full advantage of the leash by going for unmakable tubes and doing side slips down the face. Suddenly, Honolua was a circus.

To us, the leash went against everything we had established in surfing. It was like putting training wheels on your bike. Surfing was a thing you got good at by paying the price. A long swim made you think about what you could have done differently on a wave. You had to be good a skills such as pulling out of a wave, straightening off, rolling waves on the way out and hanging on to your board. There was a great pride in keeping a board intact all season long at the Bay, or making that long swim in from Waimea or Sunset. It was all about being a "waterman."

More than that, when the Bay (or anyplace) got big, it separated the men from the boys. There could be 25 guys in the line up, but when a 10-foot set rolled through, there were only a few that took charge. Especially when the consequences of a bad move meant swimming over a shallow reef or climbing into a cave to retrieve your board.

Looking back now, I say that the leash has changed surfing more so even than the short board. As I see it, there was the move from redwood to balsa (before my time), the move from balsa to foam, the introduction of wet suits, the long board to short board revolution and then the leash. Of all those significant innovations, the leash stands out in my mind as the one that changed surfing the most.

Probably inevitable, of course, but with leashes came the hordes. The guys who wouldn't dare venture out in larger surf, would be out there in mass. It made surfing more accessible, It probably fueled the whole billion dollar surf business. It certainly took a sport that was made up mostly of very individual types and made it so just about anybody could claim to be a surfer. Okay, I've vented enough, and as I said, it was probably inevitable.

But that year, only the outsiders wore leashes at the Bay. Some of them, like Lopez and Fat Paul, were good enough to maintain their respect from the crew. And, there weren't that many who used them. They had just been invented, and certainly not perfected.

Moving On — This cover shot taken by Greg Weaver was at Kitchen Window in South Africa. I didn't know it then, but my short career as a durfer was about to come to an end. Oh well, nice way to gou out. Thanks Greg (Photo Greg Weaver, published in Surfer Magazine)

According to the story, O'neil had pioneered them and succeeded in putting his eye out with one of the early versions.   ,

The winter of 1970 and '71 was another good year. Not as good as the banner year of 1969, but an excellent year. The downrailers were taking us to new heights. Jock was doing things like dropping in straight down, jumping to the nose in a little squat, and then cranking a bottom turn while hanging five! The nose turn! Oh man, it was cool. He would come off the bottom hanging five and then maintain the position as long as possible down the line. Something to see, indeed!

Moving On
While life in the water was getting better and better, life on the beach was going in the other direction. More people (isn't that always the problem?) were moving to Maui, and everywhere else in the Islands. And not just surfers, people from all walks of life were dropping out and, well, not quite "tuning in." Some bad elements were taking hold and as is true in life, the bad can out weigh the good.

Dropping Out and Dropping In
In the spring 1971, surfing was still reinventing itself on a daily basis. If these were the days of experimentation in other genres, we were taking it literally in the waves. That was good. On the other side, life was changing for many of us. Sort of that loss of innocence stage I guess. The stage where you start seeing the world in a different perspective and discover that not all of it is good.

More and more people were dropping out of the mainland life and moving to Hawaii. Destinations such as Kauai, The North Shore and Maui all had growing populations of non-surfers, surfer want-a-bees, and people on the fringe of some new found reality. Free spirits, to be sure, but their presence created tension. And that tension changed our life in many ways.

The locals were getting more uptight with the crowded conditions. They resented the high-living haoles, the new-age lifestyles and the drugs. Sure there were drugs, I don't talk about them much because I think we, as surfers, would have been doing the same thing with drugs or without drugs. I'm not one to rant on about becoming enlightened, nor about becoming dysfunctional. Drugs were there. Drugs were not good. And that's all I have to say about that.

So whatever the case, Maui was changing fast. I felt that the older locals began fearing for their children. The young locals, for the most part, just resented being invaded by a different culture. Aloha was being challenged.

Machine Gun Mike

The big change in culture became evident for me when I got a gun stuck in my face. True. It was an afternoon after a pretty good day at the bay. Four of five of us were hanging out at a surf house in the north end of town. Just kicking back on the porch listening to some tunes and talking surf.

Our peace was interrupted when a Jeep with three guys in it pull into the yard. We recognized the Jeep and the guy driving it. A local guy named Mike who had come over from Honolulu. He was always kind of weird. Never took off his wrap-around shades. He hung with the black coral divers, although I don't think he dove. Just drove the boat and stuff.

Like I said he was always kind of weird. Scary weird and there were stories going around about him having mob connections in Honolulu. The other two guys with him were Lahaina locals, a haole guy who had grown up there and another guy who was one of the pool hall locals. They had this sort of mini-gangster thing about them, but nobody paid much attention to them.

So they pull in the yard and jump out of the Jeep before we know it. It took me a second to realize they were all carrying something wrapped in towels under their arms. The guy named Mike is first up on the porch and he pulls the towel off and he's holding a gun. I think it was an AK 47, something like that. Can you picture this? Here we are all laid back on the porch, listening to tunes and the next thing we know we have a gun pointed at us.

And not just one gun. They all had them. The haole guy had a shot gun and the pool shark had a little pistol. They herded us into the house and made us sit up against the wall. I can't remember what I was thinking, but I remember looking at this barrel pointed at my face.

They took the guy who ran the house in the bedroom and made him give them all his money and whatever else he had of value. Mike and the local guy did the robbing while the haole guy kept the rest of us up against the wall with his shot gun. It all happened fast. Maybe five minutes at the most, but it seemed like an eternity. I don't remember being scared until after. Yeah, like later that night at home thinking, "I'm out of here!"

They made off with the cash and stash and no one ever did anything about it. Mike became known from then on as "Machinegun Mike." As the story goes, the black coral guys did not approve of what came down and Machinegun Mike and his crew became outcasts. But, the Maui lifestyle had been shattered, for me at least.

New Horizons
With that, a few of us started looking at new horizons. We were hearing stories about Jefferys Bay in South Africa, and far off islands like Bali that were uncrowded and had perfect waves. Diffendiffer had left the North Shore for South Africa, so had Mike Kuntz and some others. Although life on Maui was still pretty good, those far-off places were beckoning to me, and I decided to pull out all the stops and go.

Actually, Roger Yates had already picked up and left for South Africa. Like my buddy Gaglia's letters had done a couple of years before, Roger's post cards from Jefferys were singing songs of a distant adventure in untamed surf. Somehow I gathered enough money, and in March of 1971, I headed off for South Africa.

I didn't know it at the time, but my surfing career, if you can call it that, was coming to an end. I was 23 and had seen some of the greatest advancements ever in the sport, but something else was building inside. A longing, maybe, for something different. Maybe a more stable life. Maybe I didn't want to be that "surf bum" my dad had warned me about. Only a trip out in to the world would tell.

Over the next six months, I traveled to South Africa, and to a little-known island in the Indian Ocean called Mauritius. I got some of the best surf of my life in both places. And some of the best rides, too, with no one around to see. I like that.

What an experience it was. The cultural shock of Africa made me very thankful of the life that I had been given. A surfer's life. I guess I'm an old man now, by most accounts. But, I don't feel old.

In my mind I'm still that skinny little kid who lived on 32nd Street who couldn't wait for school to get out.

Now, we sit around the camp fire and tell the stories of our friends. We sing the songs of precious days spent in the sun and in a world that only the luckiest people share. I consider myself so lucky to have lived in the time I did. To have witnessed some of the greatest times in a sport that has become a life to me. To have known some of the best, to have surfed some of the best waves, and to be able to finally write it all down.

Do I still surf? I surf everyday in my mind. I don't get out in the real waves as much as I'd like to. But, when I do, I love every second. I've gone back to being Peter Cole! Do I wear a leash? Only when I have to, which is becoming more frequent. Do I still get that butterfly feeling when I paddle out? Every time. No matter what life throws at us, redemption awaits, just outside of the breaker line.

The End

ISBN 1412009201-0

Made in the USA
San Bernardino, CA
22 December 2012